Family and Succession Law in Germany

Family and Succession Law in Germany

Fourth Edition

Saskia Lettmaier
Moritz-Philipp Schulz

This book was originally published as a monograph in the International Encyclopaedia of Laws/Family and Succession Law.

Founding Editor: Roger Blanpain
General Editor: Frank Hendrickx
Volume Editor: Walter Pintens

Wolters Kluwer

Published by:
Kluwer Law International B.V.
PO Box 316
2400 AH Alphen aan den Rijn
The Netherlands
E-mail: international-sales@wolterskluwer.com
Website: www.wolterskluwer.com/en/solutions/kluwerlawinternational

Sold and distributed by:
Wolters Kluwer Legal & Regulatory U.S.
7201 McKinney Circle
Frederick, MD 21704
United States of America
E-mail: customer.service@wolterskluwer.com

ISBN 978-94-035-4252-2

e-Book: ISBN 978-94-035-4253-9
web-PDF: ISBN 978-94-035-4254-6

The Authors

Saskia Lettmaier was born in 1979. She is currently Professor of Private Law, European Legal History, Comparative Law and Private International Law at the University of Kiel, Schleswig-Holstein, where she serves as a director of the university's Hermann Kantorowicz Institute. She is trained in both Anglo-American and German law. She obtained her BA in Jurisprudence from Oxford University in 2002, being awarded a First as well as the St. Anne's College Law Prize. She holds two German law degrees (First State Exam, 2009; Second State Exam, 2012, both with distinction), LLM and SJD degrees from Harvard University (2003 and 2015), a Doctorate in Cultural Studies from the University of Bamberg (summa cum laude, 2007), and a Dr iur.habil. from the University of Regensburg (2016). She has lectured in law at a number of German and foreign law schools and published books and articles on Anglo-American and German law as well as on the intersection between law, literature, and society. She is the author of *Broken Engagements: The Action for Breach of Promise of Marriage and the Feminine Ideal, 1800–1940* (Oxford University Press, 2010) and the editor of *Ausländisches Familienrecht* (C. H. Beck), a regularly updated, loose-leaf handbook on the family laws of a vast range of jurisdictions. Since December 2016, she has also served as a family law judge at the Higher Regional Court of Schleswig, the highest court for civil and criminal matters in the German state of Schleswig-Holstein.

Moritz-Philipp Schulz was born in 1996. He holds a German Law degree (First State Exam, 2020, with distinction). While a law student at Kiel University, he worked as a university research assistant and (until 2017) served as Secretary General of the Kiel division of the European Law Students' Association (ELSA). He has a keen interest in the historical and comparative dimensions of private law, in particular family and succession law. He is currently a doctoral candidate with Professor Lettmaier at the University of Kiel. His research focuses on notarial instruments and the practice of testation in Germany in the first half of the twentieth century.

The Authors

Table of Contents

List of Abbreviations

AG	*Amtsgericht* (Local Court)
AktG	*Aktiengesetz* (Stock Corporation Act)
Alt.	Alternative
AnwBl	*Anwaltsblatt*
Art.	Article
AufenthG	*Aufenthaltsgesetz* (Residence Act)
BayObLG	*Bayerisches Oberstes Landesgericht* (Bavarian Supreme Court)
BeurkG	*Beurkundungsgesetz* (Notarization Act)
BGB	*Bürgerliches Gesetzbuch* (Civil Code)
BGBl.	*Bundesgesetzblatt* (Federal Law Gazette)
BGH	*Bundesgerichtshof* (Federal Supreme Court)
BGHSt	*Entscheidungen des Bundesgerichtshofs in Strafsachen* (Collection of Decisions of the Federal Supreme Court in Criminal Matters)
BGHZ	*Entscheidungen des Bundesgerichtshofs in Zivilsachen* (Collection of Civil Law Decisions of the Federal Supreme Court)
BNotO	*Bundesnotarordnung* (Federal Notaries' Act)
BT-Drucks.	*Bundestags-Drucksache* (Official Records of the Bundestag)
BtG	*Gesetz zur Reform des Rechts der Vormundschaft und Pflegschaft für Volljährige* (*Betreuungsgesetz*) (Care and Control Act)
BVerfG	*Bundesverfassungsgericht* (Federal Constitutional Court)
BVerfGE	*Entscheidungen des Bundesverfassungsgerichts* (Official Collection of Decisions of the Federal Constitutional Court)
cf.	Compare With

List of Abbreviations

D.	Digest
EC	European Community
ECHR	European Convention on Human Rights
ed.	Edition/Editor
e.g.	For Example
EGBGB	*Einführungsgesetz zum Bürgerlichen Gesetzbuche* (Introductory Act to the Civil Code)
EheG	*Ehegesetz* (Marriage Act)
EheschlRG	*Eheschließungsrechtsgesetz* (Formation of Marriage Act)
1. EheRG	*Erstes Gesetz zur Reform des Ehe- und Familienrechts* (First Reform Act on Marriage and the Family)
EinigV	*Einigungsvertrag* (Treaty on German Reunification)
ErbR	*Zeitschrift für die gesamte erbrechtliche Praxis*
ErbStG	*Erbschaftsteuer- und Schenkungsteuergesetz* (Inheritance and Gift Tax Law)
etc.	Et Cetera
et seq.	Following Page/s or Paragraph/s
EU	European Union
Eur. Ct. H.R.	European Court of Human Rights
FamFG	*Gesetz über das Verfahren in Familiensachen und in Angelegenheiten der freiwilligen Gerichtsbarkeit* (Act on Proceedings in Family Matters and in Matters of Non-contentious Jurisdiction)
FamRZ	*Zeitschrift für das gesamte Familienrecht*
FGB	*Familiengesetzbuch* (Family Law Code, GDR)
Gbl.	*Gesetzblatt der Deutschen Demokratischen Republik* (Law Gazette of the German Democratic Republic)
GBO	*Grundbuchordnung* (Land Registry Act)
GDR	*Deutsche Demokratische Republik* (German Democratic Republic)
GenG	*Genossenschaftsgesetz* (Co-operative Societies Act)
GG	*Grundgesetz* (Basic Law)
GmbH	*Gesellschaft mit beschränkter Haftung* (Limited Liability Company)

GmbHG	*Gesetz betreffend die Gesellschaften mit beschränkter Haftung* (Limited Liability Company Act)
GVG	*Gerichtsverfassungsgesetz* (Judicature Act)
HGB	*Handelsgesetzbuch* (Commercial Code)
HeimG	*Heimgesetz* (Nursing Home Act)
Hs.	*Halbsatz* (independent clause linked to another by a semicolon, in the plural *Halbsätze*)
i.e.	That Is
IntErbRVG	*Internationales Erbrechtsverfahrensgesetz* (International Inheritance Law Procedure Act)
JGG	*Jugendgerichtsgesetz* (Juvenile Courts Act)
JZ	*JuristenZeitung*
KG	*Kommanditgesellschaft* (Limited Partnership)
KindRG	*Kindschaftsrechtsreformgesetz* (Child Law Reform Act)
KindUG	*Kindesunterhaltsgesetz* (Child Support Act)
LG	*Landgericht* (Regional Court)
lit.	*littera*
LPartG	*Lebenspartnerschaftsgesetz* (Registered Partnership Act)
LSG	*Landessozialgericht* (Higher Social Court)
MünchKommBGB	*Münchener Kommentar zum Bürgerlichen Gesetzbuch*
n.	Footnote
NamÄndG	*Namensänderungsgesetz* (Law on the Change of Names)
NJW	*Neue Juristische Wochenschrift*
NJW-RR	*Neue Juristische Wochenschrift – Rechtsprechungs-Report Zivilrecht*
No.	Number
OHG	*Offene Handelsgesellschaft* (General Partnership)
OJ	Official Journal of the European Union
OLG	*Oberlandesgericht* (Higher Regional Court)
OVG	*Oberverwaltungsgericht* (Higher Administrative Court)
p./pp.	Page(s)
para./paras	Paragraph(s)
PStG	*Personenstandsgesetz* (Civil Status Act)

List of Abbreviations

PStRG	*Personenstandsrechtsreformgesetz* (Civil Status Reform Act)
RDG	*Rechtsdienstleistungsgesetz* (Legal Services Act)
RGBl.	*Reichsgesetzblatt* (Imperial Law Gazette)
RGZ	*Entscheidungen des Reichsgerichtshofs in Zivilsachen* (Official Collection of Civil Law Decisions of the Imperial Court of Justice)
Rpfleger	*Der Deutsche Rechtspfleger*
RPflG	*Rechtspflegergesetz* (Court Registrars' Act)
SaReG	*Samenspenderregistergesetz* (Sperm Donor Register Act)
sent.	Sentence
SG	*Sozialgericht* (Social Court)
SGB	*Sozialgesetzbuch* (Code of Social Law)
StAG	*Staatsangehörigkeitsgesetz* (Citizenship Act)
StGB	*Strafgesetzbuch* (Penal Code)
StPO	*Strafprozeßordnung* (Code of Criminal Procedure)
VersAusglG	*Gesetz über den Versorgungsausgleich* (Pension Sharing Act)
VerschG	*Verschollenheitsgesetz* (Missing Persons Act)
vol.	Volume
VormG	*Vormundschaftsgericht* (Guardianship Court)
VVG	*Versicherungsvertragsgesetz* (Insurance Contract Act)
ZEV	*Zeitschrift für Erbrecht und Vermögensnachfolge*
ZGB	*Zivilgesetzbuch* (Civil Code, GDR)
ZPO	*Zivilprozeßordnung* (Code of Civil Procedure)
ZVG	*Gesetz über die Zwangsversteigerung und die Zwangsverwaltung* (Act on Enforced Auction and Receivership)

General Introduction

§1. General Background of the Country (and Demographic Data)

1. The Federal Republic of Germany is a parliamentary democracy situated in the heart of Europe. As a result of reunification in 1990, the federation acquired five new states and now consists of sixteen Member States (*Länder*): Baden-Württemberg, Bavaria, Berlin, Brandenburg, Bremen, Hamburg, Hesse, Lower Saxony, Mecklenburg-Vorpommern, North Rhine-Westphalia, Rhineland-Palatinate, Saarland, Saxony, Saxony-Anhalt, Schleswig-Holstein, and Thuringia.

2. The chief executive is the federal chancellor, who is elected by the country's legislature, the *Bundestag*. The *Bundesrat* represents the German states at the national level. In some cases, it participates in legislation, alongside the *Bundestag*. The states each have their own sovereignty, elected parliament, government, and independent judiciary. They enjoy considerable lawmaking powers, primarily in the fields of culture, education, and internal security, and they represent the main administrative body for the execution of both state and federal laws.

3. Germany covers an area of about 357,000 km^2. At the end of 2019, the country had a population of close to 83 million (including about 10 million foreigners) – the largest in Europe after the Russian Federation. The population is distributed rather unevenly. Densely populated regions, such as the Rhine-Ruhr industrial area or the Rhine-Main area around Frankfurt, contrast with thinly populated areas, such as the heathlands of the North German Plain or the Bavarian Forest. Nearly one-third of the population lives in the eighty-one large cities with more than 100,000 inhabitants. Of the 83 million inhabitants, around 41 million are male and 42 million female.

4. Since the 1970s, the population in both the old and new states has been in decline. Whereas in 1950, around 1,117,000 children were born, in 2009, this number had shrunk to 665,000. These figures represented one of the lowest birth rates in the world, and in view of the demographic development of the country, they were alarming. This is why it is a positive sign that in recent years, the trend has reversed itself, with 778,000 children being born in 2019. Likewise, the number of marriages has decreased significantly since the middle of the twentieth century, although recent years have seen an increase here as well (1950: 750,000; 1998: 417,000; 2009: 378,000; 2014: 386,000; 2019: 416,000). The number of divorces has gone up in the same time span, with a new high of 214,000 divorces per year in 2004 (more recently, the numbers have been dropping again, with 186,000 divorces in 2009 and only 149,000 in 2019). At the same time, the number of couples cohabiting outside marriage has risen from 1,393,000 in 1991 to 3,256,000 in 2019.

§2. Historical Background of Family and Succession Law

5. In past centuries, family law in Germany has been strongly influenced by the Christian churches. During the Middle Ages, the Catholic Church played a decisive part in shaping the law of marriage and succeeded in establishing several basic principles still in force today (monogamy, marriage by consent of the spouses, prohibition of marriage among close relatives, indissolubility of marriage). In order to carry through these ideas, the medieval church claimed the exclusive right to legislate and administer justice in the core areas of marriage law. Even where secondary effects of marriage arose, church and state courts competed with each other.

6. Since the Reformation, Germany has been divided denominationally. The reformers proclaimed a marriage theology that differed from the traditional Catholic view, and marriage law from then on developed separately according to the denominations. This did not prevent the lasting influence of the church: in Protestant towns and states also, theological convictions continued to form the basis of marriage legislation (divorce was only available for the reasons set out in the Bible; there was a requirement of parental consent for the marriages of children, etc.).

7. The growing importance of the state as opposed to the church and the ideas that were developing during the Enlightenment led to an increasing secularization of family law from the eighteenth century onwards: even in Catholic regions, the state now claimed legal competence in the entire area of family law, including marriage law. Marriage and family law were reformed according to the principles of secular legal policy. This was mirrored in the introduction of a secular marriage ceremony (civil marriage) in the course of the nineteenth century.

8. The situation in the nineteenth century was characterized by extreme legal diversity, as the individual German states all had separate legal systems. Decisive steps on the way to German legal uniformity were the Civil Status Act (*Personenstandsgesetz*, PStG) of 1875 and the Civil Code (*Bürgerliches Gesetzbuch*, BGB) of 18 August 1896. Since then, Germany has had a uniform family law, which applies without distinction to persons of all religions. In principle, the law of the churches today is of no importance to the legal order of the state.

§3. Sources of Family and Succession Law

I. Constitution

9. Germany's Constitution is laid down in the Basic Law (*Grundgesetz*, GG) of 23 May 1949. When it became the constitution for West Germany in 1949, the name was chosen to mark the temporary nature in a situation still awaiting German reunification. Since 1990, the Basic Law has served as the constitution for all of Germany. The constitutional guarantees and regulations are of central importance for legislation and jurisprudence in all areas of civil law, and thus also for family law.

10. German family law is shaped especially by the constitutional guarantee of Article 6 GG, which places marriage and the family under the special protection of the state.[1] Likewise, the Basic Law safeguards the right to inherit, although the content and the limits of this right are determined by statute law.[2] The law of persons as well as all other areas of law have to comply with certain fundamental values laid down in the Constitution:

- The dignity of every man and woman is inviolable. To respect and protect it is the duty of all state authorities.[3]
- Everyone has the right to the free development of their personality in so far as he or she does not violate the rights of others or offend against the constitutional order or the moral code.[4]
- Everyone has the right to life and to the inviolability of his or her person. The liberty of the individual is inviolable.[5]
- All persons are equal before the law.[6]
- Men and women have equal rights. The state supports equal opportunity between men and women, and works to remove existing inequalities.[7]
- No one may be disadvantaged or favoured on grounds of sex, parentage, race, language, homeland and origin, faith or religious or political opinions.[8] No one shall be discriminated against for reasons of disability.[9]
- Freedom of faith, of conscience, and freedom of creed, religious or ideological, shall be inviolable.[10]

On this basis, the rulings of the Federal Constitutional Court (*Bundesverfassungsgericht*, BVerfG) have substantially influenced the development of family law in Germany.

---

1. Article 6 I GG, for details cf. *infra* para. 62.
2. Article 14 I GG.
3. Article 1 I GG.
4. Article 2 I GG.
5. Article 2 II GG.
6. Article 3 I GG.
7. Article 3 II GG.
8. Article 3 III 1 GG.
9. Article 3 III 2 GG.
10. Article 4 I GG.

11. The European Convention on Human Rights and Fundamental Freedoms (ECHR) of 4 November 1950 and its interpretation by the European Court of Human Rights have influenced the development of family law in Germany as well. Germany has ratified the Convention, which has to be applied by the German courts. Article 8 of the Convention, which entitles each person to respect for his or her private and family life, home, and correspondence, has been of particular importance. The non-discrimination provision enshrined in Article 14 has likewise been of fundamental importance to the development of family law.

II. Legislation

12. German family and succession law is mainly set down in the Civil Code (*Bürgerliches Gesetzbuch*) of 18 August 1896, in force since 1 January 1900. The enactment of the Civil Code ended the extreme diversity of legal rules and systems, which had lasted until the nineteenth century.

13. A new split in the legal system occurred after the Second World War with the division of Germany into the western Federal Republic of Germany and the eastern German Democratic Republic (GDR). Reflecting the Cold War split between eastern and western political systems, the two states developed very different political, economic, and social institutions, and the same was true for the legal systems. Whereas West Germany retained the Civil Code and developed it further by reforming it, the GDR abolished the BGB and instead enacted new codes in the area of civil law.[11] Following the example of other socialist countries, East German family law was completely reshaped according to socialist dogma and laid down in a new Family Law Code (*Familiengesetzbuch*, FGB).[12]

14. This division only ended with German reunification in 1990. On 3 October 1990, on the basis of the Reunification Treaty of 31 August 1990, the GDR acceded to the Federal Republic and adopted its laws. Both the Civil Code (BGB) and the Basic Law were thus (re-)introduced to the area of the former GDR and East Berlin.

15. European Regulations:

- Council Regulation (EC) No. 2201/2003 of 27 November 2003 concerning jurisdiction and the recognition and enforcement of judgments in matrimonial matters and the matters of parental responsibility, repealing Regulation (EC) No. 1347/2000 (OJ L 338/1).

---

11. *Zivilgesetzbuch der Deutschen Demokratischen Republik* (ZGB) of 19 Jun. 1975 (Gbl. I No. 27 p. 465); *Vertragsgesetz* of 25 Mar. 1982 (Gbl. I No. 14 p. 293).
12. *Familiengesetzbuch der Deutschen Demokratischen Republik* (FGB) of 20 Dec. 1965 (Gbl. I 1966 No. 1 p. 1).

- Council Regulation (EC) No. 4/2009 of 18 December 2008 on jurisdiction, applicable law, recognition and enforcement of decisions and cooperation in matters relating to maintenance obligations (OJ L 7/1).
- Protocol on the Law Applicable to Maintenance Obligations – European Parliament legislative resolution of 24 November 2009 (OJ C 285 E/30).
- Council Regulation (EU) No. 1259/2010 of 20 December 2010 implementing enhanced cooperation in the area of the law applicable to divorce and legal separation (OJ L 343/10).
- Regulation (EU) No. 650/2012 of the European Parliament and of the Council of 4 July 2012 on jurisdiction, applicable law, recognition and enforcement of decisions and acceptance and enforcement of authentic instruments in matters of succession and on the creation of a European Certificate of Succession (OJ L 201/107).
- Council Regulation (EU) 2016/1103 of 24 June 2016 implementing enhanced cooperation in the area of jurisdiction, applicable law and the recognition and enforcement of decisions in matters of matrimonial property regimes (OJ L 183/1).
- Council Regulation (EU) 2016/1104 of 24 June 2016 implementing enhanced cooperation in the area of jurisdiction, applicable law and the recognition and enforcement of decisions in matters of the property consequences of registered partnerships (OJ L 183/30).

16. For law reform pertaining to family and inheritance law, we refer to the special chapters *infra.*[13]

III. Treaties

17. Germany has ratified a number of international and European treaties with relevance to the area of family and inheritance law. Generally, an international treaty only becomes part of German domestic law upon its transformation into German Federal Law. The Basic Law provides that where a treaty relates to matters of federal legislation – as is the case in the area of family and inheritance law – it shall require the consent or participation, in the form of a federal law, of the bodies competent in the specific case to enact such federal legislation.[14]

18. Of special importance to our area are the following international treaties that Germany has ratified:

- The European Convention for the Protection of Human Rights and Fundamental Freedoms (4 November 1950).
- The Hague Convention on the Law Applicable to Maintenance Obligations towards Children (24 October 1956).

13. Family Law: *see infra* paras 59 et seq.; Inheritance Law: *see infra* paras 351 et seq.
14. Article 59 II 1 GG.

- The Hague Convention on the Recognition and Enforcement of Decisions relating to Maintenance Obligations towards Children (15 April 1958).
- The Hague Convention concerning the Powers of Authorities and the Law Applicable in respect of the Protection of Minors (5 October 1961).
- The European Convention on the Adoption of Children (24 April 1967).
- The Hague Convention on the Recognition and Enforcement of Decisions relating to Maintenance Obligations (2 October 1973).
- The Hague Convention on the Law Applicable to Maintenance Obligations (2 October 1973).
- The European Convention on Recognition and Enforcement of Decisions concerning Custody of Children and on Restoration of Custody of Children (20 May 1980).
- The Hague Convention on the Civil Aspects of International Child Abduction (25 October 1980).
- The United Nations Convention on the Rights of the Child (20 November 1989).
- The Hague Convention on Protection of Children and Cooperation in respect of Intercountry Adoption (29 May 1993).
- The European Convention on the Exercise of Children's Rights (25 January 1996).
- The Hague Convention on Jurisdiction, Applicable Law, Recognition, Enforcement, and Cooperation in respect of Parental Responsibility and Measures for the Protection of Children (19 October 1996).
- The Hague Convention on the International Protection of Adults (13 January 2000).
- The Hague Convention on the International Recovery of Child Support and Other Forms of Family Maintenance (23 November 2007).
- The Hague Protocol on the Law Applicable to Maintenance Obligations (23 November 2007).
- The German-Persian Settlement Agreement (17 February 1929).
- The Annex to Article 20 of the Consular Treaty between the German Reich and the Turkish Republic of 28 May 1929 (Probate Treaty).
- German-Soviet Consular Treaty (25 April 1958).
- The Hague Convention on the Conflicts of Laws relating to the Form of Testamentary Dispositions (5 October 1961).

IV. Case Law

19. Under German law, previous decisions of higher courts are not, as a rule, binding on lower courts. Still, important and recent decisions of high-ranking courts such as the Federal Supreme Court (Bundesgerichtshof, BGH) are regarded as persuasive and will in practice be followed, as otherwise, the decision of the lower court is likely to be reversed on appeal. Even so, courts may be willing to depart from a previous line of authority if it seems to be out of date and, in the absence of a doctrine of *stare decisis*, they are free to do so.

§4. The Courts Administering Family and Succession Law

20. With respect to the often sensitive nature of the issues in question and the important role that courts play in the area of family law, Germany – like many other countries – has entrusted family law matters to a special division of the civil courts. Thus, in 1976,[15] the 'family law courts' were introduced as a division of the local courts (*Amtsgerichte*).[16] The judge sits alone.

21. Appeals go to the Higher Regional Courts (*Oberlandesgerichte*). Here also, special senates have been established for family law matters (*Familiensenate*).[17] The next level of appeal – on points of law only – is the Federal Supreme Court, which has its seat in Karlsruhe (Baden-Württemberg).

22. The Act on Proceedings in Family Matters and in Matters of Non-contentious Jurisdiction (FamFG) of 17 December 2008[18] (in force since 1 September 2009) revolutionized family court procedure. It substantially extended the jurisdiction of the family courts. The law sets out a comprehensive list of 'family matters',[19] covering the legal relations of cohabiting, separated and divorced spouses, registered partners, as well as parents and children. The family courts are now also competent to decide ordinary civil law disputes between spouses where these are linked to separation or marriage dissolution.[20]

23. The Act on Proceedings in Family Matters and in Matters of Non-contentious Jurisdiction (FamFG) abolished the old guardianship courts. The family courts are now in charge of matters relating to the guardianship of minors. Special courts of protection (*Betreuungsgerichte*) were established for adults in need of protection.[21]

24. The most common instance in which courts are concerned with inheritance law is when an heir applies for a German or European certificate of inheritance. In both cases, the application is submitted to the probate court, which is a division of the local court. International and local jurisdiction lies with the court of last domicile of the deceased within the district. Any sufficiently interested party may file a complaint against the decision of this court with the Higher Regional Court.[22] Provided the Higher Regional Court grants leave, a further complaint on points of law

15. First Reform Act on Marriage and the Family (*Erstes Gesetz zur Reform des Ehe- und Familienrechts*, 1. EheRG) of 14 Jun. 1976 (BGBl. I 1421).
16. § 23b I Judicature Act (*Gerichtsverfassungsgesetz*, GVG).
17. § 119 II GVG.
18. *Gesetz über das Verfahren in Familiensachen und in Angelegenheiten der freiwilligen Gerichtsbarkeit* (FamFG) of 17 Dec. 2008 (BGBl. I 2586).
19. § 111 FamFG.
20. § 266 I No. 3 FamFG.
21. § 23a II No. 1, § 23c GVG.
22. §§ 58 et seq. FamFG.

may be filed with the Federal Supreme Court.[23] Inheritance law can also be the subject of litigation in ordinary civil proceedings. Claims for sums not exceeding EUR 5,000 are filed with the local court; claims for larger sums are filed with the regional court. On appeal, the case goes from the local court to the regional court and from the regional court to the Higher Regional Court. For a final appeal to the Federal Supreme Court, the claimant must obtain leave by the Court of First Appeal. If that court denies leave and the sum involved exceeds EUR 20,000, the claimant can submit a complaint against denial of appeal to the Federal Supreme Court, which may then grant leave to appeal.

25. The highest court in the country is the Federal Constitutional Court (*Bundesverfassungsgericht*, BVerfG), situated in Karlsruhe (Baden-Württemberg). It interprets the Basic Law in relation to individual rights, to disputes between states and the federation and in relation to legislation, and it may act, e.g., on reference by courts, on action by government institutions and legislatures or on constitutional complaint by private citizens. It has ruled extensively on questions of family law and has initiated law reform in many areas to ensure compatibility with the parameters of the Basic Law (e.g., with regard to legislation pertaining to joint parental responsibility for divorcees).

23. §§ 70 et seq. FamFG.

Part I. Persons

Chapter 1. The Status of a Person

§1. Definition of a Person

26. German law distinguishes between 'natural' and 'legal' persons. Every human being is a natural person. Legal persons are certain associations of persons and other organizations, to which the law ascribes personal qualities in the legal sense.

27. Every human being enjoys legal capacity (*Rechtsfähigkeit*), i.e., may be the subject of rights and responsibilities. Legal capacity also includes the ability to be a party in legal proceedings.[24] Legal capacity begins with the completion of birth,[25] i.e., foetal expulsion from the mother's body. In principle, all natural persons enjoy the same legal capacity: every human being may attain and exercise the same kinds of rights. This is true irrespective of sex, as the Basic Law guarantees men and women equal rights in all areas of law.[26]

28. The unborn child (*nasciturus*) does not enjoy legal capacity under German law. Still, the Constitution protects the human dignity and right to life of the unborn child.[27] This protection of the *nasciturus* is mainly effected by criminal-law provisions.[28] Under the civil law, however, the unborn child cannot be the bearer of rights or the subject of duties.

29. Some provisions of the Civil Code, however, do protect the interests of the unborn child if subsequently born alive: § 1923 II BGB rules that a person not yet born, but conceived, at the time of an inheritance, is deemed to have been born before the inheritance, i.e., may be an heir. The provision will only apply, however, if the child is born alive. To protect the future rights of the unborn child, a curator may be appointed.[29]

24. § 50 I ZPO.
25. § 1 BGB.
26. Article 3 II, III GG.
27. BVerfGE 88, 203.
28. Cf. §§ 218 et seq. of the German Penal Code (*Strafgesetzbuch*, StGB).
29. § 1912 BGB.

30. The legal capacity of a natural person ends with the person's death. Where the whereabouts of a person have been unknown for a long time without any information on whether he or she is dead or alive, such a missing person may be *declared dead* under certain circumstances.[30] The official declaration of death leads to a rebuttable presumption that the missing person has actually died at the time stated in the declaration. Although a person may not be the subject of rights and duties after his or her death, certain personal rights continue even after death and may be asserted before a court by a trustee named by the deceased before his or her death or by his or her relatives.[31]

31. German law recognizes the following legal persons:

(1) The *association with legal capacity* (*rechtsfähiger Verein*). An association is a collection of persons, the existence of which is not affected by a change in membership. An association whose object is not directed at economic activity acquires legal personality by being entered in the register of associations of the competent local court.[32]
(2) The *foundation with legal capacity* (*rechtsfähige Stiftung*). Under German law, this is an organization where the property assigned to the foundation is directed at a certain purpose, e.g., in the social sphere. The foundation gains legal capacity through recognition by the state.[33]
(3) The *Public Limited Company* (*Aktiengesellschaft*, AG).[34]
(4) The *Limited Liability Company* (*Gesellschaft mit beschränkter Haftung*, GmbH).[35]
(5) The *Registered Trade and Industrial Cooperatives* (*eingetragene Erwerbs- und Wirtschaftsgenossenschaft*).[36]

32. Furthermore, German law knows associations of persons with *partial* legal capacity, e.g., the *General Partnership* (*Offene Handelsgesellschaft*, OHG). Under its name, the General Partnership may acquire rights, enter into obligations, acquire property and property rights, sue and be sued. The partners are liable not only with the company property but also personally.[37] Partial legal capacity is also a characteristic of the *Limited Partnership* (*Kommanditgesellschaft*, KG).[38] Court rulings have also accorded (partial) legal capacity to civil law *partnerships* (*Gesellschaft bürgerlichen Rechts*).[39]

---

30. Missing Persons Act (*Verschollenheitsgesetz*, VerschG) of 15 Jan. 1951 (BGBl. I 63).
31. Cf. BGHZ 50, 133; BGHZ 107, 384; BVerfG NJW 2001, 2957.
32. § 21 BGB.
33. § 80 BGB.
34. Stock Corporation Act (*Aktiengesetz*, AktG) of 6 Sep. 1965 (BGBl. I 1089).
35. Limited Liability Company Act (*GmbH-Gesetz*, GmbHG) of 20 Apr. 1892 (RGBl. 477).
36. Co-operative Societies Act (*Genossenschaftsgesetz*, GenG) of 1 May 1889 (RGBl. 55).
37. § 128 Commercial Code (*Handelsgesetzbuch*, HGB).
38. §§ 161 et seq. HGB.
39. §§ 705 et seq. BGB, *see* BGHZ 146, 341; 151, 204; 189, 274.

§2. CAPACITY

I. General

33. Under German law, the ability to bring about legal effects through declarations (e.g., to enter into a contract) is termed 'capacity to enter into legal transactions' (*Geschäftsfähigkeit*). In principle, every human being is legally competent. Exceptions are made where: (1) a person has not yet reached 18 and (2) where a person suffers from a pathological mental disturbance preventing the free exercise of his or her will unless this condition is temporary in nature.[40]

II. Minors

34. Minors, i.e., persons who have not yet reached the age of 18, are either incompetent or partially competent to enter into legal transactions.

Children are *incompetent to enter into legal transactions* if they are under the age of 7.[41] Any declaration of will made by a legally incompetent person is void.[42] A declaration of will made to a person who is legally incompetent is not effective until it reaches his or her legal representative.[43]

Minors have *limited capacity to enter into legal transactions* if they have completed their seventh year, but not yet their eighteenth.[44] As a rule, a person with limited legal capacity may make declarations of will. The validity of the transaction will depend on the assent (prior consent, *Einwilligung*) or approval (later consent, *Genehmigung*) of his or her legal representative.[45] Such consent is not necessary, however, if the declaration is wholly advantageous for the minor.

35. Minors in principle have a *legal representative*. As a rule, this will be the parents, to the extent that they have parental responsibility. In other cases, a curator or guardian will act as legal representative.[46]

III. Adults

36. A person is legally incompetent if he or she suffers from a pathological mental disturbance preventing the free exercise of his or her will, unless this condition is temporary in nature.[47] Whether such a condition exists has to be determined in each case, e.g., when trying to assess the validity of a contract. Legal incompetence may exist only in relation to certain transactions (partial incompetence). Incapacity

40. § 104 BGB.
41. § 104 No. 1 BGB.
42. § 105 BGB.
43. § 131 I BGB.
44. If they are not legally incompetent under § 104 No. 1 BGB.
45. §§ 107–113 BGB.
46. § 1629 BGB.
47. § 104 No. 2 BGB.

to enter into legal transactions has to be proved by the person claiming it. As of 1992, it has not been possible to place someone under guardianship, i.e., to declare him or her to be legally incompetent for all purposes by way of court order.

Generally, a declaration of will made by a legally incompetent person is void. If such a person enters into a contract, the contract as a whole will be deemed void. But incompetent persons may enter into valid legal transactions provided they are of age and enter into a routine daily transaction that can be discharged with limited means. Such a contract will be deemed valid once the contractual obligations have been performed, e.g., once the item bought has been delivered and paid for.[48]

37. Conditions that are only temporary in nature do not lead to legal incapacity; the same is true for states of unconsciousness, although a declaration of will made in such a condition is void.[49]

38. If it is necessary to appoint a protector for a person (*see infra* paragraphs 260 et seq.), the protector represents the person under his or her care in judicial and non-judicial matters.[50] This does not limit the general legal capacity of the person under care. In order to avert substantial jeopardy to the person under care, the court may order that the prior consent of the protector shall be necessary (reservation of consent).[51] In that case, the person under care may, in specified categories of matters, only act with the consent of the protector.[52]

IV. Consent to Medical Treatment

39. Different rules apply where a person's consent to undergo medical treatment is concerned. German courts assume that legal capacity is not the decisive factor here. Instead, a person may validly consent to medical treatment if he or she has natural understanding, i.e., is able to understand the importance and the consequences of the treatment. Depending on the medical procedure in question, this might be assumed for minors as young as 14 or 16 years. However, the person having parental responsibility for the minor usually has to consent as well. Likewise, a person under care might have the necessary understanding to consent to medical treatment. The question is not regulated by statute. Accordingly, it is unclear whether, e.g., an underage woman might consent to the termination of her pregnancy without the consent of her parents.

48. § 105a BGB as modified by Act of 23 Jul. 2002 (BGBl. I 2850).
49. § 105 II BGB.
50. § 1902 BGB.
51. § 1903 BGB.
52. § 1903; §§ 108 et seq., 131 II BGB.

V. Responsibility for Tortious Acts under Civil Law

40. According to the German law of torts, a person who has not yet completed his or her 7th year is not responsible for any damage caused.[53] Where a minor causes damage to another in an accident involving certain modern means of transport (e.g., cars), the minor is not liable if he or she is under the age of 10 (except in cases of deliberate damage).[54] Other than that, a minor is only responsible for any damage caused if at the time of committing the damaging act, he or she had sufficient understanding.[55]

41. A person who was unconscious or suffered from a mental disturbance that prevented the free exercise of will is not responsible for any damage caused. This is different if he or she brought the condition upon himself or herself by alcoholic drinks or similar means.[56] A person who is not responsible under the above provisions may, however, have to pay compensation if equity so requires.[57]

VI. Criminal Responsibility

42. A child does not become criminally responsible until the age of 14.[58] A juvenile between the ages of 14 and 18 is criminally responsible if at the time of committing the criminal act he or she had sufficient mental and moral maturity to understand that the act was wrong and to act accordingly.[59] Juveniles and adults between the ages of 18 and 21 are tried before a special court (juvenile court) and according to special procedural rules.

§3. Absentees

43. An absent person of full age whose whereabouts are unknown has a curator (*Abwesenheitspfleger*) appointed for his or her property affairs as far as those need care.[60] The same applies to an absent person whose whereabouts are known, but who is prevented from returning and taking care of his or her property.[61] A missing person may under certain circumstances be declared legally dead.[62]

---

53. § 828 I BGB.
54. § 828 II BGB.
55. § 828 III BGB.
56. § 827 BGB.
57. § 829 BGB.
58. § 19 StGB.
59. § 3 Juvenile Courts Act (*Jugendgerichtsgesetz*, JGG).
60. § 1911 I BGB.
61. § 1911 II BGB.
62. *See* Missing Persons Act (*Verschollenheitsgesetz*, VerschG) of 15 Jan. 1951.

Chapter 2. Registration of Civil Status

§1. The Registrar

44. The register office records the civil status of a person and is responsible for the register of civil status.[63] These tasks are entrusted to the local authorities.[64] There are many register office districts (*Standesamtsbezirke*) across the country. Every municipality belongs to a certain register office district.

§2. Registers and Certificates

45. The registrar is responsible for keeping the following registers:

- The marriage register, in which all wedding ceremonies (as well as subsequent changes through death, divorce, etc.) are recorded.
- The *Lebenspartnerschaftsregister*, in which the establishment of registered partnerships between persons of the same sex is recorded.
- The birth register, in which the name and sex of a child, the day, hour, and place of his or her birth, and the name of his or her parents are recorded.
- The death register, which records all deaths.

On the basis of the civil status registers, the registrar issues certain documents, such as birth, marriage, and death certificates.

The civil status registers provide evidence of wedding ceremonies, births, and deaths, and further details recorded in this context, but they do not prove citizenship.[65] The evidence provided by the civil status registers may be rebutted.

63. § 1 I, II Act on Civil Status (*Personenstandsgesetz*, PStG).
64. § 1 II PStG.
65. § 54 I 2; § 15 II No. 2 PStG.

Chapter 3. Personality Rights

46. *See supra* paragraphs 26 et seq. and *infra* paragraph 48.

Chapter 4. Names

§1. Composition of a Name (First Name, Surname, Individual Name, Title of Nobility)

47. German law protects the name of a person as a part of his or her identity. Whoever legitimately bears a name may take action against others using it illegitimately or against someone who disputes his or her right to bear that name. If there is a risk of further infringement, the person concerned may seek an injunction.[66] A person injured in his or her right of name may claim compensation for the harm from the person responsible.[67]

48. Names in the above sense are mainly the first name and the surname. It should be noted that in Germany, titles of nobility are considered a part of the surname (e.g., Prinz von Adlersberg).[68] Pseudonyms, *noms de plume*, and stage names are protected as well along with coats of arms and seals that stand for a person's identity. Also protected are the names of legal entities and other associations, the business name of a merchant, and the abbreviations that have come to characterize a certain business (like BMW).

§2. Surname

I. Acquisition of the Surname

49. The surname is either the 'birth name' or the name acquired upon marriage. A child acquires his or her surname upon his or her birth either by act of law or because his or her parents or other persons having parental responsibility choose it. Because the right to name a child depends on the question of parental responsibility, the rather complicated rules governing the child's name are dealt with in Part II (Family Law), *see infra* paragraphs 173 et seq. A person's surname may change during his or her lifetime, e.g., because of marriage (*see infra* paragraphs 101 et seq.), divorce (*see infra* paragraphs 104 et seq.), or adoption (*see infra* paragraph 184).

II. Change of Surname

50. In addition to the rules under civil law, it is possible to change one's surname by an official procedure. However, a surname may only be changed in exceptional circumstances,[69] e.g., because the name causes ridicule.

---

66. § 12 BGB.
67. § 823 I BGB.
68. This finds its source in Art. 109 III 2 of the Weimar Constitution of 11 Aug. 1919 (RGBl. I 1383).
69. § 3 Act on the Change of Names (*Namensänderungsgesetz*, NamÄndG).

§3. First Name

51. A child's first name is chosen either by his or her parents or by other persons having parental responsibility (*see infra* paragraphs 189 et seq.). A child can have more than one first name. In this case, the order of the first names may later be changed by declaration before the registrar.[70] The registrar may refuse to record an unusual first name, but his or her decision may be appealed.[71] Like the surname, the first name can be changed by an official procedure.[72]

70. § 45a PStG.
71. § 49 I PStG.
72. § 11 NamÄndG.

Chapter 5. Nationality

52. German citizenship is acquired by birth or naturalization. A child acquires German citizenship by birth if one parent is a German citizen. Where only the father is a German citizen, it may be necessary to establish his paternity.[73]

If both parents are foreign nationals and the child is born in Germany, he or she is granted German citizenship if one parent has had his or her lawful residence in Germany for a minimum of eight years and is either an EU citizen or lawful EU resident with indefinite leave to remain.[74]

53. Furthermore, a child acquires German citizenship if the child is formally and lawfully adopted by a German national according to German law.[75] The child must be under 18 years at the time of formally lodging the adoption application.

The possibility to acquire German citizenship by naturalization[76] has been reformed.[77] Easier terms apply to spouses and registered partners of German nationals.[78]

73. § 4 I 2 Citizenship Act (*Staatsangehörigkeitsgesetz*, StAG).
74. § 4 III 1 StAG.
75. § 6 StAG.
76. Cf. §§ 8–16 StAG.
77. Cf. the *Gesetz zur Reform des Staatsangehörigkeitsrechts* of 15 Jul. 1999 (BGBl. I 1618); *Zuwanderungsgesetz* of 30 Jul. 2004 (BGBl. I 1950).
78. Cf. § 9 StAG.

Chapter 6. Domicile and Residence

54. German law knows both domicile or permanent residence (*Wohnsitz*) and habitual residence (*gewöhnlicher Aufenthalt*). A person who creates a permanent residence in a particular place establishes his or her *domicile* there.[79] A person's domicile is the place (the municipality) where he or she is established permanently. A subjective element is also necessary: the person must be willing to establish the centre of his or her life there (intent to reside permanently). A short stay will not create a permanent residence. The residence ends if it is abandoned with the intention of discontinuing it.[80] Domicile may exist simultaneously in several places.[81]

55. A person who is legally incompetent or who has limited capacity to enter into legal transactions may neither establish nor abandon a residence without the consent of his or her legal representative.[82] By act of law, a minor child shares the residence of his or her parents if they have parental responsibility. If neither parent has parental responsibility, the child shares the residence of whoever has parental responsibility.[83]

56. The term 'habitual residence' has a similar meaning. It means the factual centre of life,[84] and it is established by a long actual stay at a particular place.[85] Unlike with a permanent residence or domicile, it is not necessary for the habitual resident to act with the intention of establishing his or her centre of life somewhere. The habitual residence of a child thus does not automatically follow that of his or her parents.[86]

57. Whether a certain question hinges on the domicile or habitual residence of a person depends on the relevant legal provision. Habitual residence is of special importance, e.g., in the area of private international law.[87]

79. § 7 I BGB.
80. § 7 III BGB.
81. § 7 II BGB.
82. § 8 BGB.
83. § 11 BGB.
84. BGH FamRZ 1981, 135, 136.
85. BGH NJW 1983, 2771.
86. BGH FamRZ 1981, 135, 136.
87. Cf. Art. 14 II No. 1 EGBGB.

Chapter 7. Persons with Intellectual Disabilities

58. *See supra* paragraphs 36 et seq. and *infra* paragraphs 242 et seq.

Part II. Family Law

Chapter 1. Introductory Remarks

§1. The Development of Legislation in the Area of Family Law

59. German family law has undergone manifold changes since it was codified in the Civil Code of 18 August 1896. The main changes were brought about by the following legislation:

- The *Marriage Act*,[88] issued under the Hitler Regime, changed the entire system of rules relating to the marriage ceremony and divorce. In part, the Act was influenced by national-socialist ideology.
- The *Control Council Act* No. 16.[89] The Act issued by the Allied Control Council re-implemented the Marriage Act of 1938 after it had been cleared of national-socialist influences.
- The *Sex Discrimination Act*[90] aimed at restructuring family law according to the principle of gender equality, but in part retained a traditional understanding of gender roles within marriage (e.g., the legislation was modelled on the assumption that the female role within marriage would be that of housewife).
- The *Family Code*,[91] enacted by the GDR, separated family law from the general civil law in a way similar to other Eastern European countries and reshaped it to conform with socialist ideology.
- The *First Reform Act on Marriage and the Family*[92] established the family courts (*Familiengerichte*) as a special branch of the local courts.
- The *Parental Responsibility Reform Act*[93] put the legal relationship between parents and children on a new basis, strengthening children's rights. The distinction between children born in and out of wedlock was retained.
- The *Treaty on German Reunification*[94] introduced West German family law to the territory of the ex-GDR.

---

88. *Ehegesetz* (EheG) of 6 Jul. 1938 (RGBl. I 807).
89. *Kontrollratsgesetz No. 16* of 20 Feb. 1946.
90. *Gleichberechtigungsgesetz* (GleichberG) of 18 Jun. 1957 (BGBl. I 609).
91. *Familiengesetzbuch* (FGB) of 20 Dec. 1965 (Gbl. 1966 I No. 1 p. 1).
92. *Erstes Gesetz zur Reform des Ehe- und Familienrechts* (1. EheRG) of 14 Jun. 1976 (BGBl. I 1421).
93. *Gesetz zur Neuregelung des Rechts der elterlichen Sorge* (SorgeRG) of 18 Jul. 1979 (BGBl. I 1061).
94. *Einigungsvertrag zwischen der Bundesrepublik Deutschland und der Deutschen Demokratischen Republik* (EinigV), in force since 3 Oct. 1990 (BGBl. II 889).

- The *Care and Control Act*[95] abolished guardianship over adults. Instead, it introduced care and control (*Betreuung*) as a new legal framework to provide assistance for persons suffering from physical or mental disabilities.
- The *Child Law Reform Act*[96] aimed at doing away with different regimes for children born in and out of wedlock. Major adjustments were also made to parental responsibility, especially with regard to responsibility after divorce or separation.
- The *Child Support Act*[97] reformed the procedures for a child's support claim against his or her parents.
- The *Formation of Marriage Act*[98] completely revamped the law relating to the formation of marriage. At the same time, the Marriage Act of 1938 was repealed. Since then, all of the substantive rules governing family law have once again been reintegrated into the BGB (4th book: family law).
- The *Protection against Domestic Violence Act*[99] aims at improving civil law protection against violence and stalking. Spouses who have been attacked or threatened by their partners are given easier access to eviction orders from the family home.
- The *Registered Partnership Act*[100] introduced domestic partnerships for persons of the same sex. Some of the provisions are modelled on the law of marriage. Other provisions are quite different. In 2005, a Reform Act further strengthened the similarities with marriage.[101]
- The *Law Reform Act on Contested Paternity and Rights to Contact*[102] introduced the right of the biological father to contest the legally established paternity of another man. The Act further enlarged the range of persons entitled to contact with a child.
- The *Civil Status Reform Act*[103] introduced the option to keep registers of civil status in electronic form.
- The *Maintenance Reform Act*,[104] which has been in force since 1 January 2008, revamped the law of maintenance obligations as between divorced spouses and unwed parents.

---

95. *Betreuungsgesetz* (BtG) of 12 Sep. 1990 (BGBl. I 2002).
96. *Kindschaftsrechtsreformgesetz* (KindRG) of 16 Feb. 1997 (BGBl. I 2942).
97. *Kindesunterhaltsgesetz* (KindUG) of 6 Apr. 1998 (BGBl. I 666).
98. *Eheschließungsrechtsgesetz* (EheschlRG) of 4 May 1998 (BGBl. I 833).
99. *Gesetz zur Verbesserung des zivilgerichtlichen Schutzes bei Gewalttaten und Nachstellungen sowie zur Erleichterung der Überlassung der Ehewohnung bei Trennung* (*Gewaltschutzgesetz*) of 11 Dec. 2001 (BGBl. I 3513).
100. *Gesetz zur Beendigung der Diskriminierung gleichgeschlechtlicher Gemeinschaften: Lebenspartnerschaften* (*Lebenspartnerschaftsgesetz*, LPartG) of 22 Feb. 2001 (BGBl. I 266), in force since 1 Aug. 2001. *See also* the Act for the Revision of the Law of Registered Domestic Partnerships (*Gesetz zur Überarbeitung des Lebenspartnerschaftsrechts*) of 15 Dec. 2004 (BGBl. I 3396).
101. *Gesetz zur Überarbeitung des Lebenspartnerschaftsrechts* of 15 Dec. 2004 (BGBl. I 3396).
102. *Gesetz zur Änderung der Vorschriften über die Anfechtung der Vaterschaft und das Umgangsrecht von Bezugspersonen des Kindes* of 23 Apr. 2004 (BGBl. I 598).
103. *Gesetz zur Reform des Personenstandsrechts* (*Personenstandsrechtsreformgesetz*, PStRG) of 29 Feb. 2007 (BGBl. I 122).
104. *Gesetz zur Änderung des Unterhaltsrechts* of 21 Dec. 2007 (BGBl. I 3189).

- The *Law Reform Act on Ascertaining Paternity outside Paternity Contests*[105] introduced a legal procedure to establish a person's paternity without altering that person's civil status.
- The *Law on Facilitating Family Court Child Protection Measures*[106] made it easier for the family courts to take measures against parents and third parties to protect children at risk.
- The *Act on Proceedings in Family Matters and in Matters of Non-contentious Jurisdiction*[107] introduced sweeping changes to family court procedure.
- The *Pension Splitting Reform Act*[108] revolutionized pension splitting on divorce.
- The *Law Reform Act on Property Division on Divorce and Guardianship*[109] changed important aspects of the default marital property regime, the community of accrued gains.
- The *Reform Act on Parental Responsibility of Unmarried Parents*[110] makes it easier for unmarried parents to share parental responsibility for their children.
- The *Act to Improve the Rights of Biological, Non-Legal Fathers*[111] grants biological, but not legally recognized, fathers a right to contact with and information about the child under certain circumstances.
- The *Child Marriage Prevention Act*[112] outlawed marriage under the age of 18.
- The *Act to Regulate the Right to Know One's Genetic Heritage*[113] established a central donor register, which aims to provide children of sperm donors with information about their biological fathers.
- The *Same-Sex Marriage Act*[114] legalized same-sex marriage.
- The *Act on Stepchild Adoption in Non-Marital Families*[115] allows unmarried but committed partners to adopt each other's children, provided the partners share a common household.

---

105. *Gesetz zur Klärung der Vaterschaft unabhängig vom Anfechtungsverfahren* of 26 Mar. 2008 (BGBl. I 441).
106. *Gesetz zur Erleichterung familiengerichtlicher Maßnahmen bei Gefährdung des Kindeswohls* of 4 Jul. 2008 (BGBl. I 1188).
107. *Gesetz über das Verfahren in Familiensachen und in den Angelegenheiten der freiwilligen Gerichtsbarkeit* (FamFG) as part of *Gesetz zur Reform des Verfahrens in Familiensachen und in den Angelegenheiten der freiwilligen Gerichtsbarkeit* (*FGG-Reformgesetz*) of 17 Dec. 2008 (BGBl. I 2586).
108. *Gesetz zur Strukturreform des Versorgungsausgleichs* (VAStrRefG) of 3 Apr. 2009 (BGBl. I 700).
109. *Gesetz zur Änderung des Zugewinnausgleichs- und Vormundschaftsrechts* of 6 Jul. 2009 (BGBl. I 1696).
110. *Gesetz zur Reform der elterlichen Sorge nicht miteinander verheirateter Eltern* of 19 Apr. 2013 (BGBl. I 795).
111. *Gesetz zur Stärkung der Rechte des leiblichen, nicht rechtlichen Vaters* of 4 Jul. 2013 (BGBl. I 2176).
112. *Gesetz zur Bekämpfung von Kinderehen* of 17 Jul. 2017 (BGBl. I 2429).
113. *Gesetz zur Regelung des Rechts auf Kenntnis der Abstammung bei heterologer Verwendung von Samen* of 17 Jul. 2017 (BGBl. I 2513).
114. *Gesetz zur Einführung des Rechts auf Eheschließung für Personen gleichen Geschlechts* of 20 Jul. 2017 (BGBl. I 2787).
115. *Gesetz zur Umsetzung der Entscheidung des Bundesverfassungsgerichts vom 26. März 2019 zum Ausschluss der Stiefkindadoption in nichtehelichen Familien* of 19 Mar. 2020 (BGBl. I 541).

§2. Family Law and the German Constitution (Basic Law)

60. The German Basic Law[116] provides a framework against which all rules relating to family law in Germany have to be judged. The most important provisions are found in Articles 6 and 3 of the Basic Law:

- Marriage and the family enjoy the special protection of the state.[117]
- Men and women enjoy equal rights;[118] therefore, nobody may be discriminated against – or favoured – on the grounds of sex.[119] As interpreted by the Federal Constitutional Court, this principle of equal rights is applicable within marriage and the family[120] and is crucial in defining the legal structure of these institutions: it means that for legal purposes, the spouses are regarded as equals in marriage. This pertains to every aspect of married life, including the upbringing of children, the choice of married name, and the division of work between the spouses. For example, gainful employment and care for the family will be deemed equal by the courts.

It also means that the opinion of neither spouse takes automatic precedence; both spouses enjoy the same rights. As a result, any legislation conferring a casting vote on, e.g., the husband in case of dispute (as was the case where the married couple could not agree on a family name) will be deemed to violate Articles 3 II, 6 I GG. The principle of equality also applies to other family relationships, e.g., to the relationship between sons and daughters.

61. Article 6 GG also includes the following provisions:

- Caring for and bringing up their children are the parents' natural right and a duty primarily incumbent upon them.[121] It is the community's responsibility to ensure that they perform this duty.[122] Parental rights and duties are further specified in Article 6 III GG: children may not be separated from their families against the will of their parents or guardians, save in accordance with law in cases where the latter fail in their duty or there is danger of the children being seriously neglected for other reasons.
- Every mother is entitled to the protection and care of the community.[123]
- Finally, Article 6 V GG also makes it the state's duty to ensure that children born outside marriage are provided by law with the same opportunities for their physical and mental development and for their place in society as are enjoyed by those born within marriage.[124]

---

116. *Grundgesetz* (GG) of 23 May 1949 (BGBl. I 1).
117. Article 6 I GG.
118. Article 3 II GG.
119. Article 3 III GG.
120. BVerfGE 3, 225.
121. Article 6 II GG.
122. Article 6 II 2 GG.
123. Article 6 IV GG.
124. Article 6 V GG.

62. The Federal Constitutional Court has further clarified the threefold function of these constitutional guarantees:[125]

- First, Article 6 GG grants *individual rights* to married persons, parents, mothers, and illegitimate children in the mode of classic civil liberties, thus shielding the private sphere from undue interference by the state.
- Second, Article 6 GG contains a guarantee of marriage and the family *as institutions* (*Institutsgarantie*). In this capacity, according to the BVerfG, it protects only the essential features of marriage and the family, and sets out the standard with which family law has to comply (e.g., the principles of monogamy and freedom of marriage).
- But according to the BVerfG, the function fulfilled by Article 6 GG goes even further. Article 6 GG also constitutes a fundamental norm, i.e., an imperative value to be observed in the entire area of private and public law as regards marriage and the family. The implications are twofold. On the one hand, it means that the state is prohibited from harming or impairing the institutions of marriage and the family. On the other hand, the state is under a positive obligation to support both institutions by appropriate means and actively to protect them from impairment by other forces. The BVerfG emphasizes, however, that this duty to support and protect does not give any specific claims to individuals, e.g., to be reimbursed for all financial burdens incurred by having a family.[126]

63. Changing patterns of life have opened traditional definitions of terms like 'marriage' and 'family' for discussion. According to earlier Constitutional Court decisions, the term 'marriage' referred exclusively to the registered union between one man and one woman, lasting, in principle, for life.[127] However, more recently, this traditional understanding of marriage has come under challenge, and in a 2016 decision, the Constitutional Court defined marriage as a legally recognized relationship entailing mutual duties of care and responsibility, but did not specifically reference a difference in sex.[128] 'Family' refers to the community between parents (or one parent) and his or her child or children, embracing illegitimate children, adopted children, and stepchildren. The relationship between the biological, non-legal father and his child constitutes a 'family' if a de facto social-familial relationship (*sozial-familiäre Beziehung*) exists between them.[129] In recent cases, the courts have also held that relationships between other relatives, like those between grandparents and grandchildren, may be covered by the term 'family' if close familial ties exist.[130]

---

125. Cf. BVerfGE 6, 55, 71; 24, 119, 135.
126. Cf. BVerfGE 28, 104, 113; 107, 205.
127. BVerfGE 53, 224.
128. BVerfG FamRZ 2017, 666.
129. BVerfGE 108, 82, 112.
130. BVerfGE 136, 382 paras 22 et seq.

Chapter 2. Marriage

§1. Engagement

I. Promise of Marriage

64. Under German law, the term 'engagement' has a twofold meaning, describing both the promise of marriage between two people and the legal relationship that is established thereby. The engagement is contracted by a mutual promise supported by the intention to be bound. This promise can be given expressly or by conduct implying such an intent. Historically, German law knew complex actions for breach of promise of marriage. Today, only limited rights attach to an engagement.

65. The exact legal nature of the promise of marriage has long been a subject for discussion in Germany. In any case, however, the Code spells out that an engagement does not give a claim for specific performance of the promise.[131] A judgment to that effect would not be enforceable anyway.[132] Any contractual penalties agreed upon are void.[133]

II. Termination of an Engagement

66. Where an engagement is broken off, the gifts exchanged between the betrothed can be reclaimed according to the rules of unjust enrichment, §§ 1301, 812 et seq. BGB.

Should a fiancé(e) provoke the breach without good reason, he or she is liable for damages, §§ 1298, 1299 BGB. A good reason will be found lacking by the courts if the responsibility for the termination of the engagement lies solely with that party, for example, in case of infidelity or serious misconduct.

Under § 1298 I 1 BGB, the other fiancé(e), his or her parents or any other third party may ask to be reimbursed for expenses incurred in preparing for the wedding, like paying for the wedding reception, the future joint household, etc. The fiancé(e) may also recover damages for any financial or professional arrangements made for the benefit of the forthcoming marriage under § 1298 I 2 BGB. For example, the fiancé(e) may have given notice to an employer or sold assets. Only such expenses or other damages are recoverable, however, as it was appropriate to incur under the circumstances, § 1298 II BGB. Thus, the partner who calls off the marriage will not be liable for ill-considered or disproportionate expenses incurred by the other party.[134]

131. § 1297 BGB.
132. *See* § 120 III FamFG.
133. § 1297 II BGB.
134. Cf. BGH FamRZ 1961, 424.

67. As a result of the *Formation of Marriage Act 1998*, it is no longer possible to claim damages for non-pecuniary losses resulting from the termination of the engagement.

68. Aside from the claims spelled out in §§ 1298 et seq. BGB, German law acknowledges that the engagement creates a special bond between the betrothed. As a result, the engagement has implications for other areas of law: e.g., engaged persons may enter into marriage contracts. As far as contracts of inheritance are concerned, they are treated like spouses. Also, there are special civil and criminal procedure rules for engaged couples.[135]

§2. Capacity to Marry

I. Competence to Enter into Legal Transactions (*Geschäftsfähigkeit*)

69. Under the doctrine of freedom of marriage,[136] restrictions relating to the capacity to marry have to be based on compelling reasons. As far as declarations upon celebration of the marriage are concerned, the general rules on competence to enter into legal transactions (§§ 104 et seq. BGB) have, therefore, been modified.

70. A person who is incompetent to enter into legal transactions (§ 104 BGB) may not marry, § 1304 BGB. The wording of § 1304 BGB is misleading, however, in so far as a marriage entered into – contrary to the provision – will not be void but only voidable, i.e., valid unless annulled with *ex nunc* effect, § 1314 I No. 2 BGB.

It should also be noted that incompetence to enter into legal transactions within the meaning of § 104 BGB may be only partial. It may thus be possible for a person who is legally incompetent in other respects to contract a valid marriage. Annulment proceedings can be initiated by either spouse or, in some instances, the competent administrative authority, § 1316 BGB. The legal representative acts for the incompetent spouse. An annulment is no longer possible, however, if the incompetence has ended and the formerly incompetent spouse has made it known that he or she wants to continue the marriage, § 1315 I 1 No. 2 BGB.

71. The same rules apply to persons who are unconscious or temporarily deranged when making the declaration, § 1314 II No. 1 BGB.

II. Majority

72. As a rule, minors cannot marry. Until 2017, the family court could, on application, grant a dispensation if the applicant had completed his or her 16th year, and the applicant's intended spouse was of full age. However, this dispensing option was removed in 2017 by the Child Marriage Prevention Act.

135. *See* § 383 I No. 1 ZPO; §§ 52 I No. 1 StPO, 11 I No. 1 lit. a StGB.
136. Article 6 I GG.

73. The registrar is required to refuse to participate in a marriage ceremony that would violate § 1303 BGB. If the marriage goes ahead regardless, it is voidable if the minor partner was 16 or 17 years of age at the time of the marriage, § 1314 I No. 1 BGB. Where the minor partner was under the age of 16, the marriage is absolutely void, § 1303 sent. 2 BGB. An annulment cannot be obtained if the minor spouse indicates that he or she wants to continue the marriage on reaching majority or if the annulment would constitute grave and serious hardship for the minor spouse, § 1315 I No. 1 BGB.

III. Failure of Intention

74. The declarations of will made by the partners upon celebration of the marriage may be vitiated by various failures of intention that may lead to the annulment of the marriage. Under the new law,[137] the number of failures giving rise to an annulment has been drastically curtailed. An exhaustive list is set out in § 1314 II BGB. The general rules of §§ 116 et seq. BGB are not applicable to marital declarations.

75. An annulment may only be sought where the declaration is tainted by fraud, intimidation, or mistake. Mistake only constitutes a ground for annulment if the spouse at the time of the marriage ceremony did not know that he or she was getting married at all, § 1314 II No. 2 BGB. This may lead to surprising results: as long as the mistaken spouse knows he or she is taking part in any kind of marriage ceremony, it does not matter, as far as the validity of the marriage is concerned, if he or she did not intend to make a declaration of marriage, or if he or she was mistaken as to the identity of the other spouse. Also, as of 1 July 1998, a mistake as to the personal characteristics of the other spouse no longer constitutes grounds for annulment.

IV. Fraud and Threats

76. Fraud renders a marriage voidable if one spouse was induced to enter the marriage by fraud concerning such conditions as would have kept him or her from entering the marriage had he or she known the real state of affairs and correctly appraised the nature of the marriage. Fraud in this context means the same as fraud within the meaning of § 123 BGB, but the Code expressly exempts deceit concerning financial circumstances, § 1314 II No. 3 Hs. 2 BGB. Also, where the fraud was perpetrated by a third party, it only provides grounds for annulment under § 1314 BGB if the other spouse had positive knowledge of the fraud, § 1314 II No. 3 BGB.

It is important to note that according to the established jurisprudence of the courts, concealment of relevant facts may be fraudulent if there was a duty of disclosure.[138] Since mistake as to the character of the other spouse no longer forms a

137. In force since 1 Jul. 1998.
138. BGH FamRZ 1958, 314.

separate ground for annulment, this jurisprudence has increased in importance. Finally, a spouse may petition for an annulment where he or she was induced to enter the marriage by illegal threats, § 1314 II No. 4 BGB.

77. An annulment petition may be filed by the wronged spouse and, in some instances, a state authority or prior marriage partner (in bigamous marriage cases), § 1316 I BGB. The action must be brought within one year from the time when the relevant facts became known to that spouse, § 1317 I BGB (in case of threats within three years). In any case, an annulment is no longer possible if the spouse after the termination of the threat or the discovery of the fraud/mistake has made it known that he or she wants to continue the marriage, § 1315 I BGB.

V. Fictitious Marriages

78. The *Formation of Marriage Act 1998* introduced explicit rules about how to deal with fictitious marriages, i.e., marriages contracted for the sole purpose of achieving secondary benefits (financial, residential, etc.).[139] According to § 1314 II No. 5 BGB, a marriage is voidable where the partners agreed never to live in conjugal community with each other. The registrar is supposed to refuse to participate in the marriage ceremony where such an intent is obvious to him or her. Where necessary, the registrar may interview the partners and ask for further evidence, § 13 II PStG. Should he or she be in any doubt, he or she may apply to the court[140] for a decision.[141]

79. A marriage voidable on the grounds of § 1314 II No. 5 BGB can be annulled by a court order. The order will be effective *ex nunc* only. Applications for such an annulment order may be made by the spouses themselves or by the relevant administrative authority, § 1316 I No. 1 BGB. No order can be made, however, if the spouses – even if contrary to their original intention – have actually lived together in conjugal community, § 1315 I 1 No. 5 BGB, even if they did so only for a short period of time.

VI. Impediments to Marriage

80. In the light of Article 6 GG and the principle of freedom of marriage, legal impediments to marriage require special justification. Accordingly, only the last remnants of a once-extensive system of marital impediments remain. The Code distinguishes between impediments that lead to the marriage's voidability (with *ex nunc* effect only) and impediments that do not affect the validity of the marriage:

---

139. For example, under §§ 27 et seq. AufenthG.
140. *Amtsgericht* (local court).
141. § 49 II PStG.

(1) § 1306 BGB provides that no marriage may be contracted as long as one partner is still married to a third party, even if this other marriage is voidable. This is only different in cases where a divorce has already been pronounced, but has not yet become absolute.
With the exception of this one case, any second marriage contracted contrary to § 1306 BGB will be voidable, except where there was a false declaration of death. In such a case, the new marriage may only be annulled if both partners to it knew the supposedly dead spouse to be still alive, § 1319 BGB.
An impediment to marriage also exists where one of the parties has previously entered into a registered domestic partnership. When registered domestic partnerships were introduced in 2001, this impediment was not provided for. Thus, it would have been possible for someone living in a registered partnership subsequently to enter into a marriage. The legislature has now rectified this unhappy situation.[142]
(2) Consanguinity constitutes an impediment insofar as it prevents the marriage between persons related in the direct line and between siblings, § 1307 BGB. Thus, today, an uncle and his niece or two first cousins are free to marry. Violation of § 1307 BGB will result in the marriage being voidable, i.e., valid unless annulled.
(3) Affinity no longer forms an impediment to marriage. Since the *Formation of Marriage Act 1998*, even the marriage between a step-parent and a stepchild will thus be valid, § 1590 I BGB.
(4) The same rules apply to adoptive kinship as long as the adoption order is in place, § 1308 BGB, with one exception: although the registrar is supposed to refuse to solemnize the marriage, the marriage will be valid if it is in fact concluded in violation of § 1308 BGB.

VII. Annulment

81. Annulment of a marriage is by court order, § 1313 I BGB and effective for the future only (*ex nunc*). Jurisdiction lies with the family court, and the procedure is initiated on the application of the relevant party or local authority, § 1316 BGB. An annulment will only be granted on the grounds described *supra*, §§ 1313 sent. 3, 1314 I, II BGB. The annulment becomes effective when the court order can no longer be appealed.

82. Like divorce, the annulment of a marriage may lead to claims for maintenance, equalization of accrued gains, and pension splitting, § 1318 BGB. These claims follow special rules, however:

– Maintenance may be claimed by the injured party in a number of circumstances set out in the Code, e.g., in case of fraud or intimidation, § 1318 II No. 1 BGB, or where there were grounds for annulment according to §§ 1306, 1307 or 1311

142. *See* the Act for the Revision of the Law of Registered Domestic Partnerships (*Gesetz zur Überarbeitung des Lebenspartnerschaftsrechts*) of 15 Dec. 2004; BVerfGE 105, 313, 342.

BGB and both partners knew this. Even in the absence of such knowledge, maintenance claims may be brought where children of both parties are being looked after, § 1318 II 2 BGB.

- Equalization of accrued gains and pension splitting may not be claimed where such claims would seem grossly inequitable, § 1318 III BGB.
- Allocation of the family home and of household effects follows the same rules as on divorce, § 1318 IV, § 1568a, § 1568b BGB.[143]
- As far as any children of the annulled marriage are concerned, parental responsibility, contact, etc., will follow the rules for separation and divorce. As in the case of divorce or separation, no automatic change in parental responsibility is effected by the annulment of the marriage.
- In inheritance law, the decree of nullity is allowed a certain retroactive effect. Under §§ 1318 V, 1931 BGB, a spouse may be excluded from the right to intestate succession if the marriage was annulled for violations of §§ 1304, 1306, 1307, 1311 or § 1314 II No. 1 BGB as described *supra* and if he or she was aware of the marriage's voidability.

§3. Marriage Formalities

I. General

83. Freedom of marriage is a right guaranteed by the German Constitution.[144] Nevertheless, the Constitution entitles the legislature to lay down certain rules and formal requirements for solemnization. Since the *Formation of Marriage Act 1998*, these rules can once again be found in the BGB, the previous *Marriage Act*[145] having been repealed.

84. The celebration of marriage in Germany is a civil ceremony conducted before the registrar. No other marriage ceremony (e.g., a religious one) has any legal effect. The Code lays down further requirements relating, e.g., to the parties' capacity and marriage formalities. Where these requirements are not adhered to, the marriage will be either non-existent (*Nichtehe*), meaning that no valid marriage ever existed and no annulment proceedings need to be instituted, or *voidable* (*aufhebbare Ehe*), meaning that the marriage is valid unless dissolved. It is important to note, however, that such dissolutions have *ex nunc* effect only since German law, as it stands today, does not allow retroactive dissolutions. The term 'voidable', therefore, is used here to describe a marriage that – although suffering from certain defects at the formation stage – is valid, but may be dissolved with effect for the future.

143. *See infra* paras 132 et seq.
144. Article 6 GG.
145. *Ehegesetz* (EheG), first introduced in 1938.

II. The Marriage Ceremony

85. The celebration of marriage is preceded by a preparatory procedure before the local registrar. The parties must give notice to the registrar of their intent to marry. Such notice must be accompanied by official documents proving the parties' civil status, domicile or residence, and citizenship.[146] The registrar will enquire into any lawful impediments to the proposed marriage and may ask for further relevant proof, e.g., for a decree of divorce or a 'no impediments' certificate in foreign law marriages. Where the registrar is not satisfied that the parties are free to marry, he or she must refuse to participate in the marriage ceremony. The registrar's decision may be appealed.[147] All of the above formal requirements are directory only, meaning that their violation will not hinder the validity of the marriage.

86. The marriage is concluded by the two partners declaring before the registrar that they want to marry each other, §§ 1310 I 1, 1311 BGB. A marriage concluded without the participation of a registrar is non-existent, except where the conditions set out in § 1310 II or III BGB apply, i.e.:

- where a person has acted who, although not a registrar, has publicly exercised the official functions of a registrar and has entered the marriage in the marriage register, § 1310 II BGB; or
- where the declarations were not made before the registrar, but a registrar has entered the marriage in the marriage register and the partners have lived in conjugal community for at least ten years (or five years if one of them has subsequently died), § 1310 III No. 1 BGB. For further similar exceptions cf. § 1310 III Nos 2–3 BGB.

87. The declarations have to be made in person, with both parties present at the same time. They may not be conditional or subject to a stipulation as to time, § 1311 BGB. A violation of § 1311 BGB will lead to the marriage being 'voidable', i.e., dissolvable with *ex nunc* effect, § 1314 I No. 2 BGB. This does not include situations where no declaration is made at all. In this case, the marriage is non-existent. However, purely internal or prior reservations that did not emerge in the declaration do not affect its validity.[148] After the parties have made their declarations, the registrar proclaims that they are now legally united in lawful wedlock. The registrar then records the celebration of the marriage in the marriage register, § 15 PStG.

§4. Effects of Marriage

88. Unlike cohabitation, marriage constitutes a legal status and brings with it an extensive set of rights and duties that mutually bind the spouses. These duties and rights are based on the idea of conjugal community as spelled out in § 1353 I 1

146. § 12 II PStG.
147. § 49 I PStG.
148. But *see supra* paras 74 et seq.

BGB: thus, marriage is for life. This does not preclude divorce, but means that a marriage may not be dissolved at will and that some effects of marriage may well continue after divorce (e.g., there may be a continuing duty of support).

I. Duty of Consortium

89. According to § 1353 I 2 BGB, the spouses are mutually obliged to live in conjugal community – although the legal enforceability of this obligation is limited[149] – and they bear responsibility for each other. Apart from that – and in contrast to, e.g., the maintenance duties, which are quite minutely set out – the Code refrains from any further definition of the 'conjugal community' in which the spouses shall live.

The courts have interpreted conjugal community as a *consortium omnis vitae*, relating to many aspects of the spouses' life, including, where possible, the setting up of a joint home, the duty of marital fidelity and joint responsibility for common tasks such as the household or the raising of children.[150] It further includes permission for the other spouse to make use of household effects, except for those effects destined exclusively for the personal use of one spouse. On moving in together, joint possession of household effects takes place irrespective of legal ownership.[151]

Joint possession will also arise in relation to the matrimonial home, again irrespective of legal ownership or tenancy agreements.[152] The right to joint use and joint possession continues until the spouses separate and one of them moves out or until the family judge accords sole use to one of the spouses.[153]

90. During marriage, the spouses are expected to support[154] and respect each other.[155] This may become legally relevant in a variety of situations, e.g., in determining whether a spouse may follow a chosen career path contrary to the other spouse's wishes. Here, conjugal community has been understood as granting a right to be kept informed by the other spouse.

Under the doctrine of equality,[156] marriage is understood as a partnership of equals. Thus, no spouse's point of view will be given priority in a legal dispute. Courts do not exercise jurisdiction over disputes between spouses other than in limited instances, e.g., in matters relating to parental responsibility. Unlike in the past, today's Code refrains from setting out models for the division of the spouses' respective tasks and leaves this to the partners' discretion.

§ 1356 BGB merely provides that the management of the household is arranged between the spouses by mutual consent.[157] If the management of the household is

149. Cf. § 120 III FamFG.
150. BGH NJW 1960, 141.
151. BGHZ 12, 380.
152. BGHZ 71, 216, 223.
153. BGHZ 71, 216, 223; cf. §§ 1361b, 1568a BGB.
154. Cf. BGHSt 2, 150, BGH NJW 1954, 1818; BGH FamRZ 2010, 269, 270.
155. Cf. BGH NJW 1994, 1726; BGH NJW 2001, 815; BGH FamRZ 2015, 32 para. 16.
156. Article 3 II, III GG.
157. Cf. § 1356 I 1 BGB; BGH FamRZ 1960, 21.

left to one of the spouses, he or she alone is in charge. Such internal agreements are not without legal effect, as they define what is expected of each spouse. This may become important in the context of § 1579 No. 7 BGB when it has to be decided in divorce proceedings whether or not a spouse has severely failed in his or her conjugal duties as agreed upon by the partners.

91. § 1356 II BGB grants both spouses a right to be gainfully employed. In the choice and pursuit of this occupation, each spouse has to give proper consideration to the interests of the other spouse and those of the family. A legal duty to work in the profession or business of the other spouse does not exist, save in exceptional circumstances, e.g., under § 1360 sent. 1 BGB, if such work constitutes the sole means of safeguarding the family income, or under § 1356 II 2 BGB, if it is required as proper consideration.

Where such cooperation has been provided by one spouse, problems may arise as to the remuneration for the work.[158] This will be especially relevant when the couple divorces. The ways found by the courts to deal with the (frequent) lack of express arrangement are varied and complicated, relying, e.g., on ideas drawn from corporate law.[159]

II. Enforcing Marital Duties

92. To what extent the marital duties outlined *supra* should be legally enforceable is a difficult question. Modern law strikes a balance by separating out essentially 'personal' duties, e.g., the duty to cohabit, on the one hand, and 'economic' duties, like the duty to maintain, on the other.

As far as 'personal' duties are concerned, a spouse may bring an action before the family court claiming their violation and asking for their performance. For example, the spouse might demand that the other spouse continue to cohabit or remain faithful.[160] Owing to the personal nature of the claim, however, a court order may only declare the violation of the duty. The duty will not be legally enforceable.[161] The order may still appeal to the other spouse's sense of cooperation, however. Also, it might have indirect consequences in divorce proceedings as proof of the violation of marital duties by the other spouse.[162] The violation of marital duties of a personal nature does not give rise to a damages claim by the injured spouse.[163]

Duties of an 'economic' nature, on the other hand, are enforceable in the courts. These include maintenance claims or duties under § 1353 I 2 BGB, such as the right to joint use of the matrimonial home.[164] Where applicable, claims may also be made

158. Cf. BVerfGE 13, 290; BGH NJW 1995, 3383; BGH FamRZ 1999, 1580; BGH FamRZ 2006, 607; BGH FamRZ 2012, 1789.
159. For example, *Ehegatteninnengesellschaft*, cf. BGH FamRZ 1975, 35; BGH FamRZ 1990, 973 and 1219; BGH FamRZ 1999, 1580; BGH FamRZ 2006, 607.
160. By way of the *Herstellungsklage* (marriage enforcement action).
161. § 120 III FamFG.
162. Cf. §§ 1565 II, 1579 Nos 3–7, 1381 BGB, § 27 VersAusglG.
163. Cf. BGH FamRZ 2013, 939 paras 15 et seq.
164. Cf. BGH FamRZ 1988, 143.

under the general rules of tort law (§§ 823 et seq., 1004 BGB, etc.). Where 'economic' or general duties are violated, it is questionable whether claims for damages, removal, or an injunction can be successful because these might interfere with the special nature of the conjugal community. Claims based on the violation of general rules such as §§ 823, 1004 BGB will be successful, where absolute personal rights are concerned, for example, the right to bodily integrity, the right to one's name, or the right to privacy[165] or dignity.

93. Courts have also recognized that the matrimonial home is a specially protected sphere,[166] the violation of which – e.g., by a lover moving into the home – may give rise to compensation claims under §§ 823, 1004 BGB against the other spouse or the third party responsible for the violation.[167]

94. Where damages are claimed from the other spouse on whatever grounds,[168] a limitation of liability applies, § 1359 BGB. Spouses are thus answerable to each other for the discharge of their marital obligations only for such care as they are accustomed to exercise in their own affairs. However, § 277 BGB provides that this limitation does not exempt one from liability for gross negligence.

Beyond those based on infringement of the matrimonial home, possible claims against third parties for violation of the conjugal community have been widely discussed, but are not generally accepted by the courts. The BGH recognizes a right not to be disturbed in one's conjugal community,[169] but this is regarded as, essentially, a private matter, which, if it is not a matter of protecting the 'physical sphere' of the matrimonial home, is not open to interference by the state.

III. Duty to Maintain

95. The spouses are mutually obliged to support the family adequately, § 1360 sent. 1 BGB. This obligation is characterized by a strongly 'personal' element and by special consideration for the individual standard of living. The rules relating to maintenance among relatives (§§ 1601 et seq. BGB) are only applicable where this is expressly provided for.[170]

The spouses are obliged to apply all means at their disposal towards their own and their minor children's maintenance, § 1603 II 1 BGB. This support must come from both property and work if property alone cannot safeguard the family income. In cases of need, the spouse will be required to take up any lawful form of employment to meet his or her support obligation. Where the management of the household is entrusted to one of the spouses, that spouse's obligation to contribute to the support of the family is generally discharged thereby.[171]

165. BGH FamRZ 1990, 846.
166. *Räumlich-gegenständlicher Bereich der Ehe.*
167. Cf. BGHZ 6, 360.
168. For example, § 823 I BGB.
169. BGH FamRZ 1973, 295, 296.
170. For example, §§ 1613–1615 BGB.
171. Cf. § 1360 sent. 2 BGB; BGH NJW 1957, 537.

96. The support obligation includes everything required for the individual spouses and children. Both household expenses and personal needs must be covered, §§ 1360, 1360a I BGB.[172] Means required for the support of the family have to be made available a reasonable period in advance, § 1360 II 2 BGB. This becomes important where only one spouse has a regular income. It is important to note that future claims for maintenance cannot be waived, §§ 1360a III, 1614 I BGB. Also, if a spouse contributes more to the support of the family than he or she is obliged to, there is a presumption that this spouse did not intend to claim it back, § 1360b BGB.

IV. Transactions for Necessaries (*Schlüsselgewalt*)

A. General

97. § 1357 BGB sets out special legal consequences for transactions for necessaries made by a spouse. Where a spouse enters into such a transaction, the spouse also binds the other spouse. Both spouses thus acquire rights and obligations under the contract.

The provision was introduced not only to enable housewives to manage the household independently but also to protect creditors by making the husband jointly liable for his wife's debts. Since the *First Reform Act on Marriage and the Family 1976*,[173] § 1357 BGB has applied to both spouses irrespective of who actually manages the household. A transaction thus binds the other spouse:

- if it concerns the appropriate provision of necessaries;
- if circumstances do not indicate differently;
- if the spouses are not separated;
- and if the spouses have not agreed to limit or exclude the consequences arising from § 1357 BGB in a marriage contract and this fact is known to the third party or has been registered in the register of marital property.

98. There has been (and still is) much discussion about what kind of transactions come within § 1357 BGB. To give a brief outline of points widely agreed upon: § 1357 BGB is only concerned with transactions that are closely connected to everyday family consumption,[174] e.g., the provision of food and clothing or the purchase of household goods. It does not extend to transactions that fundamentally affect or alter the family's living conditions.[175] In the latter case, one spouse may not act alone with the power to bind the other, but both spouses have to act jointly for both to be bound.

Thus, § 1357 BGB does not cover the purchase of land or the termination of the lease of the family home. Transactions relating to the administration of property or

172. For example, *see* BGH FamRZ 1960, 225; BGH FamRZ 1985, 353.
173. *Eherechtsreformgesetz* (1. EheRG).
174. Cf. e.g., BGH FamRZ 1985, 576 (medical treatment).
175. For example, in BGH FamRZ 1989, 35.

to a spouse's professional career are also excluded. Medical treatment[176] will be included where the couple's children are concerned, and § 1357 BGB may also apply to treatment received by one spouse (meaning that the other spouse will be liable for the cost) where such treatment seems necessary and appropriate.[177]

The family is understood to comprise the spouses and such of their children as are entitled to support, including adult children still living at home. Provisions will be deemed appropriate if the actual expenses seem adequate for an average family with a comparable income and standard of living. Credit transactions will only be considered appropriate within the meaning of § 1357 BGB if the obligations entered into do not unduly burden the family budget.

B. Effects

99. A transaction coming within the terms of § 1357 BGB automatically binds the other spouse, irrespective of the other party's knowledge of the acting spouse's marital status, unless the parties agree otherwise. Both spouses are jointly liable for any obligations arising from a contract thus concluded, § 421 BGB. Correspondingly, both are entitled to enjoy the rights flowing from the transaction.

Whether § 1357 BGB covers the transfers or conveyances necessary to discharge the obligations incurred (*Verfügungsgeschäfte*) is another matter. The Federal Supreme Court (BGH) denies that the provision has this effect.[178] In practice, this leads to the curious result that – since under German law obligation and disposition require two separate transactions – a husband may be liable for the purchase price, but may – at the same time – only ask for the property to be conveyed to his wife (and not himself). In today's context, § 1357 BGB mainly works as a protection for creditors.

V. Presumption as to Ownership

100. Questions of ownership between spouses are determined both by matrimonial property rules and by the general provisions of the civil law. Under the statutory regime of community of accrued gains,[179] the property of the spouses – whether acquired before or during marriage – does not become joint property. Joint property only arises where the spouses purchase jointly. Especially where movables are concerned, who actually owns what may often be a difficult question to answer for third parties and for the spouses themselves.

§ 1362 BGB, therefore, contains a twofold presumption relating to property ownership during marriage. In favour of the creditors of each spouse, it is presumed that movables in possession of either spouse belong to the debtor spouse only. This presumption does not apply if the spouses have separated, and if the items concerned

176. Cf. BGHZ 47, 75, 81.
177. BGH FamRZ 1985, 576.
178. BGH FamRZ 1991, 923.
179. *Zugewinngemeinschaft*, §§ 1363 et seq. BGB, cf. *infra* paras 316 et seq.

are in the possession of the spouse who is not the debtor. Items typically intended for the exclusive personal use of one spouse are presumed – between the spouses and in relation to creditors – to belong to the spouse for whose use they are intended.

VI. Marital Name

101. Under German law, special rules exist as to the name a person might lawfully bear. Traditionally, spouses in Germany bear the same family name (married name). For a long time, this was the husband's name. Today,[180] especially under the influence of rulings by the Federal Constitutional Court,[181] a married couple enjoys considerable choice over whether to adopt a joint family name at all and, if so, which one, § 1355 BGB. A brief outline of the many – and rather complicated – rules and possible variations may suffice here.

102. As their joint name, the spouses may choose: the birth name of either, or the name either of them bears at the time they adopt the joint family name, § 1355 II BGB. This means that a name acquired from a previous marriage may be chosen as the new family name. This option had been excluded by the law as it stood, but the Federal Constitutional Court forced the legislature to include it.[182] However, it is not possible to choose a hyphenated surname. The chosen joint name automatically becomes the name of any children born of the marriage.

Where spouses choose a joint family name, the spouse whose name is not chosen may add his or her name to the chosen name in any order. This added name may be that spouse's birth name or the name he or she bore at the time the family name was chosen, § 1355 IV BGB. This will be a personal name for this spouse only, and it cannot be passed on to any children of the marriage or to the other spouse.

Any choice of name is made by declaration before the registrar, § 1355 IV 1, II BGB. If the couple does not choose a joint name, both spouses keep their old names, § 1355 I 3 BGB.[183] A spouse's name continues unaltered after divorce, § 1355 V 1 BGB. He or she may, by another declaration before the registrar, reassume his or her birth name or the name he or she bore at the time of the marriage, § 1355 V 2 BGB. The divorced spouse might also add either of these names to the married name in any order.

180. Since the Family Name Act (*Familiennamensrechtsgesetz*) of 16 Dec. 1993 (BGBl. I 2054), in force since 1 Apr. 1994.
181. BVerfGE 84, 9.
182. *Gesetz zur Änderung der Vorschriften über die Anfechtung der Vaterschaft und das Umgangsrecht von Bezugspersonen des Kindes* of 23 Apr. 2004; Decision of the Federal Constitutional Court of 18 Feb. 2004, FamRZ 2004, 515.
183. For the children's name in this case cf. *infra* para. 174.

§5. VOID AND VOIDABLE MARRIAGES

103. *See supra* paragraphs 69 et seq.

Chapter 3. Divorce

104. According to German law, other than by death, a valid marriage can only be dissolved by a judicial decision rendered upon the application of one or both spouses, § 1564 BGB. The marriage is dissolved as soon as the judgment becomes final. The legal status previously existing between the parties ends, although there might be ongoing rights and duties under the law of divorce or any contractual provisions they have entered into.

§1. Grounds

105. The *First Reform Act on Marriage and the Family 1976*[184] based the German law of divorce on the principle of marital breakdown. Questions of fault are no longer considered by the courts except under §§ 1565 II, 1568 BGB. There is now only one ground for divorce: the failure of the marriage, § 1565 BGB. The law considers the marriage to have failed if the matrimonial community of the spouses no longer exists and there is no expectation that the spouses will restore it, § 1565 I 2 BGB.

The family court has to analyse the current state of the marriage and make a prediction as to the likelihood of reconciliation.[185] To avoid prying into the privacy of the married couple, the Code presumes failure of the marriage in two sets of circumstances. First, according to § 1566 I BGB, there is an irrebuttable presumption that the marriage has failed if the spouses have been living apart for a year and both spouses petition for divorce, or one party applies and the other party consents. Second, according to § 1566 II BGB, there is an irrebuttable presumption of failure if the spouses have been living apart for three years.

106. Even where a failure of the marriage has been established, this will not always be enough for a divorce: where divorce is sought under § 1565 I 2 BGB and the spouses have been living apart for less than a year, the marriage can only be dissolved if continuing the marriage would result in unreasonable hardship for the petitioner owing to causes attributable to the other spouse, § 1565 II BGB. 'Unreasonable hardship' – as the courts define it – means hardship resulting from the mere legal tie between the parties.[186] Responsibility has to lie with the other spouse. Most courts hold § 1565 II BGB to be applicable to all divorces, even to divorces by mutual consent.

A spouse may have a legitimate interest in continuing the marriage even after it has failed. § 1568 BGB, therefore, lists two scenarios in which a failed marriage may not be dissolved:

---

184. *1. Eherechtsreformgesetz* (1. EheRG), in force since 1 Jan. 1977.
185. Cf. BGH FamRZ 1978, 671; BGH FamRZ 1979, 422, 1003; BGH NJW 1995, 1082, 1083.
186. Cf. BGH FamRZ 1981, 127, 129.

(1) if, and for as long as, it is necessary to uphold the marriage for special reasons in the interests of minor children of the marriage. The interests of the child or children have to be considered ex officio by the court and might in theory also prevent a consensual divorce;
(2) if, and for as long as, the divorce would result in exceptional hardship to the party opposing the application. The courts have been applying this provision very narrowly.[187] They regard it as a protection from exceptional hardship arising specifically from the act of divorce.[188]

107. The 1977 law on divorce set up an obstacle to consensual divorce by providing, in § 1566 I BGB, that a divorce may usually only be granted if the parties had made certain arrangements for the future. These arrangements included agreements on child custody, visitation rights, child support and alimony, the family home, and household effects. This obstacle was removed by the FamFG, which entered into force on 1 September 2009. While the spouse filing for a divorce still has to disclose whether such agreements have been made (§ 133 I No. 2 FamFG), it is now perfectly possible to obtain a divorce without having reached an agreement on these matters.

§2. Procedure

108. Special procedural rules apply in divorce.[189] Jurisdiction lies with the family court.[190] Proceedings are instituted by petition, §§ 124, 133 FamFG, and they are conducted under the inquisitorial, not the adversary, system, § 127 FamFG.[191] In divorce proceedings, representation by a lawyer is compulsory.[192] Divorce and ancillary matters (e.g., for support) must generally be heard jointly if they are filed during the pendency of the divorce proceedings.[193]

§3. Effects

I. Duty to Maintain

A. General

109. In principle, upon divorce, the spouses are required to support themselves from their own income and assets. Where this is not possible, German law does not follow a strict clean-break doctrine, but recognizes that the spouses continue to be responsible for each other even after divorce. Support duties between divorced

187. Cf. BVerfGE 55, 134; BGH FamRZ 1981, 1161; BGH FamRZ 1985, 912.
188. BGH FamRZ 1979, 422, 423.
189. *See* §§ 121–150 FamFG.
190. §§ 23a I 1 No. 1, 23b I GVG; §§ 111 No. 1, 121 No. 1 FamFG.
191. But *see* § 127 II, III FamFG.
192. § 114 FamFG, *see also* § 138 FamFG.
193. § 137 FamFG.

couples have been severely limited by the *Maintenance Reform Act* of 12 December 2007. §§ 1570–1576 BGB define the conditions under which a divorced spouse may be entitled to maintenance and set out seven different grounds on which maintenance may be claimed.

B. Grounds for Maintenance

1. Child Care, § 1570 BGB

110. First, a divorced spouse may claim maintenance from the other for as long and to the extent that he or she cannot be expected to pursue gainful employment by reason of having to care for or to educate a child common to both, § 1570 BGB. The claim can be made irrespective of who has parental responsibility, as it is based solely on the fact of caring for the child. The support duty exists for a minimum of three years after the birth of the child, § 1570 I 1 BGB. It may continue thereafter, to the extent that this is equitable, special consideration being given to the best interests of the child and to the existence of adequate childcare services, § 1570 I 2, 3 BGB.[194] The duration of the marriage and the roles assumed by the spouses during marriage (homemaker/primary caretaker?) might also result in a longer duty of support, § 1570 II BGB.[195]

2. Age, § 1571 BGB

111. A divorced spouse may also be entitled to maintenance in so far as he or she cannot be gainfully employed on account of his or her age. The relevant date for making the claim is either the divorce (§ 1571 No. 1 BGB), the discontinuation of care for a child common to both (No. 2), or the termination of a maintenance claim pursuant to §§ 1572 and 1573 BGB.

3. Infirmity, § 1572 BGB

112. Further grounds for maintenance are physical or mental illness or other infirmity or weakness, § 1572 BGB. The relevant date for making the claim is the same as described *supra.*

194. Cf. BGH FamRZ 2009, 770 paras 23 et seq.; BGH FamRZ 2011, 1209 para. 22.
195. Cf. BGH FamRZ 2012, 1040 para. 24.

4. Gross Inequity, § 1576 BGB

113. If none of the above grounds apply, a spouse may still be entitled to maintenance under § 1576 BGB, if he or she cannot be expected to work for other reasons, and if a denial of maintenance would seem grossly inequitable taking into account the position of both spouses.

5. Inability to Find Work, § 1573 I BGB

114. Even where under the rules set out in §§ 1570–1572, 1576 BGB, a spouse is expected to support him or herself, he or she may not be able to find employment. In this case, § 1573 I BGB provides that the spouse can claim maintenance for as long as and to the extent that he or she is unable to find 'suitable employment'. What work is 'suitable' may be a difficult question, and there is extensive case law on this point.[196] The spouse's abilities and his or her level of training are generally important considerations.

As with §§ 1570, 1571 and 1572 BGB, the claim can only be made within a certain time after the divorce. The spouse must have been unable to find suitable employment reasonably soon after the divorce or after the spouse has ceased to receive maintenance under §§ 1570–1572 BGB.

Maintenance may be granted for a limited period only. In deciding for how long maintenance payments will be made, the courts will take into account the duration of the marriage, the household structure, and the provision of care for a mutual child.

6. Additional Maintenance, § 1573 II BGB

115. Where a spouse is obliged to provide for himself or herself and has indeed secured employment, he or she may claim additional maintenance if his or her own income is insufficient to support him or her. In such a case, the spouse may claim the difference between his or her actual income and full maintenance.[197]

7. Education/Retraining, § 1575 BGB

116. Finally, a divorced spouse may claim support for further education or (re-)training in order to become able to support himself or herself. Such support may be claimed if the spouse decided to forego or interrupt his or her training because of the marriage, or where further training seems necessary to offset disadvantages that arose in the context of the marriage. Training must be likely to be successful.

196. Cf. BGH NJW-RR 1992, 1282.
197. BVerfGE 57, 361, 389.

Also, the claim only covers the usual training time and does not take into account any delays the marriage itself may have caused.

C. Amount of Maintenance

117. The level of support is determined by the following criteria:

(1) It has to cover all basic needs (§ 1578 I 2 BGB), including the cost of adequate health, long-term care and old-age insurance (§ 1578 II, III BGB).
(2) The level of support is set at the standard of living established and maintained during the marriage (§ 1578 I 2 BGB),[198] i.e., by the financial circumstances of the spouses at the time of divorce. The level is that part of their income that the spouses spent on their day-to-day affairs. Where higher incomes are concerned, however, the courts do take into account that usually a portion of the income will be invested.

118. Fixing the level of maintenance at the living standard established during the marriage has come in for criticism, which is why the courts have adopted a flexible approach. The Federal Supreme Court has ruled that income fluctuations arising *after the divorce* affect the standard of living established during the marriage.[199] Thus, the standard may be lowered if the payor spouse's income drops after the divorce or if he or she acquires new support obligations (doctrine of changeable marital living conditions). For example, if the payor spouse has another child after the divorce, the newly acquired support obligation will reduce the level of maintenance of the divorced husband or wife.[200] According to the Federal Supreme Court, this is true even if the divorced spouse remarries and puts forward the support obligation to the new spouse as a defence to the ex-spouse's maintenance claim.[201] However, the Federal Supreme Court has been overturned by the Constitutional Court on the grounds that the court's jurisprudence departs too far from the legislative scheme.[202] The Constitutional Court has stressed that the level of support is determined by the financial conditions that existed during the marriage. Changes arising after the divorce can only be considered if they were foreseeable.

119. The *Maintenance Reform Act* of 12 December 2007 introduced § 1578b BGB, which enables the court to cut down maintenance payments to a divorced spouse, thereby ameliorating the effects of divorce on the financially stronger spouse. Payments may be *reduced* where maintenance at the standard of living enjoyed by the couple before the breakdown of the marriage (§ 1578 I BGB) would be *inequitable*, § 1578b BGB. Special account is taken of how the roles taken on during the marriage may have affected the ability of the payee spouse to maintain

198. *Eheliche Lebensverhältnisse.*
199. BGHZ 175, 182; 179, 196; 183, 197.
200. BGHZ 175, 182; 179, 196.
201. BGHZ 177, 356; BGHZ 179, 196; BGH FamRZ 2010, 111.
202. BVerfGE 128, 193.

himself or herself. Marriage-related disadvantages (affecting, e.g., the homemaker wife) weigh against a reduction. Courts also have to take into account other equitable factors as well as the welfare of any children or the long duration of marriage. On the same grounds, a court might make a *fixed-term* maintenance order (§ 1578b II BGB, e.g., a maintenance order that ends five years after the divorce). It is also possible to combine reduced payments and time limits. For example, a court might make a fixed-term financial order granting full support for three years and reduced support for a further period of three years.[203]

D. Claimant's Lack of Means

120. Maintenance may be claimed while and to the extent that a spouse is unable to support himself or herself from his or her own income and assets, § 1577 I BGB, irrespective of the assets' origins. Culpable failure to generate income may result in a fictitious attribution of income.[204] The claimant is not required, however, to sell his or her assets, where such sale would be financially unwise or inequitable considering the spouses' financial circumstances, § 1577 III BGB.

E. Financial Capability of the Debtor

121. Full maintenance can only be paid if the payor spouse's income is sufficiently high. The payor spouse's financial capability may, therefore, place a restriction on the claim.

As a rule, the courts assume that both parties have an equal right to the available income,[205] but award a small bonus to the working spouse. To ensure some uniformity in the application of the law, the German courts issue tables[206] and guidelines[207] setting out the amount of maintenance granted by them.

Frequently, a person having to pay support finds himself or herself faced with several claimants. Where there are insufficient resources to cover the payor's own needs as well as the needs of those entitled to support (lack of means cases), the *order* in which claims should be met becomes relevant. Claims may be of *equal rank*, in which case they must be satisfied proportionately. However, one claim may also *take precedence over* another. The law ranks claims in the following order (§§ 1582, 1609 BGB):

- First in rank are the claims of the payor's minor children and those of unmarried children under the age of 21 who still live at home.
- Second in rank are parents who are entitled to support (or would be so entitled in case of divorce) because they are taking care of a child. This includes claims of

203. § 1578b III BGB.
204. Cf. BGH FamRZ 1981, 539.
205. So-called *Halbteilungsgrundsatz*.
206. For example, the *Düsseldorfer Tabelle*, for 2021 *see* FamRZ 2021, 93.
207. Called *Leitlinien* or *Richtlinien*.

unwed mothers. If there are several claimants entitled to support because of child-care, they are of equal rank. Spouses (including divorced spouses) who have been married for a long time are also ranked in the second category.
- Third in rank are spouses and divorced spouses who are not in the second rank.
- Fourth in rank are any other (i.e., adult) children.
- Fifth in rank are grandchildren and other descendants.
- Sixth in rank are the payor's parents.
- Seventh in rank are other relatives in the ascending line (e.g., grandparents).

F. Gross Inequity

122. The post-marital duty to maintain often places severe financial restrictions on the payor. § 1579 BGB allows the claim to be denied, reduced, or limited in time where burdening the payor would be grossly inequitable. When making such a ruling, the court will also consider the interests of a mutual child entrusted to the debtor. § 1579 BGB lists seven specific grounds and one general provision for determining gross inequity. The payment of maintenance may thus be grossly inequitable if:

- the marriage was of short duration, § 1579 No. 1 BGB. A marriage is generally assumed to have been short where the parties have been married for less than three years. When calculating the duration of the marriage, the time during which a claim could be made under § 1570 BGB (taking care of a mutual child) has to be taken into account;
- the payee cohabits with a new partner, § 1579 No. 2 BGB;
- the claimant is guilty of a crime or another serious intentional offence[208] against the debtor or the debtor's close relatives, § 1579 No. 3 BGB;
- the claimant wilfully caused his or her own destitution, § 1579 No. 4 BGB. Wilfulness in this context does not necessarily mean intent; recklessness may suffice;[209]
- the claimant wilfully disregarded important property interests of the debtor, § 1579 No. 5 BGB; or before the separation grossly, and for a protracted period, violated his or her own duty to contribute to the support of the family, § 1579 No. 6 BGB;
- if the claimant is guilty of obvious and serious misconduct against the debtor, § 1579 No. 7 BGB. Serious matrimonial offences, but also any behaviour seriously disapproved of by people in general, have been held to constitute such misconduct; or
- if there is some other serious ground of comparable weight as the grounds set out in Nos 1–7, § 1579 No. 8 BGB.

208. Cf. § 12 StGB.
209. *See* BGH FamRZ 1988, 375.

123. Depending on the circumstances, the extinction of a maintenance claim under § 1579 No. 8 BGB may only be temporary, i.e., it may revive if the new relationship ends.[210]

G. Modes of Payment

124. Maintenance is provided by monthly payments made in advance (§ 1585 I 1, 2 BGB), and in case of exceptional necessity whenever that necessity arises (§ 1585b I, III BGB). The payee spouse may ask for a capital settlement instead of periodic payments if there are substantial reasons for this (§ 1585 II BGB).

125. The maintenance claim is extinguished:

- where the conditions for the claim cease to apply;[211]
- on the remarriage or registered partnership of the person entitled;[212]
- on the death of the person entitled.[213] Upon the death of the debtor, by contrast, the obligation to provide maintenance devolves on the heirs as a liability of the estate (§ 1586b I BGB);
- on the payment of a lump sum or capital settlement;[214]
- where the maintenance claim is waived.

126. § 1585c BGB allows the spouses to make agreements about post-divorce maintenance. The claim may even be waived altogether, as § 1614 I BGB does not apply to post-divorce maintenance. The courts have substantially curtailed the possibilities of waiver. According to the Federal Constitutional Court, the courts are under a duty to review marriage contracts and divorce agreements and to determine whether these were procured by the unilateral dominance of one spouse. If they were so procured, the courts have to vet the contents of the contract according to the general clauses of the civil law (equity rules, § 138 BGB, good faith, § 242 BGB) and, where appropriate, correct them.[215] The Federal Supreme Court has ruled that marriage contracts and divorce agreements may not result in evidently one-sided burden-sharing, where this is not justified by the actual living conditions and would be unacceptable for the disadvantaged spouse. Post-marital maintenance waivers may be against public policy or represent a *mala fide* abuse of rights.[216] This is especially true for childcare-based maintenance (§ 1570 BGB), but may also be true for maintenance on account of old age or infirmity (§§ 1571, 1572 BGB).[217]

---

210. BGH FamRZ 1987, 689.
211. But *see* § 1573 IV BGB for a possible revival.
212. § 1586 I BGB, but *see* § 1586a I BGB.
213. § 1586 I BGB.
214. *See supra.*
215. BVerfGE 109, 89; FamRZ 2001, 985.
216. BGH FamRZ 2004, 601; 2005, 691; 2006, 1359, 2011, 1377; 2013, 195; 2014, 629; 2015, 824.
217. BGH FamRZ 2005, 691; 2014, 629.

II. Equalization of Support (Pension Splitting)

127. Since the 1976 *First Reform Act on Marriage and the Family*, the equal-sharing principle that applies to the distribution of assets accumulated during the marriage has also been applied to rights acquired under a pension scheme for future support in the event of old age, disability, or incapacity. To implement this principle, the German legislature has created a special legal mechanism, called *Versorgungsausgleich* (pension sharing), which was completely overhauled in 2009. The equal sharing of rights under a pension scheme is set out in § 1587 BGB as well as in the *Pension Sharing Act* of 3 April 2009.[218] The sharing principle is applied to benefits under private as well as public pension schemes (e.g., pension plans for state and local government employees; public old-age pension schemes; private pension funds). The division of pensions is triggered by the divorce; there is no sharing of rights under a pension scheme during the duration of the marriage.

128. The sharing principle only applies to benefits under a pension scheme earned or maintained *during* the marriage. Pension rights earned before the marriage are not subject to division. The beginning and the endpoint of a 'marriage' are clearly defined. The first day of the month in which the marriage ceremony took place marks the beginning of the marriage, and the last day of the month before divorce was filed marks its end.

129. The Reform Act of 2009 made the process of sharing much easier. Previously, the sum total of pension rights accumulated during the marriage had to be calculated for each spouse. The spouse who had accumulated more rights had to transfer half of the surplus to his or her partner. After the 2009 reforms, there is no longer any need for this. Rather, the pension rights each spouse has earned during the marriage are split 'in kind' (internal division), with each spouse getting one-half of the pension rights the other has accumulated over the course of the marriage. If both spouses have earned pension rights, as is very often the case, then both are entitled to a share (e.g., the wife gets half of the husband's civil service pension and the husband gets half of his wife's pension rights as a doctor). This is the general rule, which is only departed from where division in kind is not practicable or where the parties have agreed on a different arrangement. If both spouses are already retired, e.g., one spouse might have to pay a share of his or her pension, corresponding to the amount that was gained during the marriage, to the other spouse (*schuldrechtlicher Versorgungsausgleich*).

130. The law on the division of pension rights on divorce is complex and complicated. During or even before marriage, spouses can agree to modify the legislative scheme or even opt out of it altogether. Contractual modifications and opt-outs are subject to court supervision, however. A court might invalidate, or find non-binding, agreements that are grossly unfair. Agreements have to be signed in the presence of a notary or recorded in a court settlement.

---

218. *Gesetz über den Versorgungsausgleich* (*Versorgungsausgleichsgesetz*, VersAusglG) of 3 Apr. 2009.

131. Proceedings are in the family court. Pension splitting is usually ordered by the judge even when the parties are not asking for it (equalization ex officio). The court is authorized not to make a pension adjustment or to deviate from the principle of equal division, where (equal) sharing would be grossly inequitable.

III. Household Effects and the Matrimonial Home

132. The formal termination of the marriage by divorce makes it necessary to divide the household effects, and to determine the future use of the matrimonial home. Where the parties cannot agree, these matters are resolved by the family court on application.[219] The law on the allocation of household effects and the family home was remodelled by legislation dating from 6 July 2009 (§§ 1568a, 1568b BGB).

133. The allocation of household effects follows title:

- Property belonging to only one spouse remains with that spouse upon divorce.
- Jointly owned property may be redistributed upon divorce. Each spouse may ask for a transfer of items that he or she needs more than the other spouse, § 1568b I BGB. The welfare of children has to be taken into account. Allocation is largely discretionary.
- There is a presumption that household effects acquired during the marriage for the family home are jointly owned; the presumption may be rebutted by the spouse claiming sole ownership, § 1568b II BGB.

134. Allocation of the family home in case of divorce is addressed, in fairly complicated fashion, in § 1568a BGB:

- The basic principle is the following: one spouse may ask to remain in the matrimonial home if he or she needs it more than the other spouse. The welfare of any children living in the household has to be considered, § 1568a I BGB. Other equitable reasons may also justify permitting one spouse to stay. The principle is applied differently, depending on whether the home was rented or not.
- In the case of a *rented home*, the lease is adjusted by court order; the spouse to whom the home is allocated becomes the sole tenant, § 1568a III BGB.
- If one spouse is the *sole owner*, the other spouse may only ask to remain in the home where it would be grossly inequitable to evict him or her, § 1568a II BGB. He or she cannot ask for a transfer of title. Rather, if the conditions are met, a lease between the owner and the non-owner spouse is established by court order, § 1568 V BGB. The terms of the contract are those usual in the area; where the spouses cannot agree, the court decides. The same principles apply where the spouse who is required to turn over the property owns the home jointly with third parties or has a real right in the property short of full ownership. Depending on the individual facts, the lease may only run for a limited period of time.

219. §§ 23a I 1 No. 1, 23b I GVG; §§ 111 No. 5, 200 FamFG.

- Where the spouses are *joint owners*, a contract of rent is concluded in favour of the spouse to whom the court grants possession of the home, § 1568a V BGB. For example, if the wife is awarded possession, she becomes a tenant; at the same time, she, along with her ex-husband, becomes the lessor by virtue of her continuing ownership rights in the property.

§4. Separation

135. Separation causes legal problems similar to the ones arising upon divorce. For divorces under § 1566 BGB, the law requires the spouses to have lived apart for at least one year (§§ 1565 II, 1566 I BGB). Therefore, a legal framework for separation is needed, and is provided in the Code. Separation, as defined in § 1567 BGB, has objective and subjective elements. The spouses are living 'apart' if there is no longer any household community between them and if at least one spouse manifestly refuses to restore it, because he or she rejects the conjugal community.

According to § 1567 I 2 BGB, living apart can be accomplished within the conjugal home. Frequently, the financial situation of the spouses is such that it does not allow separate households for any length of time. Accordingly, separation within the conjugal home is sufficient where no joint household exists and where any contact between the spouses has its reason in the spatial proximity, rather than in the personal relations between them.

Since the requirement of separation should not act as a curb on the possible reconciliation of the parties, § 1566 II BGB provides that living together during a short period of time for the purpose of effecting a reconciliation does not interrupt or stop the periods in § 1566 BGB.

136. The legal consequences arising from the spouses' separation are similar to those following divorce:

- Parental responsibility is altered on application only, § 1671 I BGB. Where the parents continue to exercise joint parental responsibility, the resident parent is invested with sole responsibility for day-to-day matters, § 1687 I BGB.
- A spouse can claim reasonable support from the other at the living standard of the spouses, § 1361 I 1 BGB. Where a spouse was not gainfully employed before the separation, he or she can only be required to work for his or her own support thereafter if this is reasonable having regard to his or her personal circumstances. In considering this matter, the court takes into account any earlier gainful employment, the duration of the marriage, and the financial circumstances of each spouse, § 1361 II BGB. Housewives (and house-husbands), in particular, will thus be protected from having to find employment immediately after separation.

137. § 1361 BGB leads to a fundamental shift in the relations between the spouses:

- In place of the mutual obligation to maintain, we now find a unilateral monetary claim for support, which can no longer be discharged by managing the household.[220] The claim established by § 1361 BGB is similar, but not identical to the maintenance claim arising after divorce.
- Household effects may be divided by court order according to § 1361a BGB, if the parties cannot agree, although title remains unaffected. Each spouse is entitled to ask for household items that belong to him or her. He or she is, however, also obliged to leave these items in the possession of the other spouse for that spouse's use to the extent that the other spouse needs them for the separate household, but only if so leaving them seems equitable. Jointly owned items are divided according to equitable principles by the court.
- The court may grant one spouse the sole right to use the family home or a part thereof if this is necessary to avoid undue hardship (this is new, the previous formulation was grave hardship; *see* § 1361b I 1 BGB). It is enough that the welfare of any children would suffer without the allocation, § 1361b I 2 BGB. The court also has to consider title when making the order. Although an order made under this provision does not affect title, but only regulates the use of the property, the losing spouse may demand compensation where this seems equitable, § 1361b III 2 BGB. Where the use of the family home has been allocated to one spouse by court order, the other spouse is directed to refrain from anything that could impair this use (§ 1361b III 1 BGB; e.g., he or she may not terminate the lease if he or she is the sole tenant). The courts often assign the family home to spouses who have been maltreated or deprived of their freedom of movement by their partners, or threatened with such behaviour or with injury to life, § 1361 II 1 BGB. In these cases, the entire family home is assigned to that spouse's sole use. Additionally, a spouse who has been the victim of domestic violence may invoke the Protection against Domestic Violence Act (*Gewaltschutzgesetz*), which also allows for an – often temporary – assignment of the family home to one spouse's sole use.

220. Cf. § 1360 sent. 2 BGB.

Chapter 4. Cohabitation Outside Marriage

§1. Introduction

138. German law does not have express legislation for unmarried couples. Recent legislative innovations, e.g., in child law, suggest, however, that legal solutions – at least in some areas – will increasingly be sought regardless of the parents' marital status. As the law stands, however, the rules on marriage are generally neither applicable outright nor can they be applied by analogy. The relevant legal rules for unmarried cohabitation may, therefore, be found:

- in some provisions relating to marriage, which are, as an exception, applied by analogy;
- in general statutory provisions, applicable without the requirement of marriage; and
- in contract law based on the express or implied agreement of the parties.

§2. Rules Relating to Marriage

139. There are some exceptions to the general rule that the norms governing married couples are not applicable to unmarried partners. First, they might apply where the norm in question expressly refers to both marriage and cohabitation.[221] It should be noted, however, that the legislative impetus in these cases has generally not been to grant privileges to unmarried cohabitants, but rather to avoid discriminating against married couples and hence to protect the institution of marriage as demanded in Article 6 GG.[222]

140. Second, there are cases where statutory provisions have indeed been applied to unmarried cohabitants by analogy. This has been advocated most strongly in cases where the legislature's primary aim was to acknowledge the impact of a close personal relationship or of living together. Although they have not laid down a general rule, the courts have treated cohabitants as falling within the scope of § 1969 BGB, e.g., thus entitling the surviving cohabitant to thirty days' maintenance and to use of the communal home after the partner's death.[223]

Also, where one partner moves in with the other and the landlord or landlady refuses to give his or her permission, the courts have decided to apply § 553 BGB by analogy. In the case of a long-term relationship, the tenant generally has a right to such permission unless the landlord or landlady can give special reasons against it.[224]

---

221. For an example, *see* § 20 SGB XII.
222. Cf. BVerfGE 9, 20.
223. OLG Düsseldorf FamRZ 1983, 274. For the right to enter into the lease cf. BGH NJW 1993, 999 and BVerfGE 82, 6.
224. Cf. BGH FamRZ 1985, 42; OLG Hamm NJW 1982, 2876.

§3. General Rules of Civil Law

141. The general rules of civil law apply to unmarried partners as they do to everyone else. During the relationship, each partner manages his or her property independently. There is no statutory equalization upon separation. In some cases, this may lead to unsatisfactory results, especially where one partner has made financial or other contributions that significantly exceed anything provided by the other in return.

Subsequent claims for equalization or for damages run into considerable legal difficulties, although German law knows a number of general civil law provisions on which such claims might theoretically be based. These include the law of gifts, the law of restitution, mandate, and the concepts of actual or undisclosed partnership. Application of these doctrines in the individual case is complex. As a general rule, it might be said that the courts tend to deny compensation where the contribution was intended for the communal partnership, but they have upheld claims where contributions were made for the benefit of only one of the partners.[225]

§4. Explicit and Implicit Contractual Agreements

142. It is widely accepted today that cohabitants may freely enter into contracts regulating their legal relations. These contracts will not be deemed to contravene public policy (§ 138 BGB) except under special circumstances. They might be against public policy, e.g., where the contractual provisions unduly interfere with a partner's private life or curtail his or her right to self-determination – as in the case of entering into an obligation to use contraceptive methods or to continue the relationship – or where such provisions gravely violate legitimate interests of close family members.

143. In the majority of cases, the partners do not enter express contractual agreements. This does not necessarily mean that no legal relationship exists between them, since, under the general rules of contract, there may be an implied contractual agreement. The courts have been slow to acknowledge the existence of implied agreements, however. From the Federal Supreme Court's point of view, in the absence of an express agreement, it should generally be assumed that the partners intentionally refrained from setting up a legal framework for their relationship, and that any provisions made for the benefit of the other or the partnership were made without any intention of claiming them back later.[226] As of 2008, the Federal Supreme Court has started to change its jurisprudence. If one unmarried cohabitant gives property to the other expecting to continue to benefit from it as part of the non-marital unit, the unexpected termination of the relationship can undermine the basis of the transfer and give rise to a claim for adjustment (§ 313 BGB), e.g., to financial compensation or a return of the property.[227] Where the transfer served a purpose

225. Cf. BGH NJW 1997, 3371; BGHZ 77, 58; BGH FamRZ 1992, 408.
226. BGH FamRZ 1981, 530.
227. BGHZ 177, 193; BGH FamRZ 2010, 277; 2011, 1563; 2012, 1789; 2013, 1295.

beyond the scope of the cohabiting unit (e.g., where it was intended to start a company), claims might arise from an implied partnership agreement if the partners' separation terminates the cooperation.[228] A claim for a return of property upon separation may also arise from the law of unjust enrichment.[229]

§5. Registered Partnerships

144. Effective from 1 August 2001, the concept of 'registered partnership' was introduced into German law by the *Act to End Discrimination against Same-Sex Partnerships* of 16 February 2001. Since Article 6 I GG was considered to prohibit same-sex marriage, Parliament introduced a complex new concept that combines marital elements with new solutions. The Federal Constitutional Court[230] has found that the introduction of a registered partnership for same-sex couples does not infringe the Basic Law. The legislature has further amended the law on registered partnerships in 2004[231] and aligned it largely with the law of marriage; many provisions of the *Registered Partnership Act* (LPartG) now merely refer to the rules applicable to marriage. This is especially true for:

- the rules on names, § 3 LPartG;
- the property regimes, §§ 6, 7 LPartG;
- maintenance during the partnership, § 5 LPartG;
- the concept and the consequences of separation, §§ 12–14 LPartG;
- maintenance during separation, § 12 LPartG;
- maintenance after the termination of the partnership (as for spouses after divorce, § 16 LPartG);
- pension splitting, which is performed in the same way upon the termination of a registered partnership as upon divorce, § 20 LPartG;
- inheritance law, § 10 LPartG.

However, some instances remained where the rules differed from marriage. In order to remove these differences, the German legislature opened the institution of marriage itself to same-sex couples in 2017.[232] As of the effective date of this Act, same-sex couples may get married and registered partnerships may no longer be concluded, Article 3 III. Same-sex partnerships already in existence at that date may be converted into regular marriages by a personal declaration of the couple given in each other's presence, § 20a I LPartG. A partnership thus converted entails the same

228. BGHZ 177, 193; BGH FamRZ 2010, 277.
229. BGHZ 177, 193 para. 33; BGH FamRZ 2009, 849 para. 15.
230. BVerfGE 105, 313.
231. Registered Partnership Reform Act (*Gesetz zur Überarbeitung des Lebenspartnerschaftsrechts*) of 15 Dec. 2004. *See* further *Gesetz zur Bereinigung des Rechts der Lebenspartner* of 20 Nov. 2015 (BGBl. I 2010).
232. *Gesetz zur Einführung des Rechts auf Eheschließung für Personen gleichen Geschlechts* of 20 Jul. 2017.

rights and duties as regular marriage, § 20a IV LPartG. Registered partnerships that are not converted continue as registered partnerships with their own set of rights and duties.

145. The enforceability of these duties tracks the enforceability of marital duties, except that there is no action to enforce living together in marital community. Thus, there is a general distinction between duties of a 'personal' and duties of an 'economic' nature and the violation of general rules such as §§ 1004, 823 BGB. For details, *see supra* paragraphs 92 et seq. Where damages are claimed, the same limitation of liability as in marriage applies (§ 4 LPartG; *see supra* paragraph 94).

146. Registered partnerships are characterized by mutual solidarity. In particular, the following effects apply to the registered partnership:

- § 10 LPartG gives a statutory right to inheritance and to a compulsory portion.
- According to § 11 I LPartG, the registered partner is a 'family member' unless otherwise stated. He or she has the same evidentiary privileges as a spouse or fiancé(e), § 52 I No. 2a StPO; § 383 I No. 2a Civil Procedure Act (*Zivilprozessordnung*, ZPO).
- Registered partnerships create a relationship of affinity between the partners and their relatives, § 11 II LPartG.
- Important consequences follow from registered partnerships in the area of citizenship and the laws concerning aliens. Here, similar privileges as for married couples apply.

147. Registered partnerships are generally concluded for life. Once validly established, a partnership may only be terminated with *ex nunc* effect by an act of court, the so-called *Aufhebung* (termination), § 15 I LPartG. Jurisdiction for actions arising from a registered partnership lies with the family court, §§ 23a I 1 No. 1, 23b I GVG, § 111 No. 11 FamFG.

148. The reasons for terminating a registered partnership have been substantially modified by the 2004 Reform Act and are now modelled on the law of divorce. There are now five reasons for a termination:

(1) The registered partnership is terminated on request if the partners have been separated for one year and both state that they want the termination, § 15 II 1 No. 1 lit. a LPartG.
(2) The partners have been separated for one year and it is not to be expected that a domestic partnership will be resumed, § 15 II 1 No. 1 lit. b LPartG.
(3) The termination will be granted without further enquiry if the partners have been living apart for at least three years, § 15 II 1 No. 2 LPartG.
(4) The registered partnership is terminated on the request of one partner if the continuation of the partnership would result in unreasonable hardship to the petitioner owing to causes attributable to the other partner, § 15 II 1 No. 3 LPartG. In this case, no separation is necessary.

(5) Finally, a registered partnership may be terminated if there were 'vices of consent' within the meaning of § 1314 II Nos 1–4 BGB (§ 15 II 2 LPartG; e.g., wilful deception or threats against one of the partners). Where other requirements are violated, no effective registered partnership comes into existence.

149. The termination may be defended with the negative hardship clause of § 15 III LPartG: according to this provision, the registered partnership shall not be terminated, even if the partners have been living apart for more than three years, provided the termination would constitute a hardship so severe for the opposing partner that continuing the partnership – after due consideration of the interests and concerns of the applicant – seems necessary by way of an exception.

The consequences of termination are generally the same as on divorce.

Chapter 5. Parent and Child

§1. Mother and Father of a Child

I. Mother

150. Prior to the *Child Law Reform Act 1997*, the BGB did not contain a definition of motherhood. In response to modern developments in artificial reproduction, the Reform Act now clarifies the situation: from the law's point of view, when a woman gives birth to a child, she alone is the child's mother, irrespective of the child's genetic origins. The BGB thus refuses to split motherhood between the genetic and the gestational mother. There is no way to contest maternity nor are agreements between the egg donor and the gestational mother valid. The (gestational) mother's identity is usually known. However, under the confidential birth legislation, passed in August of 2013,[233] her identity (though registered) remains undisclosed, until the child requests disclosure at a later point.

II. Father

151. When attributing paternity, the law still draws distinctions according to the marital status of a child's parents. § 1592 BGB declares the child's father to be the man:

- who was married to the mother at the time of the child's birth;
- who has formally acknowledged the child; or
- whose paternity has been established by a court order.

152. These three possibilities are mutually exclusive. Only paternity established by marriage or acknowledgement may be contested.[234]

A. Marriage to the Child's Mother

153. If the parents are married at the time of the child's birth, no further act of recognition is necessary or even possible. The BGB follows the Roman law maxim '*pater est quem nuptiae demonstrant*'.[235] The mere possibility of a prospective annulment (with *ex nunc* effect) is irrelevant. This is different where the marriage was never valid to begin with (*Nichtehe* or non-marriage). Here, no paternity will be established.

---

233. *Gesetz zum Ausbau der Hilfen für Schwangere und zur Regelung der vertraulichen Geburt* of 28 Aug. 2013 (BGBl. I 3458).
234. *See* §§ 1599 I, 1600 BGB.
235. D. 2,4,5.

The relevant moment at which the parents have to be married is the child's birth. The *Child Law Reform Act 1997* abolished the concept of legitimation by subsequent marriage. Accordingly, the parents' later marriage does not change the child's status. It is important in another respect, however, since it automatically establishes joint parental responsibility (§ 1626a I No. 2 BGB), even where the mother had sole parental responsibility before (§ 1626a III BGB).

154. No paternity arises where the child is born after the marriage is annulled (with *ex nunc* effect) or after the parents' divorce, even if the child was conceived during the marriage. The rationale behind this rule is that where a child is conceived shortly before a divorce or annulment, the husband is not the most probable father. His paternity can only be established by court order or by his own acknowledgement, § 1592 Nos 2 and 3 BGB.

The situation is different where the marriage is ended by the death of the husband. Here, the law sees no reason to doubt the husband's paternity. Any child born to the widow within 300 days of the husband's death is legally considered to be his (§§ 1593 sent. 1, 1592 No. 1 BGB). Where the child is known to have been conceived more than 300 days before its birth, the period is extended accordingly, § 1593 sent. 2 BGB.

155. There is yet another situation where the law departs from the rule that marriage at the time of the child's birth decides paternity: if a child is born during divorce proceedings and another man formally acknowledges the child, this man may be recognized as the father if the husband consents, § 1599 II 2 BGB. The formal acknowledgement can be made before the child's birth, although it only becomes valid upon the dissolution of the marriage.[236]

B. Acknowledgement of Paternity

156. In the absence of an established paternity, a man who is not married to the mother at the time of the child's birth may be recognized as the father if he formally acknowledges the child to be his.[237]

To be valid, the acknowledgement of paternity must be publicly and officially recorded by a qualified person, usually a notary, § 1597 I BGB. It can only be made in person, § 1596 IV BGB. According to § 1595 I BGB, the child's mother must consent, subject to the same formalities (§§ 1595–1597 BGB). Should she refuse, paternity can only be established by a court order, § 1592 No. 3 BGB.

Even under the new law, the child's consent is only required if the mother does not have parental responsibility, § 1595 II BGB. This has been criticized for treating the child as a mere object, whose status may be determined by the mother and the prospective father at will.

236. *See* §§ 1599 II 1 Hs. 2, 1594 IV, 1599 II 3 BGB.
237. §§ 1592 No. 2, 1594–1598 BGB.

157. As soon as the required formal declarations have been made, paternity is established with all the resulting consequences. No act of court or public authority is required. The father is recorded in the register of births, although this is not a condition of validity. The effect is generally *ex nunc* only, § 1594 I BGB. An exception applies to maintenance duties.[238]

C. Contesting Paternity

158. Paternity – whether established by marriage or by acknowledgement – may be contested by bringing an action in the family court.[239]

The following persons have a right to contest paternity: (1) the man recognized as the father because of marriage or acknowledgement, (2) the mother and (3) the child (§ 1600 I Nos 1, 3, 4 BGB). The man's parents or other relatives do not have such a right.

As the result of a ruling by the Federal Constitutional Court,[240] the law now also grants a right to contest paternity to (4) any man who could be the child's father because he had intercourse with the mother at the time of the child's conception (§ 1600 I No. 2 BGB). However, the potential father's right to contest paternity is hedged about by a number of restrictions (§ 1600 II, III BGB):

- the potential father has to make a declaration on oath stating that he had intercourse with the mother at the time of conception;
- the right to contest paternity is excluded by a 'familial relationship' (*sozial-familiäre Beziehung*) between the child and the man until then considered the father (§ 1600 II BGB). A 'familial relationship' will be assumed if the legal father has or has had 'actual responsibility' for the child. Such actual responsibility will generally be found where the legal father is married to the mother or has lived with the child in a joint household for an extended period of time (§ 1600 III BGB). If the legal father is deceased, the question to ask is whether a familial relationship existed at the time of his death;
- finally, the contestant has to be the actual genetic father of the child (§ 1600 II BGB).

The rationale behind this complicated rule is to protect the child from the destruction of established family ties.

159. An Act of 13 March 2008[241] granted state authorities the right to contest paternity (§ 1600 I No. 5, III BGB). The Act was passed as a reaction to cases where men falsely acknowledged paternity in order to get a residence permit for the child's mother or German citizenship for the child. This is why the authority's right only existed where there was no familial relationship between the child and the legal

---

238. Cf. § 1613 II No. 2 lit. a BGB, *see infra* paras 279 et seq.
239. For the procedure *see* §§ 169–185 FamFG.
240. BVerfGE 108, 82.
241. *Gesetz zur Ergänzung des Rechts zur Anfechtung der Vaterschaft* of 13 Mar. 2008 (BGBl. I 313).

father, and where the acknowledgement of paternity led to a right of entry or of residence for the parent or the child. In 2013, the Constitutional Court invalidated the provision, holding that the state authorities' right to contest paternity was unconstitutional.[242] The provision has now been removed.[243]

160. A paternity contest is instituted by bringing an action in the family court. The child, the father, and the mother are all necessary parties to the suit. Problems may arise where the child is the contesting party and has not yet come of age. According to § 1600a II BGB, the proceedings will in this case be conducted by the child's legal representative. § 1600a IV BGB provides that the legal representative may only bring the action if it is in the best interests of the child to do so.

161. Paternity can only be contested within two years of the contestant becoming aware of the facts leading to the challenge, § 1600b I, II BGB. The two-year period does not start until the child's birth or the acknowledgement of paternity, § 1600b II 1 BGB.

A special rule applies where the child is contesting paternity: even if the legal representative has allowed the two-year period to elapse, the child may bring an action after coming of age. The two-year period runs from the child's own knowledge of the relevant facts, starting no earlier than the child's majority, § 1600b III BGB. Even after the two years have passed, the child may contest paternity where special circumstances have arisen that would render remaining under the current status intolerable for the child, § 1600b VI BGB.

162. An action that satisfies the above formal requirements will be successful if the court considers the claim to be legally justified. The court must be convinced that the man to whom the child is attributed is not in fact the child's genetic father. The action is a purely negative one. It is not necessary to establish who the child's genetic father is – although this may be the subject of subsequent paternity proceedings. The situation is different where the potential father is contesting; here – as was shown above – it is imperative that he be the genetic father. In such a case, a successful action results in the positive affirmation of the potential father's paternity (§ 1592 No. 3 BGB, § 182 I FamFG).

A successful court action ends with the *ex nunc* termination of the paternal relationship by order of the court, dating back to the time it has first arisen (e.g., the child's birth in the case of paternity established by marriage). The court's decision is binding on everyone, not just *inter partes*.[244] Maintenance previously paid for the child now lacks a cause, and intestacy claims lack legal justification. The same goes for citizenship based solely on paternity: the child attains the status it would have had if the (contested) paternity had never existed.

---

242. BVerfGE 135, 48.
243. *Gesetz zur besseren Durchsetzung der Ausreisepflicht* of 20 Jul. 2017 (BGBl. I 2780).
244. § 184 II FamFG.

163. Where paternity is successfully contested, the previous 'father' may have been maintaining the child presumed to be his for years. Recovery of those payments from the child under the law of restitution is rarely possible since § 818 III BGB prohibits repayment of money actually spent. §§ 1613 II No. 2 lit. a, 1607 III 2 BGB, therefore, lift the ban on claiming maintenance for the past. These provisions allow the former father to seek reimbursement from the child's actual genetic father – once he has been established as such.

Damages claims against the child's mother will only succeed in exceptional circumstances, e.g., where the mother wilfully used the alleged paternity to trick the man into marriage or to prevent him from contesting paternity.[245]

D. Establishing Paternity by Judicial Decision

164. In the absence of paternity by marriage or official acknowledgement, or after such paternity has been successfully contested, a person may apply to the court to establish paternity, § 1600d I BGB. Exclusive jurisdiction lies with the family court.[246] The application is successful if the man in question is the child's genetic father (by procreation or sperm donation). The court will enquire into the matter ex officio.[247] Paternity is established to the satisfaction of the court if the evidence points beyond reasonable doubt to the alleged father.

165. The law works from the presumption that paternity can normally be inferred from the fact that a man had sexual intercourse with the mother at the time of the child's conception, § 1600d II 1 BGB. The statutory period of conception runs from 181 to 300 days before the date of the child's birth – unless a different time span is proved, § 1600d III 2 BGB. Intercourse during that time has to be established. The presumption is rebutted by serious doubts as to the man's paternity, § 1600 II 2 BGB. It is also possible to obtain a negative declaration of paternity.[248] Where the child was conceived in a medically assisted procedure with sperm donated to a sperm bank, the sperm donor cannot be established as the child's legal father, § 1600d IV BGB. Sole jurisdiction for affiliation proceedings is with the family court.

The court's declaration is binding on everyone.[249] All claims arising from the parent-child relationship – e.g., maintenance claims – can be based on the court's decision, even claims for past maintenance, § 1600d V BGB.

245. BGH FamRZ 1990, 367, 369; 2013, 939.
246. §§ 23a I 1 No. 1, 23b I GVG; §§ 111 No. 3, 169 No. 1 FamFG.
247. §§ 26, 177 II FamFG.
248. § 169 No. 1 FamFG.
249. § 184 II FamFG.

E. Artificial Reproduction

166. Artificial reproduction is not generally prohibited by German law. However, the *Protection of Embryos Act 1990*[250] places restrictions on certain techniques that are considered abusive. Under the current law, artificial reproduction is left out of account in determining the child's legal mother: the birth mother is regarded as the legal mother, whether she is the child's genetic mother or not. Maternity thus established cannot be challenged.[251] Agreements between the genetic and the gestational mother about the transfer of the child to the genetic mother or any other woman are prohibited and legally void.

167. The situation is different where the child's father is concerned. Here the genetic father may become the child's legal father by using the processes presented *supra*. However, if the genetic father is a sperm donor who donated his sperm to an official sperm bank (rather than privately) and if the child is conceived in a medically assisted procedure, the donor may not be established as the child's legal father by a court order, § 1600d IV BGB. This provision does not preclude the donor from becoming the child's legal father by an acknowledgement of paternity, however, if the mother consents.

It has long been disputed whether a husband, who has consented to the heterologous insemination of his wife, can, after the birth, contest paternity.[252] The legislature decided this issue in 2002:[253] where a child is conceived with the consent of the husband and the wife by using the sperm of a third man, neither the husband nor the wife can contest paternity, § 1600 IV BGB. The sperm donor is not caught by this provision. Accordingly, he may have a right to contest since the Federal Supreme Court considers sperm donation to be 'intercourse' with the mother within the meaning of § 1600 I No. 2 BGB.[254] However, the donor's right is excluded where a familial relationship exists between the child and its legal father, § 1600 II BGB. Also, the courts generally find that the donor has waived his right to contest paternity if the child's conception was the result of an agreement between the donor and the child's legal parents.[255] If the child has no legal father (e.g., because its mother is lesbian), the donor's right to have his paternity established by a court order may be excluded pursuant to § 1600d IV BGB.[256]

168. The legal position of the sperm donor flows from the rules outlined *supra*: where no other man is recognized as the child's legal father or where the legal father's paternity has been successfully contested, the sperm donor may acknowledge the child to be his or seek a paternity order, § 1592 Nos 2, 3 BGB.

---

250. *Embryonenschutzgesetz* of 13 Dec. 1990 (BGBl. I 2746).
251. *See supra* para. 150.
252. *See* BGHZ 87, 169; BGH NJW 1995, 2921.
253. Act for the further Protection of Children's Rights (*Gesetz zur weiteren Verbesserung von Kinderrechten*) of 9 Apr. 2002 (BGBl. I 1239).
254. BGH FamRZ 2013, 1209.
255. BGH FamRZ 2013, 1209.
256. BGH FamRZ 2013, 1209.

In most cases, however, sperm donors will be more interested in safeguarding their anonymity. Here, German law provides little protection.[257] An Act of 2017 establishes a donor register,[258] to which any person who suspects that he or she may have been conceived in a medical procedure using donor sperm may apply for information about the donor's identity, § 10 SaRegG. Once a donor has been established as the child's father, he is under the same legal obligations – e.g., to maintain the child – as every father. The mother may not waive these claims on behalf of the child, § 1614 I BGB.

III. Knowledge of One's Genetic Origins

169. As of 2008, German law has provided a procedure, whereby biological parentage may be established without changing a child's legal status. According to the Constitutional Court, the child has a right, derived from the right of personality (Article 2 I in conjunction with Article 1 I GG), to know his or her genetic origins. This means that available information must not be kept from the child.[259] The Constitutional Court went even further and recognized a legal father's right to know if a certain child is his biological offspring.[260] The German legislature has introduced a legal mechanism through which biological parentage may be established without having to contest paternity.[261] The new § 1598a BGB gives a right to demand consent to genetic tests and to the collection of blood and saliva samples to establish (or disprove) genetic paternity. This right only applies *between certain persons*:

- the legal father has a right against the mother and the child;
- the mother has a right against the legal father and the child;
- the child has a right against both legal parents.

Not included in this list is the potential genetic father.[262] Also not included are other relatives such as grandparents and siblings. Jurisdiction lies with the family court.[263] The above-mentioned duties may be enforced. The court does not itself establish paternity, but allows the applicant to do so by means of genetic samples. The proceedings may be followed by a formal contestation of paternity, but this is not obligatory. Legal *parenthood* may thus be maintained, even though it has been conclusively established not to correspond to biological *parentage*.

170. § 1598a BGB does not help when it comes to positively establishing genetic parentage (except where the legal father turns out to be the biological father). Hence, the courts have had to decide whether a child has a right as against the mother to be informed of the identity of the (potential) father. Although this right

257. *See infra* paras 169 et seq.
258. Sperm Donor Register Act (*Samenspenderregistergesetz*, SaRegG) of 17 Jul. 2017.
259. BVerfGE 79, 256; 90, 263; 96, 56.
260. BVerfGE 117, 202.
261. *Gesetz zur Klärung der Vaterschaft unabhängig vom Anfechtungsverfahren* of 26 Mar. 2008.
262. Accepted by the Constitutional Court, BVerfG FamRZ 2008, 2257.
263. §§ 23a I 1 No. 1, 23b I GVG; §§ 111 No. 3, 169 No. 2, 3 FamFG.

is generally thought to exist, the courts see a conflict between the child's right to know his or her genetic origins and the mother's right to respect for her private life; the conflicting interests have to be balanced on a case-by-case basis.[264]

171. A child also has a right to know its birth mother. This right may come into conflict with a mother's wish to remain anonymous. In 2013, the German *Bundestag* introduced confidential birth legislation.[265] In a confidential birth, the mother gives birth under a pseudonym. However, a record of origin (*Herkunftsnachweis*) is created and enclosed in a sealed envelope bearing the mother's pseudonym and the child's place and date of birth. On reaching sixteen, the child has a right to inspect the record of origin. The mother can file objections. If she does so, the child has to take the case to the family court, which will balance the child's right to know its genetic origins against the mother's interest in maintaining her anonymity.

§2. The Position of the Child (General)

I. The Child's Name

172. German law has a set of intricate rules regulating a person's name. Parents thus have only limited freedom as far as the child's name is concerned. They may choose the child's first name, but only as long as the child's welfare is not jeopardized by their choice.[266] Registration of the name will be refused, e.g., where the name would subject the child to ridicule. If the parents cannot agree on a first name, the dispute will be resolved by the courts, § 1628 BGB.

173. Complicated rules govern the child's surname: where the child's parents are married and share a family name (§ 1355 I 1, II BGB), the child will acquire this name automatically, § 1616 BGB. Where the spouses do not have the same name (§ 1355 I 3 BGB), they can choose either of their surnames as the child's last name, § 1617 BGB. This choice is binding for any future children of the couple (§ 1617 I 3 BGB).

174. Since the right to choose the child's surname springs from parental responsibility, similar rules apply where the parents are not married, but share parental responsibility.[267] If the parents cannot agree on the child's surname within one month of the birth, the registrar will notify the court. The court will grant the right to choose a name to one of the parents.[268]

264. BVerfGE 96, 56.
265. *Gesetz zum Ausbau der Hilfen für Schwangere und zur Regelung der vertraulichen Geburt* of 28 Aug. 2013.
266. BVerfGE 104, 373, 385.
267. Following the rules set out in §§ 1594 IV, 1626b II BGB.
268. § 1617 II BGB.

Where one parent has sole custody, the child bears that parent's name (§ 1617a I BGB). Where both parents agree – and the child, if over five, consents (§ 1617a II 2 BGB) – the child may also be named after the other parent (§§ 1617a II; 1617c I BGB).

175. A child's last name can only be changed in exceptional circumstances, e.g., where the parents later assume a joint family name (§§ 1355 III, 1617c I BGB) or acquire joint parental responsibility (§ 1617b II BGB). The law also grants the right to change a child's last name if it is established that the man whose name the child bears is not the genetic parent, § 1617b II BGB.

II. Assistance and Due Consideration

176. § 1618a BGB spells out a general rule for the parent-child relationship: parents and children owe each other assistance and due consideration. Although this provision cannot in itself be the basis for claims between children and parents, it has to be considered by the courts where the interpretation of legal rights and duties within the family is concerned. Thus, maintenance claims may be forfeited by a violation of § 1618a BGB.[269] The courts have also used the principle to limit the liability of (adult) children who guarantee their parents' debts: the guarantee may be invalid if the parents secured it in violation of the principle of assistance and due consideration, and if the creditor exploited the violation.[270]

269. Doctrine of *Rechtsmissbrauch* (abuse of rights).
270. *See* BGH NJW 1994, 1341; 1997, 52.

Chapter 6. Adoption

177. The German BGB regulates the adoption of minor children in detail (§§ 1741 et seq. BGB). Adult persons may also be adopted, but only where the adoption is 'morally justified', § 1767 I BGB. Generally, adult adoptions are governed by the same rules as adoptions of minors, § 1767 II BGB. However, as a rule, their legal effects are more limited, § 1770 BGB. It is only in exceptional cases that the adoption of an adult may be given the same legal effects as the adoption of a minor child, § 1772 BGB.

§1. Application and Consent

178. Under German law, adoption is performed by a court order, made on the application of the prospective parent(s) (§ 1752 BGB), and with the consent of a number of specified parties.

The initiative lies with the adoptive parent(s). The application has to be notarized, and it can only be made in person, unconditionally and without time limits, § 1752 II BGB. The applicant has to be at least 25 years old. Twenty-one years are enough in the case of in-family adoptions or where the applicants are married and one spouse has reached the age of 25, § 1743 sent. 1, 2 BGB.

179. As a rule, spouses may only apply jointly for an adoption order (§§ 1741 II 2, 1754 I BGB), unless one of them is the child's natural parent (*see* § 1741 II 4 BGB for further exceptions).

One spouse may adopt the child of the other spouse with the result that the child is legally considered a child of both, §§ 1741 II 3, 1754 I BGB. Since 2005, it has been possible to adopt the biological child of one's registered partner so that the child becomes a mutual child of the (same-sex) partners and lives under their joint parental care.[271] In 2014, it was expressly provided that a registered partner may also adopt the adopted child of his or her spouse so that the adopted child becomes a mutual child of the partners.[272] As a result of a Constitutional Court decision,[273] a further exception was introduced in 2020. According to the new § 1766a BGB, an unmarried partner who lives in a committed relationship and shares a common household with the child's parent may adopt his or her partner's child. This adoption will have the same effect as a step-parent adoption by a married or registered partner; i.e., it will not sever the child's legal tie with the other unmarried partner, §§ 1766a I, 1755 II BGB. A committed relationship may be presumed, where the partners have either lived together for four years or have lived together in a marriage-like relationship with a mutual child, § 1766a II 1 BGB. A committed relationship will usually be lacking, where either partner is married to a third person, § 1766a II 2 BGB. With that one exception, persons who are not married may only

271. § 9 VII LPartG in connection with § 1754 I, III BGB.
272. *Gesetz zur Umsetzung der Entscheidung des Bundesverfassungsgerichts zur Sukzessivadoption durch Lebenspartner* of 20 Jun. 2014 (BGBl. I 786).
273. BVerfGE 151, 101.

adopt alone, § 1741 II 1 BGB. In particular, German law does not allow joint adoptions by unmarried couples or registered partners. Except where a spouse (or a registered partner) joins an adoption made by his or her partner before the marriage, a child may only be adopted once during the lifetime of the adoptive parents, § 1742 BGB.

180. The prior consent of the following people is required before an adoption order can be made:

(1) The child: where the child is under 14, the legal representative acts for the child, § 1746 I 2 BGB. Where the child has reached 14 years and has limited legal capacity, the child has to act himself or herself, albeit with the representative's approval, § 1746 I 3 BGB.
(2) The child's natural parents: their consent is needed irrespective of their marital status and of whether they have parental responsibility, § 1747 BGB. To ensure the natural parents' freedom of decision, the law provides that the consent may not validly be given until eight weeks after the child's birth, § 1747 II 1 BGB. This is different only in the case of the unmarried father, who may consent before the child's birth, § 1747 III 1 BGB. Once given, the consent is irrevocable. It loses its validity, however, if the adoption application is refused or withdrawn or if no adoption order is made within three years, § 1750 IV BGB. The sperm donor is considered a father within the meaning of § 1747 I 2 BGB, except in cases coming within § 1600d IV BGB. His consent is only necessary, however, if he adduces prima facie evidence for his paternity. To afford him an opportunity to do so, the family court is required to inform him of the adoption proceedings. The court may only refrain from doing so if he clearly has no interest in the proceedings because he waived his paternal rights.[274] In exceptional circumstances, a natural parent's consent may be dispensed with by the court, e.g., where a parent's residence is permanently unknown, § 1747 IV BGB. According to § 1747 IV 2 BGB, the residence of a mother who has given birth confidentially is considered permanently unknown until she provides the necessary information for the child's birth record. The court can also supply the consent where there is severe danger to the child's welfare. This intrusion into the very centre of parental rights requires a serious violation of parental duties, as § 1748 I BGB makes clear (e.g., major crimes against the child).
(3) The adoptive parent's spouse and the child's spouse: in the former case, the unwilling spouse's consent may be supplied by the court unless the spouse's refusal is based on legitimate conflicting interests, § 1749 I 2, 3 BGB.

274. BGH FamRZ 2015, 828.

§2. PLACEMENT PRIOR TO ADOPTION

181. Normally, an adoption order will only be made if the child has previously lived with the prospective adoptive parent for a reasonable amount of time, § 1744 BGB. § 1751 BGB provides a legal framework for such 'placement prior to adoption': as soon as the natural parents consent to the adoption, their parental responsibility and right to contact with the child are suspended.

The local Youth Welfare office (*Jugendamt*) acts as a guardian. The prospective adoptive parents become entitled to decide routine matters and to represent the child legally to that extent, §§ 1751 I 4, 1688 I BGB. They also become liable for the child's maintenance, § 1751 IV BGB.

§3. THE ADOPTION ORDER AND ITS EFFECTS

182. Jurisdiction for adoption orders lies with the family court.[275] Where the legal requirements described *supra* are met, the court will grant the order if this is beneficial to the child and if it can be expected that a true parent-child relationship will develop between the parties. Financial interests should not be decisive, § 1745 sent. 2 BGB. Once made, the order is unchallengeable and irrevocable.[276]

183. No adoption order may be granted posthumously for the deceased child, § 1753 I BGB. Adoption after the death of the prospective adoptive parent is possible, however, provided he or she filed the application or requested a notary to do so before his or her death. A posthumous adoption order has retroactive effect and dates back to the time of the applicant's death, § 1753 III BGB. The adopted child might, therefore, have a statutory right to inherit.

184. Once the order comes into effect, the adopted child is legally considered the adoptive parents' offspring and a member of their family. This includes statutory rights to inheritance, maintenance, etc., in relation to the new family. At the same time, the child's ties to the natural parents and their families are severed, § 1755 BGB.

The child's name changes upon adoption and becomes the adoptive parents' family name, § 1757 I BGB. On application and with the child's consent, the court may allow the child to bear a hyphenated name made up of the old and the new family name (in either order), § 1757 III 1 No. 2 BGB.

275. §§ 23a I 1 No. 1, 23b I GVG; §§ 111 No. 4, 186–199 FamFG.
276. But *see infra* paras 185, 186.

§4. Revocation of the Adoption Order

185. As a rule, an adoption order once granted is irrevocable and final so as to provide a stable basis for the new family. Under exceptional circumstances set out in the Civil Code, however, the law departs from this principle and allows a revocation:

(1) Where the required declarations were not (validly) given[277] or where there was a fundamental error in making the declaration.[278] Any such defects, however, are purged three years after the effective date of the adoption order, § 1762 II 1 BGB. Furthermore, even before that time, there is a ban on revocation if revocation would seriously jeopardize the child's welfare and the court discerns no overriding interest on the side of the adoptive parents, § 1761 II BGB.
(2) The family court may, on its own motion, revoke the adoption order during the child's minority if it considers this necessary to protect the child, § 1763 I BGB.

186. The revocation of an adoption order does not have retroactive effect, § 1764 I 1 BGB. Once the revocation order has become absolute, the family ties previously established by the adoption come to an end and those previously severed revive, § 1764 II, III BGB. The natural parents do not automatically regain parental responsibility, but an application for parental responsibility would be granted by the court unless contrary to the child's best interests, § 1764 IV BGB.

277. For example, lack of valid application, or of a required consent, *see* §§ 1747, 1746 BGB.
278. For example, mistake as to the child's identity or duress, *see* § 1760 II BGB.

Chapter 7. Parental Responsibility

§1. Acquiring Parental Responsibility

187. As a rule, parental responsibility (*elterliche Sorge*) – meaning all the duties and rights of a parent in relation to his or her child – belongs to both parents. Under certain conditions, however, German law also recognizes sole parental responsibility. Even then, however, the tie between the other parent and the child is not completely severed, and some rights and duties (e.g., the duty to maintain, the right to contact) remain. Parental responsibility may be acquired in three ways: by operation of law, by declaration, or by court order.

I. Parental Responsibility Acquired by Law

188. Where the parents are married at the time of the birth, both acquire parental responsibility automatically without any further act being required or even possible.[279] Parental responsibility thus acquired continues until it is ended by law (e.g., by the death of a parent) or by court order. The parents' divorce or separation has no effect on who has parental responsibility. Where a child is born out of wedlock, generally only the mother has parental responsibility, § 1626a III BGB. Joint parental responsibility arises where the parents marry (§ 1626a I No. 2 BGB) or where they file a declaration saying that they want to share parental responsibility (§ 1626a I No. 1 BGB). Where the mother refuses to share parental responsibility, the law formerly gave her sole parental responsibility without any possibility of review. According to the European Court of Human Rights, this state of the law violated the non-discrimination provisions in Articles 14 and 8 ECHR.[280] The German Constitutional Court has also found a violation of the parental rights of the father (Article 6 II GG) where a refusal on the part of the mother denies him parental responsibility and leaves him without the possibility of review.[281] In 2013, the legislature finally addressed this situation:[282] the family court may now, on the parent's application, grant parental responsibility (in all or some areas) to both parents jointly if this is not contrary to the best interests of the child, § 1626a I No. 3, II 1 BGB. *See infra* paragraph 192.

II. Parental Responsibility Acquired by Formal Declaration

189. Where the parents are not married to each other at the time of the birth, joint parental responsibility can result from a formal declaration. This declaration is only effective if made in the prescribed form. It has to be made by both partners in

279. Cf. §§ 1626, 1626a BGB.
280. FamRZ 2010, 103.
281. BVerfGE 127, 132, breaking with BVerfGE 107, 150.
282. *Gesetz zur Reform der elterlichen Sorge nicht miteinander verheirateter Eltern* of 16 Apr. 2013.

person, and it must be unconditional, § 1626b I BGB. It also has to be officially recorded.[283] It is not possible to limit the extent to which one or both parents exercise parental responsibility.

The declaration does not become legally effective until the child is born (although it is possible to lodge a declaration prior to the birth, § 1626b II BGB). There is no time limit as to when the declaration has to be made except that it has to be made before the child comes of age. Where parental responsibility for a child has been granted by a court order, there is no room for a declaration, § 1626b III BGB.

As long as the requirements spelled out in §§ 1626a–1626d BGB are adhered to, the declaration will be valid. Even a violation of general contractual rules – e.g., fraudulent misrepresentation – will not render them void, § 1626e BGB.

190. The parents' declarations do not have to be made simultaneously. They do not form a contract, but run in parallel, leading to the curious result that the father, when lodging his declaration, might not even know that the child's mother has already done so. Also, it is not necessary for the parents to cohabit. Where they do not cohabit, joint parental responsibility is exercised by granting the resident parent the sole right to decide routine matters, § 1687 I 2, 3 BGB.[284]

191. At no point in the proceedings is there any enquiry into the child's welfare. However, once a declaration of joint parental responsibility has come into effect, the parents' power of free disposition ends: any change in parental responsibility can now only be effected by court order, e.g., under § 1666 BGB, if the child's welfare is seriously endangered, or on the application of one of the parents.

III. Parental Responsibility Acquired by Court Order

192. Since 2013,[285] the family court has been able, on the application of one parent, to grant parental responsibility (relating to some or all matters) to both parents jointly if this is not contrary to the best interests of the child, § 1626a I No. 3, II 1 BGB. *See supra* paragraph 188. Joint parental responsibility is now favoured by the law. There is a presumption that joint parental responsibility is not contrary to the best interests of the child if the other parent does not advance any reasons against it and if no such reasons are otherwise apparent, § 1626a II 2 BGB. A mother's chances to resist joint parental responsibility are also lessened by current procedural rules. The family court can set a time limit for the other parent's (usually the mother's) objections, § 155a II 2 FamFG. If reasons against the grant of joint parental responsibility are neither advanced nor otherwise apparent, the court decides by written procedure, without hearing either the parents or the Youth Welfare office, § 155a III 1 FamFG. The presumption that joint parental responsibility is not against the best interests of the child must not be taken too far. The family court has to carry out a fact-based, case-by-case analysis into whether joint parental responsibility is

283. §§ 1626d I BGB, 59 I 1 No. 8 SGB VIII.
284. *See infra* para. 229.
285. *Gesetz zur Reform der elterlichen Sorge nicht miteinander verheirateter Eltern* of 16 Apr. 2013.

in fact compatible with the best interests of the child in question. If the parents cannot agree on and cooperate in basic childcare matters, granting them joint parental responsibility is generally *not* in the child's best interests.[286]

193. Unmarried fathers have not just become able to acquire joint parental responsibility, even against the mother's wishes. Since 2013, an unmarried father who is not living with the mother has also been able to apply for *sole* parental responsibility, § 1671 II BGB. If the mother consents, the application will be successful unless transferring parental responsibility to the father would be contrary to the child's best interests or the child is over 14 and objects to the transfer, § 1671 II 1 No. 1 BGB. If the mother does not consent, the application will only succeed if joint parental responsibility is not an option and if transferring parental responsibility to the father promises to be in the child's best interests, § 1671 II 2 No. 2 BGB.

194. Where parents who have previously shared parental responsibility separate, each might apply for a court order giving him or her sole parental responsibility, § 1671 I BGB. If the other parent consents, the application will succeed unless the child is over 14 years old and objects to the order, § 1671 I 2 No. 1 BGB. If the other parent does not consent (or the child over 14 objects), an order can still be made if terminating joint parental responsibility, and granting sole parental responsibility to the applicant parent, promises to be best for the child, § 1671 I 2 No. 2 BGB.

195. A court parental responsibility order must be changed if weighty reasons, having a lasting effect on the welfare of the child, demand this, § 1696 I BGB.

§2. Care for the Child's Person (§§ 1626 I 1, 1631 BGB)

196. Parental responsibility for a child is exercised in two main areas: in the personal and in the financial sphere. German law thus distinguishes between personal and financial responsibility as the duties of a parent. Care for the child's person gives to the parents' rights and duties in relation to the child and in relation to third parties. The main objective is to further the child's interests and welfare. In the area of personal care – as well as in that of financial care – the right to represent the child legally (§ 1629 BGB) plays a key role.

The right to care for the child's person includes the right to consent to the circumcision of a male child, provided the circumcision is carried out *lege artis* and does not endanger the child's welfare, § 1631d I BGB. During the first six months of the child's life, the circumcision may be carried out not only by doctors but also by the officers of a religious community provided they are specially trained and as skilled at conducting the procedure as a doctor, § 1631d II BGB.

Parents also have a right to determine the child's residence (§ 1631 BGB) and a right to physical possession enforceable against anyone who detains the child

286. OLG Koblenz FamRZ 2014, 319; OLG Brandenburg FamRZ 2014, 1856; KG FamRZ 2014, 1375.

against their wishes (§ 1632 I BGB). They also have the right to control and direct contact (§ 1632 II BGB). § 1626 II BGB points out, however, that when providing care and education, parents have to take account of the growing abilities of the child and the child's need to act independently and responsibly. Accordingly, parents are required to discuss questions of parental responsibility with the child to the extent that the child's development indicates this, and they must try to reach an agreement.

§3. The Welfare Principle

197. The guiding principle for a parent exercising parental responsibility is the child's welfare or best interests. The Basic Law gives parents the right to direct the child's upbringing;[287] thus, it is not primarily for the state to determine how the child's welfare is best achieved in practice. The state is under an obligation to intervene, however, if the child is suffering or is likely to suffer significant harm.[288]

The law lays down some guidelines as to the meaning of the welfare principle: § 1626 II BGB reminds parents to take account of the child's increasing capacity to arrive at decisions independently, and it directs them to consult with the child accordingly. This is particularly relevant where the child's education and training are concerned (§ 1631a BGB). § 1631 II BGB[289] guarantees children a right to an upbringing free of violence. Corporal punishment, mental cruelty, and other forms of humiliating treatment are not permitted.

§4. Legal Representation

198. Parents may legally represent the child in two ways: they can act for the child, and they can consent to the child's own acts. The child may also be covered by the protective effect of contracts entered into between the parents and third parties (under the doctrine of contracts with protective effects for third parties).[290]

The parents represent the child either jointly (§ 1629 I 2 BGB) or singly (§ 1629 I 3 BGB), depending on who has parental responsibility for the child.

I. Joint Parental Responsibility

199. Where the parents share parental responsibility, both parents have to act for the child, although representation may be arranged between them. If the parents cannot agree, the family court can transfer the right to decide to one parent and also grant that parent the right to represent the child alone to that extent, § 1628 BGB.

---

287. Article 6 II 1 GG.
288. Article 6 II 2 GG.
289. As laid down in the Prohibition of Violence in Education Act (*Gesetz zur Ächtung der Gewalt in der Erziehung*) of 2 Nov. 2000 (BGBl. I 1479).
290. The so-called *Vertrag mit Schutzwirkung zugunsten Dritter*.

The court might also grant one parent the sole right to decide a certain set of questions, e.g., questions relating to the child's medical treatment. Furthermore, parents can act alone in case of imminent danger, provided the other parent is informed without delay, § 1629 I 4 BGB.

200. Upon the parents' separation, the right to decide routine matters lies with the resident parent, § 1687 I 1–3 BGB.

II. The Limits of Legal Representation

201. German law knows several instances in which the parents' right to legal representation is curtailed to protect the child's best interests, or to acknowledge the child's growing capacity to make his or her own decisions. A few examples may suffice:

(1) Transactions that seem likely to jeopardize the child's interests need the consent of the family court.[291] Examples are the disposal of the child's real property (§ 1821 I No. 1 BGB), of all assets at once (§ 1822 No. 1 BGB), debts incurred in the child's name (§ 1822 No. 8 BGB), and the renunciation of an inheritance (§ 1822 No. 2 BGB). The family court decides, in accordance with the welfare principle, whether to permit the parents to enter into the transaction in question (§ 1697a BGB). It is for the parents to decide whether they want to act upon the permission.
(2) The law does not allow the parents to decide for the child where there is a conflict of interest, e.g., where the legal transaction is between the child and one or both parents or between the child and a close relative (§§ 181, 1795 II; 1795 I No. 1, 1629 II 1 BGB). These restrictions do not apply, however, if the transaction is wholly beneficial for the child.[292] If the parents act for their child in disregard of the prohibition, they act as unauthorized representatives (§§ 177 et seq. BGB). Their actions might be sanctioned by the child once the child comes of age. Also, the court may subsequently grant its permission.
(3) The Constitutional Court has decided that these restrictions are insufficient to protect the child's interests. Parents are not allowed to enter into obligations that burden the child to such an extent that the child's ability to lead a self-determined life on majority is put in danger.[293] Accordingly, the *Act Limiting the Liability of Minors*[294] introduced § 1629a BGB, which now limits the child's liability for obligations incurred by the parents on behalf of the child (§ 1629a BGB).

---

291. *See* §§ 1643 I, II; 1821 et seq.; 112 BGB.
292. BGHZ 59, 236; BGH FamRZ 1975, 480.
293. BVerfGE 72, 155.
294. *Gesetz zur Beschränkung der Haftung Minderjähriger* of 25 Aug. 1998 (BGBl. I 2487).

§5. Disagreement Between Holders of Parental Responsibility

202. Where parental responsibility is exercised by both parents, decisions have to be taken jointly and aimed at the welfare of the child, § 1627 sent. 1, 2 BGB. Disagreements that the parents cannot resolve themselves might ultimately require to be decided by the family court, § 1628 BGB. On the application of at least one parent, the court can issue an order in matters of considerable importance. By the order, the court transfers the right to decide to one parent.[295]

203. § 1628 BGB enables the court to transfer the right to decide all future questions arising in a specific area to one parent. As an exception to the rule of joint parental responsibility, such an order should only be made in special circumstances.

§6. Self-Determination of the Child

204. As the child matures, the scope of parental responsibility diminishes, § 1626 II BGB.[296] This recognition of the child's growing maturity is expressed in a number of provisions in the Code:

(1) From the age of 14, the child can determine its religious denomination, § 5 *Religious Upbringing of Minors Act*.[297]
(2) From the age of 16, the minor can draw up a will (albeit not in holographic form, § 2247 IV BGB) without the parents' consent, § 2229 I, II BGB.
(3) Consent to medical treatment depends on the level of understanding of the individual child.[298] Under what conditions the child's consent is in itself sufficient for medical treatment (e.g., an abortion) is still a matter of controversy.
(4) The child has increasing procedural rights as it grows older: a minor above the age of 14 years must always be heard in proceedings that relate to his or her personal care.[299] Younger children will be heard if the court thinks it necessary.
(5) Also, from the age of 14 the child has a right to appeal to a higher court,[300] e.g., where a parental responsibility (§ 1671 BGB) or contact order (§ 1684 BGB) is concerned.

§7. Protecting Parental Responsibility

205. Parental responsibility may need protection from the undue influence of third parties. The state guarantees to parents the undisturbed exercise of parental

---

295. Cf. *supra* para. 199.
296. *See supra* para. 197.
297. *Gesetz über die religiöse Kindererziehung*.
298. *Natürliche Einsichtsfähigkeit*, BGHZ 29, 33.
299. § 159 I FamFG.
300. § 60 FamFG.

responsibility by granting them certain rights against third parties in § 1632 BGB. Parental responsibility is also recognized as a right protected by tort law, § 823 I BGB.

I. Possession of the Child

206. According to § 1632 I BGB, the holder of parental responsibility may ask for the child to be returned to him or her by any third party provided this does not run counter to the child's welfare. The right may be exercised against the other parent as well as against third parties.

II. Contact

207. Parents also have the right to determine who may have contact with the child. Where necessary, they can apply for a court order to defend that right, irrespective of whether it is a third party or the child who desires the unwished-for contact. This might be problematic where the child is approaching majority, in view of the child's growing maturity and right to self-determination, § 1626 II BGB.

The courts cautiously weigh the interests at stake and only go against the child's express wishes where there are persuasive reasons for doing so. Courts will be especially careful where a positive relationship has been established, even if this happened against the parents' wishes. It should be noted, however, that § 1632 II BGB is not applicable where contact between the child and the non-residential parent is concerned.[301]

§8. Third Parties Caring for Children

208. As a rule, parental responsibility is strictly personal and cannot be transferred in its entirety to a third party. Parents can only invest others temporarily with certain rights in relation to the child, e.g., neighbours caring for the child.

209. The situation is different where the parents are not willing or able to undertake the child's upbringing but also do not want to give the child up for adoption. Foster parents may then be asked to become the child's social parents,[302] while parental responsibility remains vested in the legal parents. § 1688 BGB tries to balance the potentially conflicting interests between parents and foster parents. Where a child lives with a foster family for a longer period, the foster parents are entitled to make decisions regarding the child's routine matters. They may also manage the child's earnings and enforce child support duties and social security claims. In urgent cases, they become fully competent to decide and act for the child. These rights do not exist where the parents object or the court orders otherwise.

---

301. Cf. *infra* paras 240 et seq.
302. So-called *Familienpflege*.

210. Should the parents request the child's return to the detriment of the child's welfare, the family court can order the child to remain with the foster family, § 1632 IV BGB. Since this severely curtails parental rights, however, the child's welfare has to be seriously endangered for the court to make such an order.

With the parents' consent, the family court can give further rights to the foster carers to the exclusion of the parents under § 1630 III BGB.

211. Similar protections apply to stepfamilies. Where the child is living with one parent and that parent's partner or spouse, social ties might develop, the destruction of which would be detrimental to the child. Therefore, the courts may order a child to remain with his or her stepfather or stepmother if the parent having parental responsibility is planning to withdraw the child, § 1682 BGB. By way of example: after the parents' divorce, a child lives with the father and his new wife. After the father's death, the mother is granted sole parental responsibility. She now plans to take in the child and asks for the child to be handed over. A stay order will only be made if surrendering the child to the parent with sole parental responsibility would endanger the child's welfare.

If the child lives with a parent having sole parental responsibility and that parent's new spouse, the latter has certain rights: where questions of the child's daily life are concerned, the spouse can decide along with the parent having parental responsibility. In cases of imminent danger, he or she can initiate the measures necessary for the child's welfare, but has to inform the parent with parental responsibility without delay, § 1687b BGB. The foregoing also applies to the registered partner of a parent with parental responsibility, § 9 LPartG.

§9. Care for the Child's Property

212. On the financial side, the parents' care is chiefly aimed at conservation and augmentation of the child's assets. With the exception of the assets named in § 1638 BGB, these include everything the child owns and acquires, including anything purchased by the parents with the child's means.

In governing the assets, the parents are bound by the principles of prudent property management, § 1642 BGB. If they fail to observe their duties, the family court may intervene, §§ 1666, 1667 BGB. Transactions that are potentially dangerous to the child's property also require the court's prior approval, § 1643 BGB, as the parents' power to represent the child is correspondingly restricted.[303]

213. The Code also outlines how the child's assets are to be used: income is to be used for administering the property and for maintaining the child, § 1649 BGB. The principal can only be touched if the child's maintenance would otherwise be jeopardized. Any surplus income has to be reinvested. § 1649 II 1 BGB, which is based on the idea of family solidarity, allows for a limited use of surplus income for the maintenance of the parents and any minor siblings.[304]

303. *See supra* para. 201.
304. Notwithstanding the rules found in § 1602 I BGB.

§10. Claims Between Parents and Children Arising from the Exercise of Parental Responsibility

214. Parents might incur expenses in the exercise of parental responsibility that they are entitled to consider necessary under the circumstances. They can claim reimbursement from the child to the extent that they themselves are not chargeable for these expenses, § 1648 BGB. Upon termination of parental responsibility, the parents must release the child's property and, on demand, render an account of their administration, § 1698 I BGB.

215. As a rule, parents may also be held liable for breaching their parental duties. § 1664 BGB provides that parents exercising parental responsibility are only liable for the level of care that they customarily apply to their own affairs. However, the relationship of § 1664 BGB to the general law of torts and hence the exact extent of the parents' liability are matters of considerable dispute.[305]

§11. State Support

216. Parents who, for whatever reason, encounter difficulties in caring adequately for their children are entitled to rely on the state for assistance and support. This assistance is provided mainly by the family court in the form of orders and also by local authorities, acting through the local Youth Welfare office. The courts may assist by way of admonitions or warnings to the child or by granting orders, e.g., sending the child to an educational institution of the parents' choice.

Any court orders will take into account the welfare of the child. On being applied to by the parents, the local Youth Welfare office provides assistance (*Beistandschaft*) under a legal framework spelled out in §§ 1712–1717 BGB. The office supports holders of parental responsibility in paternity proceedings (§ 1712 I No. 1 BGB) and maintenance claims (§ 1712 I No. 2 BGB). Rights arising from parental responsibility are not curtailed by this assistance.

217. On the non-judicial side, the local child and youth welfare services provide help in areas relating to the upbringing and welfare of children at the request of parents.

§12. State Control

218. The Basic Law grants parents the fundamental right to raise their offspring as they see fit.[306] The state, nevertheless, has to fulfil its role as guardian of the child's own basic rights, Article 6 II 2 GG.[307] It may, therefore, be authorized to curtail parental rights in order to protect children whose carers abuse them or are

305. Cf. e.g., BGH FamRZ 1988, 267.
306. Article 6 II GG.
307. Idea of the *staatliches Wächteramt.*

unable or unwilling to look after them. § 1666 BGB enables the family court to intervene where the welfare of the child or the child's assets are at risk.

I. Personal Welfare

219. Where the child's physical, mental or psychological welfare is endangered, the family court is competent to take all necessary measures, § 1666 I BGB. This is on condition that the parents are either unwilling or unable to ward off the danger themselves. Any kind of imperilment, such as parental abuse or neglect, will suffice, even if not culpable, as well as threats posed by third parties.

220. What order the court makes depends on the facts. The legal measure has to be both necessary to ward off the danger and proportionate. Measures may take the form of a requirement to cooperate with child and youth welfare services or to ensure school attendance. The court may also prohibit a person (even a parent!) from contacting the child or entering the child's residence. The court may also, if necessary, override a parental refusal to consent to medical treatment. As a last resort, the court may terminate parental responsibility, §§ 1666 III, 1666a II BGB. Court orders may also be directed against third parties, § 1666 IV BGB. A child may only be separated from his or her parents by court order, and only if this is the only way to protect the child from harm. Orders may be changed by the court at any time (§ 1696 BGB), and the court is under an obligation to amend an order when the danger to the child's welfare is no longer imminent.

II. Management of Financial Affairs

221. § 1666 BGB also grants the court powers over the child's assets where those are put at risk by the behaviour of the parents or the conduct of third parties. The child's financial interests are endangered if the parents act in blatant disregard of economic principles, or from motives of self-interest, and thus risk diminishing or losing the child's capital, cf. also § 1666 II BGB. Again, the court has wide discretion in making orders, although it is bound by the principle of proportionality.

§13. Changing Parental Responsibility

222. Parental responsibility may be changed by the declarations of the parents – e.g., the unmarried parents, § 1626a I No. 1 BGB – themselves.[308] Changes occur by operation of law where one parent having joint parental responsibility dies or becomes unavailable, §§ 1680 I, III; 1681, 1678 I BGB. Finally, court orders may

308. *See supra* paras 189 et seq.

alter the situation in a number of cases, e.g., where the sole holder of parental responsibility dies or becomes unavailable[309] or where the child's welfare is endangered, § 1666 BGB.

I. Suspension of Parental Responsibility

223. The Code addresses several cases where parental responsibility may be suspended by court order. Suspension of parental responsibility means that the parent formally retains his or her position as a holder of parental responsibility, but may no longer exercise this right, § 1675 BGB. Suspension occurs where the court finds a long-term inability to act as a parent, § 1674 I BGB, because the parent is serving a protracted prison sentence, e.g., or has no (§ 1673 I BGB) or only limited legal capacity (§ 1673 II BGB). In the latter case, the parent may still exercise parental responsibility in some areas, *see* § 1673 II 2 BGB. Where parents share parental responsibility and the responsibility of one parent is suspended, the other parent may act alone. If this parent does not have parental responsibility, the court will transfer parental responsibility to him or her, provided this is consistent with the child's welfare.

224. The parental responsibility of a mother who has given birth confidentially is suspended until the family court finds that she has made the necessary statements for the child's birth record, § 1674a BGB.

II. The Termination of Parental Responsibility

225. Parental responsibility ends when the child comes of age. This does not mean that all responsibility for the child ends, however.[310]

226. Parental responsibility also ends when the parent dies, or when it is terminated by court order, e.g., under § 1666 BGB. Where the other parent does not yet have parental responsibility, the court will allocate parental responsibility to that parent if this is not contrary to the child's welfare, § 1680 II 1 BGB. There used to be special rules for unmarried fathers not yet vested with parental responsibility: under the former § 1680 II 2 BGB, they could be granted parental responsibility only where this would benefit the child's welfare. By the 2013 *Act to Reform the Parental Responsibility of Unmarried Parents*, however, the position of unmarried fathers was improved. The family court may now vest them with sole parental responsibility if the mother, as the sole parental responsibility holder, dies and if the grant of sole parental responsibility to the unmarried father is not contrary to the child's welfare, § 1680 II BGB. Where the other parent is unfit, the court appoints a guardian for the child, § 1773 I BGB.

309. *See* §§ 1680 II, III; 1681, 1678 II BGB.
310. Cf., e.g., the continuing duty to maintain, §§ 1603 II 2, 1609 BGB.

§14. PARENTAL RESPONSIBILITY UPON SEPARATION/DIVORCE

I. Joint Parental Responsibility

227. The law's guiding principle is that the parents' separation or divorce does not necessitate a change in their (legal) relationship with the child. When granting a divorce, the court only looks into the position of children where one or both parents apply for sole parental responsibility – and even then, the court is free to refuse the application.[311] Joint parental responsibility may thus continue unaltered despite changes in the parents' marital status.

228. The law does recognize, however, that the parents' separation brings about changes in the child's day-to-day life. Where the parents cannot agree where the child is to live, the court may grant one parent the exclusive right to decide this issue, § 1628 BGB. Separated or divorced parents who continue to exercise parental responsibility jointly can apply to the court on a number of further questions, relating to contact (§ 1684 III BGB), maintenance or upbringing, etc. (§ 1628 BGB).

229. § 1687 BGB spells out a general allocation of responsibilities between separated or divorced parents: as far as routine matters are concerned, the resident parent has the exclusive right to decide and represent the child, § 1687 I 2, 3 BGB. The non-resident parent has a similar right when the child is staying with him or her. The family court may limit these rights if the interests of the child require it, § 1687 II BGB. Important issues must be decided by both parents jointly. In cases of imminent danger, however, either parent may act alone, §§ 1687 I 5, 1629 I 4 BGB. Where to draw the line between routine and important matters is a question of considerable difficulty.

II. Sole Parental Responsibility

230. A parent wishing to exercise sole parental responsibility may apply to the family court for an order in his or her favour. The request will be granted if the other parent agrees (§ 1671 I 2 No. 1, II 2 No. 1 BGB) or if the court is convinced that allocating sole parental responsibility to the applicant parent is in the best interests of the child (§ 1671 I 2 No. 2, II 2 No. 2 BGB).

Where both parents wish to terminate their joint parental responsibility, the court may not question their parental autonomy. The only exceptions are where the child's welfare is in danger, § 1697a BGB, or where the child is over 14 years and objects.

If the other parent opposes the application for sole parental responsibility, the family court may only grant the order if it is convinced that sole parental responsibility – in general and also as exercised by the applicant parent in particular – is in the best interests of the child. This may be the case, e.g., where severe discord prevails between the parents, or where there is a history of abuse. In arriving at its

311. *See* § 1671 I BGB.

decision, the court takes account of the child's wishes. It also considers the child's best possible future development, as well as the importance of continuity in its upbringing.

231. Even if it decides to grant the order, the court may retain certain areas for joint decision-making, in effect only complying with the request for sole parental responsibility in part. The Code does not specify how parental responsibility should be divided, leaving considerable discretion to the courts to tailor individual orders. Changes to parental responsibility determined by court order can only be made by a further court order, even where the parents reconcile, § 1696 BGB.

232. Occasionally, there may be a collision between the procedures under § 1671 BGB (court order on parental application) and § 1666 BGB (ex officio order because of a risk to the child's welfare).[312] In this case, the state's duty to protect the child's welfare comes first.

III. Unwed Parents

233. Where unwed parents live apart, much depends on whether the mother has sole parental responsibility (§ 1626a III BGB) or whether parental responsibility is shared:

- Where parental responsibility is shared, the rules are the same as for children of married couples who separate: parental responsibility continues to be shared unless one parent successfully asks for sole parental responsibility, § 1671 I BGB.
- Where the mother has sole parental responsibility according to § 1626a III BGB, she continues to do so on separating from the father. Previously, this situation could not be changed without the mother's consent. According to the Constitutional Court, this unduly restricted the father's parental rights.[313] As the law now stands, the father can apply to the family court for a transfer of parental responsibility in two sets of circumstances. The first is where the mother agrees, unless the transfer would be contrary to the best interests of the child or the child is over 14 years and objects, § 1671 II 2 No. 1 BGB. The second is where joint parental responsibility is not an available option and where the transfer of parental responsibility is likely to be in the best interests of the child, § 1671 II 2 No. 2 BGB.

§15. Procedure

234. Jurisdiction over parental responsibility orders is with the family courts, §§ 23a I 1 No. 1, 23b I GVG; §§ 111 No. 2, 151 No. 1 FamFG. The principle of ex officio judicial investigation applies, § 26 FamFG. The parents and the child have to

312. *Supra* paras 219 et seq.
313. BVerfGE 127, 132.

be heard (§§ 159, 160 FamFG), as does the Youth Welfare office (§ 162 FamFG). The court is supposed to facilitate a consensual agreement where this is not contrary to the child's welfare (§ 156 I 1 FamFG), and to draw attention to counselling offered by child and youth welfare services, and to the possibility of mediation (§ 156 I 1, 2 FamFG). The court may appoint a representative for the minor child (child's attorney).

§16. Contact and Information

I. Contact Between the Child and His or Her Parents

235. § 1626 III BGB emphasizes that generally the child's welfare requires contact with both parents. The Code accordingly grants the child a right to contact with his or her mother and father, § 1684 I Hs. 2 BGB. The corresponding parental right and duty to contact with the child is constitutionally protected under Article 6 GG.[314]

Contact is achieved by different means, often limited in time (weekend visits, holidays, day visits, telephone calls, letters, etc.). Its extent and quality are mainly determined by the agreement of the parents. As the child has a right to contact with his or her parents, the child's wishes must be taken into account to the greatest possible extent.

236. The contact rights and duties exist irrespective of who has parental responsibility. Contact may become an issue:

- where sole parental responsibility is exercised by one parent. Here, the other parent is restricted to contact, which is also a right of the child;
- where parental responsibility is shared, but the child lives with only one parent. The non-resident parent has contact rights and duties in addition to his or her continuing parental responsibility;
- where the child lives in foster care, both parents have a right and a duty of contact;
- even where the parents have been divested of parental responsibility, a right to contact remains if it does not jeopardize the child's welfare.

In 2013, the biological father, who is not also the legal father of the child, was given a right to contact by the *Gesetz zur Stärkung der Rechte des leiblichen, nicht rechtlichen Vaters*. The right exists if the biological father has shown a serious interest in the child and if having contact with him benefits the child, § 1686a I No. 1 BGB. The biological, non-legal father also has a right to be informed about the child's personal affairs if he can show a legitimate interest and if giving him the

314. BVerfGE 64, 180, 188.

information is not contrary to the child's welfare, § 1686a I No. 2 BGB. Applications for contact or information are only admissible if the applicant swears an affidavit that he had sexual intercourse with the mother during the period of conception, § 167a I FamFG.

237. § 1684 III 1 BGB grants the family court the right to rule on the extent of contact, and to regulate, limit or exclude such contact. A contact order may also include third persons (e.g., the new spouse of a parent) or impose conditions, such as requiring a third person to be present while contact takes place. A complete exclusion or long-term limitation is only permissible, however, if necessary to prevent considerable harm to the child's welfare. Contact orders are generally enforceable, §§ 88 et seq. FamFG, but the child may not be compelled to have contact.[315]

When having contact with the child, parents are obliged to abstain from any behaviour that might adversely affect the child's relationship with the other parent or interfere with the child's upbringing, § 1684 II BGB. Where a parent permanently or repeatedly disregards this duty, the family court may appoint a special guardian to supervise contact (§ 1684 III 3 BGB, *Umgangspfleger*).

Usually, a contact order will be applied for by one of the parents. It is possible, however, for the child to take the initiative. The child's application may be directed against the parent who prevents contact, or against the parent who refrains from exercising contact. However, the Constitutional Court has ruled that it is usually counterproductive and against the child's best interests to compel a parent who does not wish to have contact to see the child.[316]

II. Contact with Other Persons

238. By the *Child Law Reform Act 1998*, further persons were given a legal right to contact with the child: contact rights were given to the child's grandparents and his or her siblings, § 1685 I BGB. Similar rights were given to other attachment figures who have or have had actual responsibility for the child, in particular persons who have lived with the child in the same household, such as step-parents and foster carers, § 1685 II BGB.[317] All contact must be in the best interests of the child, who, in this instance, does not have a right to contact of its own. Although it is generally for the parents to determine the child's best interests, § 1626 III 2 BGB points out that, as a rule, the child's welfare is served by contact with persons with whom it has established close personal ties.

315. § 90 II 1 FamFG.
316. BVerfGE 121, 69, 95.
317. *Familienpflege.*

III. Information

239. Effective exercise of parental responsibility depends on sufficient information about the child's welfare, especially where day-to-day care for the child is provided by one parent only. Irrespective of who has parental responsibility, § 1686 BGB grants both parents the right to demand information from each other about the personal affairs of the child if this is compatible with the child's welfare. The competent court in case of dispute is the family court. In 2013, the biological father of the child, who is not also the child's legal father, was given a right to information if he can show a legitimate interest and if giving him the information would not be contrary to the child's welfare, § 1686a I No. 2 BGB.

Chapter 8. Guardianship, Curatorship, and Care and Control

§1. Introduction

240.
- Guardianship (*Vormundschaft*) is an institution of long-standing in German law. Traditionally, guardianship meant the all-encompassing care for another person regulated by law. Since the *Care and Control Act,*[318] guardianship no longer applies in relation to adult persons, but only to minors.
- Curatorship (*Pflegschaft*) means care for another person in a limited area only. It resembles guardianship, the rules of which are largely applicable (§ 1915 BGB), but it may be used in relation to both minors and adults.
- Care and Control (*Betreuung*) is a new concept introduced by the *Care and Control Act*. It only applies to adults. Here, a protector (*Betreuer*) is appointed to care for persons who, because of physical, mental or psychological impairments, can – either wholly or partially – no longer care for themselves.

241. Guardianship, curatorship, and care and control are all concerned with both private and public law issues. Today, the state regards it as its duty to provide protection for persons unable to care for themselves. The actual care, however, is provided by individuals appointed to do so. The relation between carer and cared-for thus falls under the rules of private law, although strong public law elements remain, e.g., in the control exercised by the courts.

§2. Guardianship (*Vormundschaft*)

I. Establishment

242. As a rule, guardianship is established by an ex officio court order, § 1774 sent. 1 BGB. Guardianship by operation of law is the exception, but arises, e.g., upon the birth of an illegitimate child who requires a guardian (§ 1791c BGB) or where a child is freed for adoption under § 1751 I 2 BGB.

243. According to § 1773 BGB, a minor will be given a guardian:

- if he or she is not under parental authority (e.g., where the father has died and the mother has been deprived of parental responsibility);
- if his or her parents are not entitled to represent him or her in matters concerning both the person and the property of the child (§ 1773 I BGB, e.g., where the father has died and the mother is still a minor);
- if his or her family situation cannot be ascertained, § 1773 II BGB, e.g., in the case of a foundling.

318. *Betreuungsgesetz* (BtG) of 12 Dec. 1990.

A guardian may be appointed before the child is born, § 1774 sent. 2 BGB.

II. Choosing the Guardian

244. Where guardianship is established by court order, the court is responsible for choosing the guardian or guardians.[319] Where appropriate, the court may also additionally appoint a supervising guardian, § 1792 BGB.

245. The main problem is to find a suitable person to act as guardian. The Code presumes that guardianship will usually be exercised by relatives or friends of the family acting free of charge. Today, the reality is often different. Where no suitable individual is available to act as guardian, the court may appoint the Youth Welfare office or a society especially accredited for this purpose instead, §§ 1791a, 1791b BGB.

The law provides guidelines to be followed by the court in the act of nomination: first, the persons nominated by the child's parents are qualified, if the parents at the time of their death were entitled to personal and financial care of the child, §§ 1776, 1777 BGB. Where no such person has been nominated, the court will select a suitable guardian having regard to his or her personal and financial position, the parents' presumed wishes, relations of consanguinity and affinity, and any personal ties the ward (*Mündel*) has formed, as well as the ward's religious denomination, § 1779 II BGB.

246. A person who is incompetent to enter into legal transactions may not be appointed as guardian, § 1780 BGB; minors or persons under care and control, as well as persons excluded by the parents, are generally deemed unsuitable by law, § 1781 BGB.

247. Every German is under an obligation to accept the role of guardian proposed to him or her except where special reasons listed in § 1786 BGB apply. Should a person nevertheless refuse, he or she may be compelled by fines and may be liable for any loss or harm caused to the ward, §§ 1787, 1788 BGB.

The chosen guardian is then appointed by the family court and placed under the obligation to discharge the guardianship faithfully and conscientiously. The obligation is entered into with a handshake, § 1789 BGB.

III. Personal Care

248. Guardianship takes the place of parental responsibility. The guardian, therefore, has the full right and duty to care for the ward's property and person, including the right to represent the ward legally, § 1793 BGB. The rules relating to personal care exercised by parents apply, e.g., the duty to consider the growing

319. Only under special circumstance, cf. § 1797 BGB.

maturity of the ward.[320] The guardian may receive the child into his or her home, § 1973 I 3 BGB. Alternatively, the guardian can send the child to be cared for by an appropriate foster family or children's home, etc. In each case, the guardian is under a duty to maintain personal contact and, as a general rule, to visit once a month, § 1793 Ia BGB.

249. The family court exercises supervision over the entire activity of the guardian(s); it is assisted by the Youth Welfare office. The court is given the power to intervene where the guardian violates his or her duties by issuing appropriate orders and prohibitions, and may impose penalties, § 1837 II, III BGB. The guardian must report to the family court on the personal circumstances of the ward at least once a year, § 1840 I 1 BGB. Where the guardian's continuation in office would jeopardize the ward's interests, especially because of a breach of duty by the guardian, the court may dismiss the guardian, § 1886 BGB. Special rules apply in relation to the child's religious upbringing.[321]

IV. Legal Representation

250. As far as legal representation of the ward is concerned, the guardian is subject to stricter rules than parents: the guardian needs the family court's approval for more transactions than parents do.[322] Like a parent, the guardian is excluded from legal representation pursuant to §§ 181 and 1795 BGB.

V. Financial Care

251. In managing the ward's financial affairs, the guardian, like the parents, has to aim at the conservation, augmentation, and best possible use of the child's assets. To ensure this, the guardian has to draw up an inventory. He or she is subsequently placed under considerable and specific restrictions in relation, e.g., to the investment of money, the deposit of bearer securities, or the disposal of claims.[323] The guardian is not permitted to use the ward's property for himself or herself,[324] nor may he or she make gifts as the ward's representative, except where a moral duty or common decency require this,[325] §§ 1805 et seq. BGB.

252. The family court, with the assistance of the Youth Welfare office, supervises the financial aspects of care.[326] To this end, the guardian is requested by law

320. §§ 1800, 1631–1632 and §§ 1793, 1626 II BGB.
321. Cf. §§ 1801 I, 1909 I BGB.
322. Compare §§ 1821–1823 and §§ 1643, 1645 BGB.
323. Cf. §§ 1802 et seq. BGB.
324. Cf. § 1805 sent. 1 BGB.
325. Cf. § 1804 BGB.
326. As regulated in § 1837 II BGB, § 53 III 5 SGB VIII.

to provide information and to report to the court at least once every year, §§ 1840–1843 BGB. Again, the court may take action if the guardian violates these duties.[327]

VI. The Relationship Between Guardian and Ward

253. The relationship between guardian and ward contains strong elements of mandate (§§ 662 et seq. BGB). Where the guardian incurs expenses, he or she is entitled, according to §§ 669, 670 BGB, to advance payment or reimbursement from the ward, § 1835 BGB. If the ward is without means, the state treasury makes these payments instead, § 1835 IV BGB. Services provided by the guardian are generally not chargeable, except where they pertain to the guardian's trade or profession, § 1835 III BGB.

According to the concept of the Code, guardianship is generally performed free of charge, § 1836 I 1 BGB. As an exception to this rule, the Code allows for appropriate remuneration in the case of acknowledged professional guardianship, § 1836 I 2 BGB. Where the ward does not have sufficient means, the guardian may claim remuneration from the public purse.[328] The court may also award remuneration if the amount of work or level of difficulty justify this, and if the ward has adequate means, § 1836 II BGB.

VII. Ending Guardianship

254. Guardianship ends upon the lapse of the conditions that originally led to it being established, §§ 1882, 1773 BGB, e.g., where the ward reaches majority. Likewise, it ends with the ward's death.[329] It should be noted that the end of guardianship does not necessarily coincide with the term of office of any individual guardian. As it relates to the capacity of the ward, guardianship continues through a change of guardian. The guardian may also be dismissed by the family court if the ward's best interests are jeopardized by his remaining in office, § 1886 BGB.

255. Upon termination of office – for whatever reason – the guardian must deliver the administered property to the ward and account for his administration to the ward and the family court, §§ 1890 et seq. BGB.

---

327. *See supra* and §§ 1837, 1886 BGB.
328. § 1 II 2 *Gesetz über die Vergütung von Vormündern und Betreuern.*
329. Cf. § 1884 BGB for details.

§3. Curatorship (*Pflegschaft*)

I. General Matters

256. Curatorship constitutes a special legal framework for the care of a person or financial entity.[330] Grounds for an order establishing curatorship can be found throughout private and public law. Here, we will only look at those forms of curatorship that are closely connected with family law.

257. Structurally, curatorship over a person resembles guardianship. The main difference is that the curator's range of responsibilities is not all-encompassing, but strictly limited. Still, the provisions governing guardianship are applicable *mutatis mutandis*, unless the law provides otherwise. Such differing provisions include:

- no supervising curator will be appointed, § 1915 II BGB;
- the rules as to qualification for a guardian do not apply, §§ 1916, 1917 BGB;
- termination of curatorship is different, §§ 1918 et seq. BGB.

258. Curatorship is established by law or by court order (family court, where minors are concerned, or the *Betreuungsgericht*, court for care and control).[331]

II. Forms of Curatorship

259. The law knows different forms of curatorship. Of special importance to the family lawyer is supplementary curatorship as described in § 1909 BGB. Supplementary curatorship does not replace parental responsibility, but is provided where and to the extent that parents are unable to attend to matters relating to the child. Appointment does not follow the rules for guardianship (§ 1916 BGB); the court may, therefore, make an appointment without being bound by parental suggestions.

A curator can also be appointed for the unborn child (§ 1912 BGB) where such support seems necessary for the protection of the child's future rights. Finally, curatorship is available for where the conditions for a guardianship order exist, but no guardian has been appointed. Here, curatorship fills the gap (§ 1909 III BGB).

§4. Care and Control (*Betreuung*)

260. The *Care and Control Act*[332] abolished several legal institutions: declarations of incompetence, guardianship over persons who have reached majority, and curatorship over persons suffering from physical infirmity. In place of these, the Act introduced the concept of 'Care and Control' (*Betreuung*). Jurisdiction concerning

330. For example, an estate, § 1961 BGB.
331. Cf. § 1915 I 3 BGB.
332. *Betreuungsgesetz* (BtG) of 12 Dec. 1990, in force since 1 Jan. 1992.

care and control lies with a special court for care and control (*Betreuungsgericht*), which operates under the rules for non-contentious matters.[333]

I. Appointment of a Protector

261. The Code describes the grounds on which a protector may be appointed in rather general terms: an appointment will be made if a person of full age is at least partially unable to take care of his or her affairs because of psychological ailments or physical, mental, or psychological impediments. For a person who is capable of making decisions, no protector may be assigned against his or her wishes, § 1896 Ia BGB.[334]

262. The appointment may only be made where and to the extent that it is required. This 'requirement principle' is further developed: care and control is not necessary where affairs can be taken care of just as efficiently by a person with powers of attorney or by other assistants. The law thus leaves room for private-law solutions.

The requirement principle, furthermore, demands that care and control be restricted to areas in which the person concerned is indeed in need of assistance. Only in special cases will a protector be invested with all-encompassing powers of representation; usually, the powers will be specific and restricted to health care matters, management of financial assets, etc.

263. Orders are also limited in time: when making the order, the court has to set a date for review, which can be no more than seven years from the making of the order.[335]

II. Forms of Protectorship

264. Finding suitable protectors can be difficult. This explains the considerable variety of appointment options that the law provides for. The starting point is the private natural person who will – ideally – act pro bono. As such a person is often not available, care and control may also be performed for remuneration and by associations or authorities. Even then, however, the new law strives to retain some personal element: where possible, it is not the association or authority that functions as protector, but an individual member within this institution, § 1900 II 1, 2 BGB.

Appointments will be made according to suitability and capacity to represent the person under care adequately. Priority is given to any nomination made by the person under care, unless appointing the nominee would be contrary to the welfare of

333. § 23c GVG; §§ 271 et seq. FamFG.
334. This principle, which had been recognized by the courts, was expressly included in the BGB in 2005 by way of Second Act to Amend the Law of Care and Protection (*Zweites Gesetz zur Änderung des Betreuungsrechts*) of 21 Apr. 2005 (BGBl. I 1073).
335. § 295 II FamFG.

the person under care, § 1897 IV BGB. Likewise, the refusal of the person under care to accept a certain protector is taken into consideration as are aspects of kinship, family ties, and possible conflicting interests, § 1897 V BGB. A professional protector should only be appointed if no other suitable person is willing to act on a voluntary basis, § 1897 VI 1 BGB.

III. The Protector's Rights and Duties

265. In carrying out his or her duties, the paramount consideration for the protector is the welfare of the person under care. The new law places special emphasis on preserving a maximum degree of self-determination for the person under care. Thus, the protector has to consult with the person under care and where possible comply with his or her wishes, § 1901 II, III BGB.

266. To enable the protector to carry out his or her duties efficiently, the law invests him or her with the right to represent the person under care in judicial and non-judicial matters (§ 1902 BGB); this right may be flanked by further rights, e.g., the right to determine contact and residence.

267. The right to legal representation is subject to numerous restrictions. First, most of the restrictions applicable in the law of guardianship apply via § 1908i I 1 BGB. Second, the special provisions of care and control contain a number of further restrictions. For example, in order to consent to certain medical procedures, the protector needs the permission of the court for care and control, §§ 1904, 1905, 1906a I, II BGB. The same is true of measures involving deprivations of liberty, § 1906 I, II, IV BGB.

268. Third, it is important to note that even where the protector enjoys the right of representation and decision-making, the person under care still retains full power to enter into legal transactions, unless he or she is in fact legally incompetent within the general rules set out in § 104 No. 2 BGB.[336] This overlap of responsibilities may cause problems where the protector and the person under care act in the same matter, but in conflicting ways. As a rule, the earlier act is valid, but where both acts can be valid independently of each other, both will be valid.

269. The law recognizes that there are, nevertheless, limits to the principle of self-determination, in the best interests of the person under care. Therefore, where necessary to prevent substantial harm, the court may order that any declaration made by the person under care needs the protector's consent, § 1903 BGB.

336. *See supra* para. 36.

IV. Termination

270. A protector may be dismissed by the court for various reasons, e.g., if his or her qualification is no longer assured (§ 1908b I 1 BGB), or if the person under care suggests someone equally qualified (§ 1908b III BGB). The dismissal does not end care and control, but only terminates the individual protector's office. A new protector will then have to be appointed.

271. Care and control as a whole may be terminated only if the conditions for it cease to exist (§ 1908d BGB), e.g., if the person under care no longer suffers from the relevant impediment. Such termination may be applied for by the person under care himself or herself. If the care and control order was made on the person's own application, the wish for termination has to be obeyed by the courts unless a care order would now have to be made ex officio (§ 1908d II BGB).

Chapter 9. Financial Support among Relatives

§1. General

272. The right to be maintained by another person may be based on statute or on contract. Under German law, statutory rights to maintenance can arise between (divorced) spouses, between relatives in the direct line, and between the unmarried parents of a child. An action may be directed at future support[337] or at information in respect of the payor's financial capability prior to the actual claim for maintenance. Jurisdiction lies with the family court.[338]

273. In addition to civil law maintenance claims, there is the system of social security, which is also directed towards provision in cases of need. Difficult problems may arise from this juxtaposition since as a general rule, civil law maintenance can only be claimed if there are no other sources of provision. § 2 II SGB XII resolves this conflict. It sets out that social security benefits are subsidiary to civil law maintenance and that the state may recover any payments made from the payee.[339]

§2. Financial Support among Relatives

274. According to § 1601 BGB, only relatives in the direct line are obliged to furnish maintenance to each other, e.g., parents to their children, grandparents to parents and their offspring, and vice versa. Siblings are not obliged to maintain each other under German law. The maintenance duties of parents in relation to their minor children are a special type of maintenance among relatives and follow special rules, which are set out in the next chapter. The maintenance duties of spouses and unwed parents towards each other are also dealt with separately by the law.

Generally, a claim for maintenance may be made on two conditions: the payee's lack of means and the payor's financial capacity.

I. Lack of Means

275. Only a person who is unable to support himself or herself is entitled to maintenance, § 1602 I BGB. This means that the claimant must have insufficient income from either gainful employment or property or the sale of assets. Employment may be deemed suitable even if it is 'beneath' the claimant's educational level or living standard. Even care for a child does not per se free the claimant from the obligation to pursue at least part-time employment where this seems equitable.

337. § 258 ZPO.
338. §§ 23a I 1 No. 1, 23b I GVG, § 111 No. 8 FamFG.
339. Cf. also § 94 SGB XII.

II. Financial Capability

276. A person is deemed to be of sufficient financial capability where – taking into account his or her other obligations – he or she is able to provide maintenance without jeopardizing his or her own appropriate maintenance, § 1603 I BGB. The courts will not only regard the payor's actual income but also consider what income he or she could reasonably have available to him or her (imputed income). Assets only have to be used if the obligor is left with enough for his or her own maintenance, including in old age.[340] Both lack of means and financial capability may only be partial, resulting in a reduced claim.

III. Maintenance Claim

277. Maintenance includes the necessities of life, including expenses for appropriate training or – where needed – education, § 1610 II BGB. It does not include maintenance that the claimant would have to pay to his or her own needy relatives, nor does it include the cost of old-age provision.

The level of maintenance is measured by the claimant's standard of living and thus is not necessarily limited to the bare necessities of life. However, it also, to some extent, depends on the obligor's standard of living, as this has to be taken into account when determining the obligor's financial capability, § 1603 I BGB.

278. Maintenance is provided by periodic payments, made monthly in advance, § 1612 I 1, III BGB. Where special reasons justify this, the obligor may be allowed to provide maintenance in kind. On top of the monthly payments, the claimant may ask for further financial assistance in case of exceptional and unusually expensive needs, § 1613 II BGB.

279. The relationship that gives rise to the maintenance claim as such is not subject to prescription (§ 194 II BGB), but each individual claim prescribes in three years (§§ 195, 197 II BGB). Importantly, past maintenance may only be claimed in special circumstances, to protect the obligor, who might not be aware of his or her duty, from high and unexpected arrears. Retrospective performance can only be demanded from the time the claim was filed, the obligor was required to give information relating to the claim, or was given notice of default, § 1613 I 1 BGB.

280. An exception from these limitations is made by § 1613 II BGB, where the obligor seems unworthy of the protection, i.e., if the claimant was prevented from making the claim by legal or certain factual reasons. Even in that case, the obligor is protected by a hardship clause in § 1613 III BGB: no (or at least no full) claim can be made if this would impose undue hardship on the obligor. Expenses for past exceptional needs under § 1613 II are fully claimable, § 1613 II No. 1 BGB.

340. BGH FamRZ 1986, 48; 2013, 203 paras 35 et seq.

IV. Restrictions

281. The duty to maintain may be reduced or removed entirely where maintenance payments would seem inequitable in the light of serious misconduct on the part of the claimant. According to § 1611 BGB, this may be the case where the person entitled to maintenance:

- became indigent as a result of his or her moral fault;
- grossly neglected his or her own maintenance obligation towards the person liable for maintenance; or
- intentionally committed severe misconduct against the person liable for maintenance, or a close relative of the person liable for maintenance.

282. The maintenance claim expires on the death of either party. Only where retrospective payments or damages for such payments are concerned, or where prospective claims had already fallen due, may claims be made after the death of one party. Also, where the claimant's heirs are unable to meet the funeral expenses, that bill has to be footed by the obligor, § 1615 II BGB.

283. The statutory duty to maintain can be modified by contract, but only within the limits set by § 1614 BGB: most importantly, this means that claims to future maintenance may not be waived.

V. Ranking

284. Difficult questions of ranking arise where the person in need might bring claims against several obligors: the claimant's spouse is liable before the relatives, § 1608 BGB. The relatives are, however, liable to the extent that the spouse – because of limited means – is unable to meet the cost.

Among relatives, the claimant's descendants are liable before relatives in the ascending line, § 1606 BGB. Within each group, closer relatives are liable before more remote ones, § 1606 II BGB. Several equally close relatives are liable in proportion to their earnings and property, § 1606 III 1 BGB. Where a relative is exempted from the duty to maintain because of a lack of funds, the relative next in line becomes liable, § 1607 I BGB.

285. Similar problems arise where a person has maintenance duties towards several needy claimants, but is unable to provide maintenance for all of them, § 1609 BGB. *See supra* paragraph 121.

VI. Reimbursement

286. A relative or parent may have paid maintenance even though he or she was not – or only subsidiarily – liable. In that case, the payor can seek repayment from the recipient under the general rules of restitution according to § 812 I BGB.[341] The payor may, however, prefer to seek reimbursement from the person actually liable. The maintenance claim of a child passes to the payor:

- where the payor relative was only liable for maintenance because bringing the maintenance claim in Germany against the relative primarily liable was not possible or met with considerable difficulty, § 1607 II BGB;[342]
- where the payor maintained the child believing himself to be the child's father and § 1607 III BGB applies. In that case, the payor may seek repayment from the child's natural father. An obstacle to prosecution within the meaning of § 1607 II BGB exists where the child's paternity has not been challenged, with the result that the child does not (yet) have a claim against the natural father. In this case, maintenance may even be claimed for the past.[343] However, the father may find it difficult to ascertain the biological father's identity. In the absence of a special legislative provision, his right to information against the mother is based on the general clause of § 242 BGB. The Constitutional Court has ruled that the mother's right not to reveal a sexual relationship with a third person is covered by her personality right and that this right may not be interfered with on the basis of the general clause of § 242 BGB alone.[344]

§3. The Parents' Duty to Maintain Their Children

I. General

287. Special provisions apply to one particular maintenance duty among relatives: the parents' duty to provide for their children. In relation to minors, the duty to maintain flows from the principle of parental responsibility. This interdependence of parental responsibility and the duty to maintain is reflected in the fact that – unlike other obligors – parents may meet their obligation to contribute to the maintenance of the minor child by providing care and upbringing, § 1606 III 2 BGB.[345]

288. The situation is different for children who have come of age. They are generally presumed to be self-reliant. But even here the parental relationship may imply a continued duty to maintain where the child has not yet reached 'economic independence', e.g., because the child is still completing his or her education.

341. But cf. § 814 BGB for limitations.
342. Cf. §§ 1607 II, III, 1608 BGB for a similar *cessio legis* in relation to spouses or parents.
343. *See* § 1613 II No. 2 lit. a BGB.
344. BVerfGE 138, 377.
345. *See infra* para. 295.

289. Where the special statutory provisions relating to maintenance claims of children against their parents do not apply, the maintenance duties follow the general rules for maintenance between relatives set out *supra.*[346]

II. The Child's Lack of Means

290. In contrast to other claimants, the minor child is not required to use his or her assets to provide for his or her maintenance, cf. § 1602 II BGB. Also, the minor is under no obligation to seek gainful employment, as education and training take precedence. This is true even for a child who has come of age, but still pursues an education, unless continued maintenance is inequitable in light of the parents' precarious financial situation and the ready availability of education-related work for the child.

III. The Parents' Financial Capability

291. Unlike other obligors, parents may not claim reduced financial capability because of their own standard of living. They have to apply all the means at their disposal for their own and the child's maintenance in equal measure, § 1603 II 1 BGB. Since the *Child Support Act 1998*, this obligation has existed not only in relation to the parents' minor children but also in relation to any unmarried children under 21 years who are still living at home and going to school, § 1603 II 2 BGB.

Even in strained financial circumstances, the parents are thus committed to solidarity with their children, including adult children who are still going to school. Parents can claim financial incapability only if there is another relative who is obliged to provide maintenance or if the child can be maintained from the principal of his or her own property, § 1603 II 3 BGB.

292. § 1603 II BGB even requires parents to sell assets. In light of these demands, the courts have developed a system (laid down in tables) to prevent parents from having to rely on social security because of their extensive support duties. Even in relation to a child, parents are thus always entitled to a certain minimum retention (e.g., in 2021: EUR 1,160 per month for an employed person in relation to a minor child; EUR 1,400 in relation to a child who is of age).[347]

IV. The Maintenance Claim

A. Level of Maintenance

293. The level of maintenance is determined according to the general rule of § 1610 BGB. Again, the courts use tables based on the parent's income and the

346. *Supra* paras 274 et seq.
347. *Düsseldorfer Tabelle 2021*, FamRZ 2021, 93, 94.

child's age to ensure relative uniformity of decisions. The Code provides for statutory standard rates (*Mindestunterhalt*),[348] and the possibility to seek a suitable percentage of those rates, in a special simplified procedure.[349]

The cost of education or training is of special importance in the maintenance of children. Parents are under an obligation to provide education for a suitable length of time, even after the child has reached majority. Individual circumstances have to be taken into account to determine the extent of this obligation, and extensive case law exists on this point. The child, however, is under an obligation to follow his or her studies purposefully and may lose the claim if this obligation is not met.[350]

294. The courts are rather restrictive as regards the amount of maintenance awarded to children who have come of age. Even where the parents' standard of living is very high, they usually grant amounts only slightly in excess of public education grants.[351]

B. Mode of Provision

295. Maintenance for minor children can take the form of care and upbringing, § 1606 III 2 BGB. Furthermore, if parents have to provide maintenance for an unmarried child, they are under no obligation to meet the claim by monthly payments. It is for them to determine in what manner and for what period maintenance is provided in advance, § 1612 II 1 BGB. With minors, fulfilment in kind is the rule, but parents may also choose in-kind fulfilment for an older child, provided they take into account the child's interests, § 1612 II 1 BGB.

296. The restriction or removal of the duty to maintain spelled out in § 1611 BGB does not apply to maintenance provided by parents to their minor children, § 1611 II BGB. In exceptional cases – e.g., where the child has attempted to kill a parent – the claim may be forfeit according to the general rules of equity, § 242 BGB.

V. Procedure

297. Statutory maintenance claims can be pursued before the ordinary civil courts. Jurisdiction lies with the family court.[352] Some special procedural rules apply, however,[353] to ensure that the court has sufficient inquisitorial powers. For

348. § 1612a BGB and *Mindestunterhaltsverordnung* of 3 Dec. 2015 (BGBl. I 2188).
349. Cf. §§ 1612a–1612c BGB and §§ 249 et seq. FamFG.
350. BGH FamRZ 1998, 671; 1987, 470; 2011, 1560 para. 15.
351. *Düsseldorfer Tabelle*: EUR 860 per month for students, *see* FamRZ 2021, 93, 94.
352. §§ 23a I 1 No. 1, 23b I GVG; § 111 No. 8 FamFG.
353. §§ 231 et seq. FamFG.

maintenance claims by minor children against a non-resident parent, a simplified procedure exists to ensure speedy and effective realization of the child's rights.[354]

§4. Special Provisions for Unmarried Parents

298. Since the 1998 child law reforms,[355] the provisions on maintenance have been applied to all children irrespective of the marital status of their parents. A few wrinkles, however, remain for children of unmarried parents.

299. Even before the child is born, the court may make an interim child support order for the first three months after birth, § 247 I FamFG. The same applies to the mother's support claim (interim support orders for six weeks before and eight weeks after birth). A presumption of paternity under § 1600d II, III BGB is a sufficient basis for such an order. Apart from this provision, interim support orders for the mother or the child can only issue if paternity is established or affiliation proceedings are pending, § 248 FamFG.

300. Second, the Code grants a limited maintenance claim to the child's mother against the father, § 1615l BGB. The legislation has systematically increased the scope of this claim over the years:

- Without having to meet any further criteria, the mother can claim maintenance for six weeks prior to and eight weeks after the child's birth, as well as birth- and pregnancy-related expenses, even if these were incurred outside this time period, § 1615l I BGB.
- Further maintenance can only be claimed if the mother is unable – or only partially able – to pursue gainful employment as a result of a pregnancy- or birth-related illness or because the child cannot otherwise be cared for, § 1615l II BGB. To meet this situation, the same rules as in the case of a divorced spouse seeking maintenance under § 1570 BGB apply.[356]

301. This claim (§ 1615l II BGB) is also limited in time. The father's duty to maintain begins no earlier than four months before the confinement. It exists for a minimum of three years after the birth of the child, § 1615l II 3 BGB. It may continue thereafter to the extent that this is equitable, special consideration being given to the best interests of the child and the existence of adequate childcare services, § 1615l II 4, 5 BGB.

302. The general rules for maintenance between relatives apply (§ 1615l III 1 BGB); the claim, therefore, depends on the mother's lack of means and the father's

354. §§ 249 et seq. FamFG.

355. Child Law Reform Act (*Kindschaftsrechtsreformgesetz*) of 16 Feb. 1997 and Child Support Act (*Kindesunterhaltsgesetz*) of 6 Apr. 1998.

356. *See supra* paras 109 et seq.

financial capability. The level of maintenance is determined by the mother's living standard. Future maintenance claims cannot be waived.[357] For questions of ranking, *see* § 1615l III BGB.

303. Where the unmarried father cares for the child, he is entitled to similar claims, § 1615l IV BGB.

357. § 1614 BGB. This is different where a divorced spouse raises a claim, *see supra* paras 109 et seq.

Part III. Matrimonial Property Law

§1. Introduction

304. The German Civil Code does not set out a compulsory property regime for married couples. The spouses are – within limits – free to regulate property matters in a binding marriage contract, § 1408 I BGB.

In §§ 1408 et seq. BGB, the Code sets out guidelines for these contractual property rights and presents two model contractual regimes, separate property (*Gütertrennung*) and community property (*Gütergemeinschaft*). Where – as in the majority of cases – no agreement is made, the statutory regime of community of accrued gains (*Zugewinngemeinschaft*) applies, as does pension splitting.

The liberty of the spouses to regulate their property relations by contract has been curtailed by recent court rulings (*see supra* paragraph 126). According to the Federal Constitutional Court,[358] the courts must check marriage contracts to see whether they are the result of unilateral dominance and unequal bargaining positions. In this case, the courts are asked to review the contents of the contract, in accordance with the general clauses of civil law (equity rules, § 138 BGB; good faith, § 242 BGB). Where appropriate, they must intervene and correct the contract terms. The Federal Supreme Court has ruled[359] that marriage contracts and divorce agreements may not result in an evidently one-sided distribution of marital burdens, which is not justified by the actual living conditions and unacceptable to the disadvantaged spouse. This line of cases is especially relevant when the spouses have chosen a separate-property regime. While spouses may choose this property regime, the certifying notary has to make sure that neither spouse is unduly burdened; an undue burden may be found where one spouse relinquishes rights he or she would need for his or her own support after divorce. Waivers of maintenance or of pension splitting are especially suspect.

358. BVerfGE 103, 89; BVerfG FamRZ 2001, 985.
359. BGH FamRZ 2004, 601; 2005, 691.

Chapter 1. The Contractual Matrimonial Property Regimes

§1. Separate Property

305. Separate property arises where the spouses formally agree on this regime or agree to forego the statutory property regime, § 1414 BGB.

Under separate property, each spouse manages his or her own property. No limitations as to management or disposal result from the marriage. There will be pension splitting, however, unless this is separately excluded. Joint property only comes into being according to the general rules, e.g., where the spouses jointly enter into a transaction. Often, one spouse transfers property or other assets to the other spouse during the marriage. Should the marriage be dissolved at some later point, problems may arise if the transferor wishes to regain the assets. The law does not provide special rules for this case. If the parties have not settled this point either, claims for restitution or compensation might arise under the general law. For example, the transferor spouse might seek to recover under § 531 II BGB (revocation of a gift).[360] If the law of gifts does not apply, other possible avenues of redress include partnership, frustration of contract, and unjust enrichment (*see infra* paragraphs 342 et seq.).

§2. Community Property

306. Where the spouses formally agree on a regime of community property, the rules found in §§ 1415–1482 BGB apply: all assets become the joint property of the spouses (common property). Property passing into the ownership of either spouse during the marriage automatically and instantly becomes joint property as long as the property regime is not changed. There is no need to transfer individual items by a separate transaction. Upon entering the regime, community property comes into existence by universal succession, § 1416 II BGB. Where necessary, the land register has to be amended accordingly, § 1416 III BGB.

307. Certain exemptions are made from the rule of automatic community property. Each spouse still acts independently and as the sole owner in the case of:

- Special property (*Sondergut*), § 1417 BGB, comprising non-transferrable items (e.g., a usufruct).
- Separate property (*Vorbehaltsgut*), § 1418 BGB. This comprises items: (1) that are declared to remain separate in a marriage contract or (2) that a spouse receives *mortis causa* or by way of gift from a third party who has declared them to constitute that spouse's separate property or (3) that are received in lieu of an item belonging to the spouse's separate property.

360. But cf. the problems arising from the court's restrictive interpretation of donations among spouses (*ehebedingte Zuwendungen*), *see infra* para. 342.

308. In relation to the community property, both partners enjoy the same rights and duties unless otherwise agreed upon. Considerable mutual restrictions apply: according to § 1419 I BGB, no spouse may dispose of his or her share of the community property or of the individual items belonging to it. The community property is managed jointly unless the spouses agree otherwise in their marriage contract, § 1421 BGB.

This means that the spouses are under a mutual obligation to cooperate (§ 1451 BGB), and as a rule may only act jointly, when disposing of or litigating with respect to their community property.[361] This obligation to act jointly complicates legal transactions. Sole property management by one of the partners, which the spouses may agree upon in their marriage contract, implies considerable dependence for the non-managing spouse, however.[362]

309. Creditors may demand satisfaction from the community property for obligations entered into by either spouse, §§ 1459 I, 1437 I BGB.[363] Additionally, the spouses are personally liable with their special and separate property for their respective personal obligations. If they have agreed on joint management, the special and separate property of each spouse is also liable for the community property obligations, § 1459 II BGB.

310. Each spouse may institute proceedings for the dissolution of the community by act of court, §§ 1447 et seq., 1469 et seq. BGB. Community property further ends with the dissolution of the marriage unless otherwise agreed; cf. §§ 1483 et seq. BGB for the possible continuation of community property after the death of one spouse.

§3. Formalities

311. Where the spouses agree to regulate their property relations by marriage contract, they must observe certain formal requirements and limitations:

- The marriage contract must be signed in the simultaneous presence of both parties and must be recorded by a notary, § 1410 BGB.
- The matrimonial property regime may not be determined by reference to a foreign law or a law no longer in force, § 1409 BGB. Foreign legal provisions may nevertheless govern the marriage under the rules of conflict of laws, where applicable.[364]
- After getting married, the spouses are free to cancel or alter the property regime, § 1408 I BGB.

361. For exceptions *see* §§ 1450 II, 1454, 1455 BGB.
362. Cf. §§ 1422, 1423–1432 BGB.
363. For exceptions from this rule *see* §§ 1460–1462, 1438–40 BGB.
364. Cf. Art. 229 § 47 II No. 2, 15 II EGBGB and Council Regulation (EU) 2016/1103 of 24 June 2016 implementing enhanced cooperation in the area of jurisdiction, applicable law and the recognition and enforcement of decisions in matters of matrimonial property regimes.

312. In addition to agreeing on or excluding one of the property regimes, the spouses may also alter provisions within one of the regimes, or simply opt out of pension splitting. In the absence of an express agreement, opting out of the statutory property regime leads to a presumption of separate property, § 1414 BGB.

313. To what extent the spouses should be free to regulate their property relationships in ways different from the models set out in the Code (i.e., community of accrued gains, separate property, and community property) is a matter of dispute. There seems to be no justification, however, for restricting the spouses' freedom of contract further than demanded by the rules set out *supra* and the general rules of civil law.

§4. The Register of Marital Property

314. To make their property agreements enforceable against third parties, the spouses may apply for registration in the register of marital property at the local court, § 1558 BGB. Agreements concerning property may be registered where they vary from the statutory property regime and where this divergence might affect the interests of third parties.

315. The register enjoys negative publicity only,[365] meaning that provisions in an unregistered agreement may not be invoked against a third party, like a creditor, unless the relevant provision was actually known to that party. However, non-registration does not affect the validity of the property arrangements as between the spouses.

365. So-called *negative Publizität.*

Chapter 2. The Statutory Matrimonial Property Regime

316. If the spouses have not formally agreed otherwise, the statutory property regime of community of accrued gains applies. In this case, each spouse manages his or her property independently during the marriage, and it is only when the marriage has ended that an equalization of accrued gains is achieved, §§ 1363 et seq. BGB.

Still, some restrictions apply during the marriage. Independent management is limited in several ways to protect the other spouse's interests effectively: §§ 1365, 1369 BGB.

§1. Disposing of Property in Its Entirety, § 1365 BGB

317. According to § 1365 BGB, a spouse may bind himself or herself to dispose of his or her property in its entirety only with the consent of the other spouse. If he or she enters into such an undertaking without the requisite consent, he or she may discharge the obligation only if the other spouse consents.

318. Defining the term 'disposal of property in its entirety' meets with considerable difficulties:

- The courts have pointed out that the term has to be interpreted from an economic point of view. Therefore, even the disposal of *one* item of property may suffice if this item constitutes the entire property of the spouse or at least nearly the entire property (less than 10%–15% remaining).[366]
- What a spouse receives in return for the transaction is not taken into account.
- The acting spouse does not have to be aware of the fact that he or she is disposing of his or her entire property. The Federal Supreme Court (BGH) has set out another important requirement, however, substantially curtailing the reach of § 1365 BGB: the other party to the transaction must have positive knowledge that (almost) the entire property of the spouse is involved in the transaction, or this must have been evident from his or her knowledge of the couple's financial situation. Where the other party does not have the requisite knowledge, § 1365 BGB does not apply and no consent is required.[367]

319. Where the transaction falls within the scope of § 1365 BGB, consent is required for the obligation entered into as well as for the actual transfer of the property.

366. BGH FamRZ 2013, 948 para. 8 (10% in case of large assets).
367. BGHZ 43, 174.

§2. Disposing of Household Items, § 1369 BGB

320. § 1369 BGB limits the spouses' power to dispose of household items. A spouse living under the statutory property regime may only dispose of items in the conjugal household that belong to himself or herself – or enter into an obligation to do so – if the other spouse consents. It does not matter in this context whether the item in question is owned jointly or solely by the acting spouse. Items serving only the personal use of one spouse are not covered by § 1369 BGB.

§3. Consent

321. Where consent is required pursuant to § 1365 or § 1369 BGB, the other spouse is free to consent to the transaction or not. Should he or she unreasonably refuse his or her consent, the family court may, upon the application of one spouse, supply the consent. The same applies where the other spouse is prevented from making a declaration by ill health or absence, §§ 1369 II, 1365 II BGB.

A unilateral transaction carried out without the requisite consent is ineffective, § 1367 BGB. A bilateral contract made without that consent may, by contrast, be effective if the other spouse ratifies it, § 1366 BGB.

322. The other party to the contract is entitled to revoke the contract until ratification, § 1366 II 1 BGB. Revocation is excluded if this party knew that the spouse was married, unless the spouse untruthfully claimed to have the necessary consent, § 1366 II 2 BGB. If the other party demands ratification, only the consenting spouse can grant the ratification; any prior ratification will be ineffective. Ratifications have to be made within two weeks from the receipt of the demand; otherwise, ratification is deemed to have been refused, § 1366 III 2 BGB. Where ratification is refused, the contract is ineffective, § 1366 IV BGB.

323. To prevent the acting spouse from continuing with the (ineffective) transaction by refusing to reclaim the transferred property, § 1368 BGB grants the other spouse the right to enforce the rights arising from the ineffectiveness of the disposition against the third party.

324. In the absence of the required consent, no good-faith acquisition is possible as §§ 1365, 1369 BGB constitute absolute restraints on alienation.[368]

368. Cf. BGHZ 40, 218.

Chapter 3. Equalization of Accrued Gains

325. The statutory property regime may terminate in various ways. Upon the death of one spouse, the ensuing equalization of accrued gains is achieved by increasing the surviving spouse's intestate share by one quarter (§§ 1371 I, 1931 BGB), irrespective of whether the deceased spouse actually made a gain in the individual case.[369]

326. Upon divorce, annulment, contractual opting-out, or death without the surviving spouse being either heir or legatee, an equalization claim is granted according to §§ 1371 et seq. BGB.

§1. Accrued Gains

327. If the gains one spouse made during the marriage exceed those of the other spouse, the latter is entitled to one-half of the difference as an equalization claim, § 1378 I BGB.

328. Which spouse is entitled to this claim and what it amounts to is determined by comparing the spouses' assets at the beginning ('initial assets', § 1374 BGB) and at the end ('final assets', § 1375 BGB) of the statutory property regime. In divorce, the relevant date for determining the final assets is set at the date when the divorce application becomes pending, § 1384 BGB. 'Accrued gains' thus means the amount by which a spouse's final assets exceed his or her initial assets, § 1373 BGB. A spouse's initial and/or final assets might also be negative (§§ 1374 III, 1375 I 2 BGB), e.g., where the spouse's debts exceed his or her assets. Even in such a case, there might still be a gain since a spouse might have reduced his or her debts during the marriage.

329. It may be difficult for a spouse to know what his or her partner's initial and final assets actually amount to. Accordingly, § 1377 BGB presumes that where the spouses have jointly compiled an inventory of the contents and value of their respective initial assets, this inventory is accurate. Each spouse can call on his or her partner to join in drawing up this inventory, § 1377 II BGB.

Where no inventory has been drawn up – as is usually the case – § 1377 BGB further presumes that the final assets of a spouse represent his or her accrued gains (§ 1377 III BGB), i.e., that no initial assets existed. As a result, each spouse bears the burden of proving the existence and the amount of his or her initial assets.

330. The burden of proof rests with the spouse advancing an equalization claim.[370] Matters are complicated by the fact that the spouse in question may have imperfect knowledge about the financial circumstances of his or her partner. This is

369. *See infra* paras 345 et seq.
370. Cf. BGH FamRZ 1986, 1196.

why the law grants spouses mutual information rights. Information rights are triggered by the mere act of *petitioning* for divorce. Each spouse is then entitled to be informed of the financial circumstances of the other insofar as these might be relevant to calculating the other spouse's initial and final assets, § 1379 I 1 No. 2 BGB. The information pertains to the other spouse's initial asset balance, later additions thereto according to § 1374 II BGB (*see infra*), the spouse's final assets and even to dissipated assets (these might increase the final assets balance, *see infra*). Claims to information can be enforced in the family courts.

Additionally, the law grants spouses mutual information rights regarding the property each spouse owned *at the time of separation* (§ 1379 I No. 1 and § 1379 II BGB) in order to uncover unfair transactions carried out after separation with a view to manipulating the size of the equalization claim.

§2. Adjustments

331. The Code allows for several adjustments to the actual amount of initial and final assets in order to achieve an accurate equalization of accrued gains.

332. The law treats assets acquired by gift or through inheritance (including lifetime transfers motivated by future inheritance rights) after the beginning of the statutory property regime as independent of the conjugal community, and as bearing no connection with the spouses' contributions during the marriage. § 1374 II BGB, therefore, treats them as if they had been acquired before the beginning of the statutory property regime. They are, after deducting liabilities, classed as *initial* assets.

333. A similar method is used to equalize any undue diminution of a spouse's final assets (he or she may try to reduce his or her surplus and thus improve his or her position in relation to the other spouse). Gratuitous transfers that were not compelled by a moral obligation or common decency, assets that were wasted, or transactions implemented with the intent to cause detriment to the other spouse will be deemed to be included in the spouse's final assets, § 1375 II BGB.

§3. The Claim for Equalization

334. The equalization claim amounts to one-half of the difference between the accumulated gains of the one spouse and those of the other spouse, § 1378 I BGB.

The law provides for a maximum amount: the payor spouse is not supposed to run up debts in order to discharge the equalization claim. This is why § 1378 II 1 BGB limits the amount of equalization to the value of the property (after deducting liabilities) that the payor spouse actually owns at the time of divorce. This means that the payor spouse does not have to give his or her partner more than he or she has left after deducting liabilities. A spouse who has disloyally dissipated assets does not benefit from this limitation, however. In dissipation cases, the statutory maximum is increased by the value of the dissipated assets, § 1378 II 2 BGB.

335. A spouse's equalization claim may be reduced according to § 1380 I BGB, if he or she received assets from the other spouse, either because such transfers were actually understood to reduce a further equalization claim or because they are presumed to have been meant in such a way because they exceed the value of occasional gifts customarily given among spouses of similar social status.

336. The equalization claim arises upon the termination of the property regime. It is heritable and transferable from this time, § 1378 III 1 BGB.

I. Gross Inequity

337. The debtor may refuse to meet an equalization claim partly or entirely if an equalization of accrued gains would seem grossly inequitable under the circumstances, cf. § 1381 BGB. The courts have been slow to find gross inequity.[371] They require an intolerable offence to natural ideas of justice and might refuse a claim where the claimant has significantly neglected his or her marital obligations.[372]

II. Contractual Modifications

338. The spouses may – even if they wish to remain under the statutory property regime as such – sign a marriage contract (§§ 1408 I, 1410 BGB) that modifies the equalization of accrued gains. They might, e.g., exclude certain items of property – such as a business[373] – from the equalization. § 1378 III 2 BGB also grants them the right to draw up modification agreements during divorce proceedings. Any agreements have to be notarized.

§4. Advance Equalization

339. Under certain circumstances, a spouse might ask for equalization before getting divorced (advance equalization). An advance equalization claim may be made where (§§ 1385, 1386 BGB):

- the spouses have lived apart for a minimum of three years, § 1385 No. 1 BGB;
- there is reason to suppose that the other spouse is disloyally dissipating funds or disposing of his or her entire property without the other spouse's consent, thereby endangering the equalization claim, § 1385 No. 2 BGB;
- the other spouse has persistently failed to meet the financial obligations of marriage (e.g., his or her duty of support), and there is reason to suppose that he or she will continue to do so in the future, § 1385 No. 3 BGB;

---

371. Cf. BGH FamRZ 1973, 254.
372. *See* § 1381 II BGB.
373. Cf. BGH NJW 1997, 2239.

– the other spouse persistently refuses to provide information about his or her assets, § 1385 No. 4 BGB.

340. In a claim for advance equalization, the relevant date for calculating final assets is that of filing, § 1387 BGB. The equalization claim is not affected by any change in the financial situation of the other spouse arising after the filing date.

§5. Further Claims for Equalization Beyond §§ 1363 et seq. BGB

341. The statutory equalization of accrued gains (§§ 1363 et seq. BGB) may not always lead to satisfactory results. Some spouses might, therefore, try to achieve more by using legal provisions from outside marriage law. Whether this is possible or prevented by §§ 1363 et seq. BGB acting as *leges speciales* has been a subject for debate. The answer depends on the grounds on which the further claims are brought and raises difficult questions as to the relationship between marital property law and the general provisions of private law.

342. Thus, alongside statutory equalization, courts have allowed claims for returns of gifts made during marriage where the donee has shown gross ingratitude towards the donor or the donor's relatives, §§ 530, 531 BGB.[374] 'Gift' is given a narrow interpretation: transfers of property that are meant to support and further the conjugal unit are not classed as gifts. For these transfers, German law has coined the expression '*transfers matrimonii causa*' (e.g., a husband might give his home-making wife a half-share in the matrimonial home).[375] *Transfers matrimonii causa* are not subject to revocation for gross ingratitude. However, there may be a claim for (partial) reimbursement under the rules of frustration of contract. Where the spouses live in the statutory matrimonial property regime, however, this claim may only be made where the statutory equalization, standing alone, would be grossly inadequate.[376]

343. Where one spouse works in the other's business without an express contract, he or she might have a partnership-based claim to a share in the profits, § 738 I 2 BGB. The courts generally infer an implied[377] partnership contract (§ 705 BGB) that only exists between the spouses inter se.[378] A partnership may also be inferred where the spouses pool their assets in the interests of a joint venture that goes beyond the scope of the marriage.[379] These partnership-based claims might exist alongside the statutory property regime.

374. Cf. BGH FamRZ 1982, 1066; 1983, 349.
375. *Ehebedingte Zuwendung, gemeinschaftsbedingte Zuwendung* cf. BGH FamRZ 1999, 1580; 2006, 1022.
376. BGHZ 115, 132, 135.
377. Cf. BGH FamRZ 1999, 1580, 1581; 2012, 1789 para. 17.
378. Cf. BGH FamRZ 1989, 147; NJW 1995, 3383.
379. Cf. BGH FamRZ 1999, 1580.

344. Finally, property transferred during the marriage might be recovered under the rules of unjust enrichment (§ 812 I 2 Alt. 2 BGB, *Zweckverfehlungskondiktion*). This requires that the transfer was made with the aim of furthering the marriage and that this aim can no longer be achieved because of the failure of the marriage.[380]

§6. Special Provisions for Equalization upon Death

345. In the majority of cases, the property regime is terminated by the death of one spouse. To avoid the complications of the equalization of accrued gains under §§ 1372 et seq. BGB, the Code provides for a generalized equalization instead.

346. Where the deceased dies intestate, the surviving spouse's intestate share is increased by one quarter, § 1371 I BGB. Where there are first-degree relatives, such as descendants, the spouse would thus be entitled to $^1/_4 + ^1/_4 = ^1/_2$ of the estate. The top-up also applies to the spouse's compulsory portion, § 1371 II BGB.

The increase of one quarter is irrespective of whether the spouses actually realized a gain during the marriage. An 'equalization' will thus be made even if the marriage only lasted for a few days and even if the surviving spouse actually accumulated more wealth during the marriage.

347. If the surviving spouse is the testate heir or legatee, no additional 'equalization' by way of increasing his or her share is made, it being assumed that any equalization intended is already provided for in the will. The spouse may always disclaim the inheritance, however.

348. Where the surviving spouse disclaims the inheritance or where he or she is neither the heir nor a legatee, equalization of accrued gains will be performed according to §§ 1373 et seq. BGB. In addition, the spouse may claim the compulsory portion. His or her suit must be filed against the heir(s).

380. Cf. BGHZ 177, 193 para. 34 – concerning unmarried couples; BGHZ 184, 190 para. 47 – concerning contributions by parents-in-law.

Part IV. Law of Succession

Chapter 1. Introduction

349. The law of succession has grown in importance in the past years. As the savings of the elder generation have not been destroyed by political or economic catastrophes, it is estimated that within the next years, assets of more than EUR 3.1 trillion will be inherited by the younger generation, the average estate having a value of more than EUR 350,000.

Whereas family law has been changed fundamentally within the past decades, the law of succession has remained rather unchanged. A broad discussion on the legitimacy of succession law[381] and its modernization[382] led to nothing but some changes with regard to the limitation of succession rights, the compulsory portion and the claim to augmentation of this portion.[383]

§1. Basic Concepts of the Law of Inheritance

I. Subject Matter of the Law of Inheritance

350. In objective terms, the law of succession comprises all norms which regulate the transfer of private proprietary rights and duties on an individual's death. In subjective terms, the law of succession describes the position of a person who has become the heir of another, i.e., the deceased.

II. Legal Sources

351. Article 14 I GG guarantees the right to succeed. The law of succession is governed by the 5th book of the German Civil Code (§§ 1922–2385 BGB), but the

381. Cf. Anatol Dutta, *Warum Erbrecht?* (2014); Anne Röthel, *Erbrecht* § 1 paras 2 et seq. (18th ed. 2020).
382. Cf. Anne Röthel, *Ist unser Erbrecht noch zeitgemäß?, in 1 Verhandlungen des 68. Deutschen Juristentags Berlin 2010* A1 (Ständige Deputation des Deutschen Juristentages ed., 2010); Hans Klingelhöffer, *'Ist unser Erbrecht noch zeitgemäß?'*, ZEV 2010, 385; Peter Rawert, *Ist unser Erbrecht noch zeitgemäß?*, AnwBl 2010, 556; Inge Kroppenberg, *Erbrechtliche Herausforderungen des demographischen Wandels*, ErbR 2010, 206; Dieter Leipold, *Ist unser Erbrecht noch zeitgemäß?*, JZ 2010, 802.
383. Cf. Wolfgang Reimann, *Die Reform des Erb- und Verjährungsrechts*, FamRZ 2009, 1633.

other books contain provisions partly relating to the law of succession as well (e.g., §§ 563 et seq., 857 BGB). Proceedings of an insolvent estate are regulated in §§ 315 et seq. InsO. The law of succession also appears in the *Law on Hereditary Farms*, which is applicable only in parts of Germany.[384] Even after reunification, succession in East Germany before 3 October 1990 is still governed by the Civil Code of the former German Democratic Republic (East Germany) (Article 235 § 1 EGBGB). If the deceased had his or her assets in both East and West Germany, the estate will be separated.

The applicable law in transnational cases has (since 17 August 2015) been regulated by Articles 20–38 of the European Regulation (EU) No. 650/2012 on jurisdiction, applicable law, recognition and enforcement of decisions – in matters of succession – of 4 July 2012.[385] Articles 25, 26 EGBGB now only contain complementary rules. The European Regulation is implemented by the *Internationales Erbrechtsverfahrensgesetz* of 29 June 2015.[386] Yet, the German-Turkish Estates Agreement of 1929,[387] the German-Soviet Consular Treaty of 1958, and the German-Persian Settlement Agreement of 1929 are still valid and have priority (Article 75(1) European Succession Regulation).[388]

III. Probate Court Rules

352. The German Civil Code mostly contains substantive law, but there are still some procedural rules. That is to say, it regulates the competence of the probate court to issue a certificate of inheritance (§ 2353 BGB). The new *Act on Proceedings in Family Matters and in Matters of Non-contentious Jurisdiction* (FamFG) of 17 December 2008 (in force since 1 September 2009) now contains very detailed rules on all relevant non-contentious proceedings in matters of succession law (§§ 342–372 FamFG).

The rules governing the documentation of wills in the law on certification[389] must also be observed when drawing up notarial wills and deeds of inheritance.

IV. Inheritance Tax

353. The private law of succession is supplemented and, at least in part, greatly influenced (with respect to the details of wills and to dispositions providing for the case of death) by the *Act on Inheritance Tax and Donation Tax*.[390] This law was partly reformed in 2008. This amendment provided for tax benefits for heirs of enterprises with the intent to preserve jobs, but the concrete benefits were held to be

384. § 1 I 1 Höfeordnung.
385. OJ 2012 L 201/107 (BGBl. I 1042).
386. *Internationales Erbrechtsverfahrensgesetz* (IntErbRVG) of 29 Jun. 2015 (BGBl. I 1042).
387. Cf. BGH FamRZ 2016, 122.
388. Cf. Peter Mankowski, *Gelten die bilateralen Staatsverträge der Bundesrepublik Deutschland im Internationalen Erbrecht nach dem Wirksamwerden der EuErbVO weiter?*, ZEV 2013, 529.
389. *Beurkundungsgesetz* (BeurkG) of 28 Aug. 1969 (BGBl. I 1513).
390. *Erbschaftsteuer- und Schenkungsteuergesetz* of 17 Apr. 1974 (BGBl. I 933).

unconstitutional.[391] After a long and highly controversial discussion, a new *Law to Adapt the Law of Inheritance Tax and Donation Tax to the Rulings of the Federal Constitutional Court* of 4 November 2016 was enacted, applicable from 1 July 2016.[392]

§2. Fundamental Terms and Principles of the Law of Succession

I. Universal Succession

354. The principle of universal succession is the starting point of the German Civil Code. All proprietary rights of the deceased go directly on his or her death to one or several successors, § 1922 I BGB. Furthermore, the heir gains possession by law, § 857 BGB. In contrast to this, strictly personal rights, like damages for breach of privacy,[393] cannot be inherited.[394] The duty of physicians, lawyers and so on, to maintain confidentiality, does not lapse on death. Apart from that, succession is not restricted to patrimonial rights, but includes (information on) accounts with social networks.[395] § 630g III BGB expressly states that the heir succeeds to the right of the deceased patient to inspect his or her file. Information about the capacity to make a will shall correspond with the presumed intent of the deceased.[396] Legal aid is not hereditable, but must be granted anew to the heir on a fresh application.[397]

If there are several heirs, they inherit jointly (joint heirs, §§ 2032 et seq. BGB), with the exception of the following: (1) shares in a partnership (OHG, KG) – a special type of succession will take place here; (2) farms inherited according to the Law on Hereditary Farms – the farm will be inherited independently of other assets by its successor; (3) a tenancy is inherited by the spouse or registered partner, alternatively by the children, family members or other persons, who shared a common household with the deceased, § 563 I, II BGB.

II. Succession to Liabilities

355. An inheritance encompasses not only the total estate but also its encumbrances, i.e., all assets and liabilities. The heir is, therefore, liable for the deceased's debts (§ 1967 BGB), but with the possibility of disclaiming the inheritance (§§ 1942 et seq. BGB) or the opportunity of limiting liability (§§ 1975 et seq. BGB; §§ 315 et seq. InsO). For his or her protection, the heir can apply for a public notice requiring creditors to file their claims within a certain period (§§ 1970 et seq. BGB).

---

391. BVerfGE 138, 136.
392. *Gesetz zur Anpassung des Erbschaftsteuer- und Schenkungsteuergesetzes an die Rechtsprechung des Bundesverfassungsgerichts* of 4 Nov. 2016 (BGBl. I 2464); cf. BT-Drucks. 18/5923, 18/6379, 18/6910 and 18/8911.
393. BGHZ 201, 45.
394. Cf. BGHZ 50, 133.
395. LG Berlin FamRZ 2016, 738.
396. BGHZ 91, 392.
397. OLG Düsseldorf FamRZ 2016, 2024.

III. Bequest of Specific Assets

356. A beneficiary who is due to receive individual items from the testator's assets in accordance with the will is termed a specific legatee. He or she will only have a personal claim against the heir or heirs, § 2174 BGB.

IV. Possible Heir

357. Every individual or legal entity can be an heir, irrespective of age and contractual capacity, § 1923 I BGB. For practical reasons, children who have already been conceived can inherit if they are subsequently born alive according to § 1923 II BGB. If a child has not yet been conceived, it can only become a reversionary heir, § 2101 I BGB.

V. Entry of Succession

358. Devolution of an inheritance occurs on the death of the decedent, indicated by the stopping of the heart and circulation, but may also occur if the testator has become brain-dead.

VI. Intestate Succession

359. Those dying intestate are succeeded by operation of law by their spouse and closest relatives or, alternatively, by the state, §§ 1924 et seq. BGB (*see infra* Chapter 2, §1).

VII. Testate Succession

360. Alternatively, the decedent can dispose of his or her assets as he or she sees fit through a last will and testament and/or succession agreement (§§ 1937 et seq. BGB) (*see infra* Chapter 2, §2). The law will only go so far as to stipulate that a compulsory portion of the estate should go to the surviving spouse and closest relatives. This gives rise to a claim under the law of obligations against the heir or heirs specified in the will equal to half of the intestate share of the compulsory heir (§§ 2303 et seq. BGB; *see infra* Chapter 2, §3).

VIII. Burial

361. The decedent can nominate a person to organize his or her burial (even against the will of his or her kin or heirs).[398] If he or she has made no such disposition, the next of kin are entitled to organize the funeral and choose the grave, even if they are not the heirs.[399] They have a claim against the heirs for costs, § 1968 BGB.

Under public law, the public authority that paid for the burial is entitled to recover the cost from the next of kin, even if they are not heirs of the deceased.[400]

398. Cf. AG Osnabrück FamRZ 2016, 491; OLG Naumburg FamRZ 2016, 1106.
399. Cf. Walter Zimmermann, *Rechtsfragen zum Thema 'Friedhof und Bestattung'*, ZEV 1997, 440; Wolfgang Küpper, *MünchKommBGB* § 1968 para. 7 (8th ed. 2020).
400. Cf. OVG Schleswig FamRZ 2016, 851; SG Karlsruhe FamRZ 2016, 1108.

Chapter 2. Passing Wealth on Death

§1. Intestate Succession

I. Relatives' Right of Succession

362. In the absence of a testamentary disposition by the deceased, his or her estate will go to his or her family by operation of law, §§ 1924 et seq. BGB. The surviving spouse and relatives of the first order are joint heirs. The term 'relative' is defined in § 1589 BGB.

A. *Primary Heirs*

363. The order in which relatives have a right to succeed is determined by §§ 1924 et seq. BGB according to an arrangement that, in essence, favours the younger generations:

(1) Primary heirs are the children of the decedent and their issue, § 1924 BGB. Secondary heirs are the parents of the decedent and their issue (brothers, sisters, nephews, nieces), § 1925 BGB.
The grandparents and their issue are tertiary heirs, § 1926 BGB. More distant relatives are excluded in favour of nearer ones, § 1930 BGB.
(2) Within the first three degrees, a system of *per stirpes* distribution applies, which, starting with the second degree, is complemented by a system of lineal heirs.
Descendants of the same degree receive an equal share of the inheritance. Each child of the intestate can be a head of a line. His or her issue (grandchildren, great-grandchildren) are related to the intestate exclusively via him or her. If the intestate dies a widower and leaves three children, e.g., the children inherit equal shares § 1924 IV BGB, independently of their marital status and of whether they have children of their own.
(3) Each *per stirpes* descendant is represented by the nearest relative ('Principle of Representation'), § 1924 II BGB. Thus, a child excludes its own children, i.e., the grandchildren, from the line of succession. If a child has predeceased the intestate, then this child's offspring inherits in its place, § 1924 III BGB. This principle of representation applies even if the nearer descendant does not become heir, be it because he or she disclaims the inheritance, is disqualified from receiving it or predeceases the intestate.

B. Secondary Heirs

364. For secondary heirs, succession is also still determined by *per stirpes* distribution, the representation principle and the right of pre-emption, § 1925 BGB. The lineage refers to the relations of a person in the ascending line to his or her parents, in reverse order.

C. Tertiary Heirs

365. Tertiary heirs are the deceased's grandparents and their offspring. According to the principle of representation, the grandparents inherit if they survive the testator, § 1926 II BGB. If they are no longer alive, the right of pre-emption comes into play once again, § 1926 III BGB. If there are no offspring on the side of one set of grandparents, that share devolves on the other grandparents and their offspring, § 1926 III 2 BGB. If one set of grandparents is no longer alive and has no offspring, the other grandparents and their offspring inherit alone, § 1926 IV BGB. The offspring's right of representation is determined by the rules governing primary heirs, § 1926 V BGB.

D. Further Heirs

366. From the fourth degree onwards, the principle of representation and the right of representation are no longer applicable. From the fourth degree, all persons who are equally close relatives of the deceased inherit equally, § 1928 II, III BGB, if the great-grandparents are no longer alive.

E. Status of Illegitimate Children

367. Nowadays, legitimate and illegitimate children inherit in the same way. The Act granting equal status to illegitimate children, passed in 1997,[401] abolished the substituted inheritance right (formerly § 1934d BGB) and the claim for advance compensation payments in lieu of future performance (formerly § 1934d BGB) without replacement for successions taking place after 1 April 1998 (Article 227 I No. 1 EGBGB). The illegitimate child can only advance inheritance rights once paternity has been established (§§ 1594 I, 1600d IV BGB). According to a further law of 1970, all illegitimate children born before 1 July 1949 were excluded from succeeding their father. After the European Court of Human Rights ruled on 28 May 2009[402] that this violated Articles 14 and 8 ECHR, the German legislature reacted with a *Second Act on the Equalization of Illegitimate Children in Succession Law*

---

401. *Gesetz zur erbrechtlichen Gleichstellung nichtehelicher Kinder* (*Erbrechtsgleichstellungsgesetz*) of 16 Dec. 1997 (BGBl. I 2968).

402. *Brauer v. Germany*, No. 3545/02, § 45, Eur. Ct. H.R. 28 May 2009.

of 12 April 2011:[403] retroactively from 29 May 2009, the day after the decision of the European Court, illegitimate children born before 1 July 1949 become legal heirs of their father if the father has died after 29 May 2009. If the father died before that date, the children are excluded from succession only if there is a reasonable relationship of proportionality between the exclusion and the aims of preserving legal certainty and protecting the 'legitimate expectations' of the deceased and his or her family.[404]

F. *Status of Adopted Children*

368. An adopted child becomes a child of the adopting parents according to §§ 1754, 1924 BGB. The relationship with, and along with it, the right to succeed the biological parents is extinguished by the adoption, § 1755 BGB. The only exception to this rule arises when dealing with the adoption of stepchildren, § 1756 II BGB. If an adult is adopted, the new relationship is only established between the adoptive parents and adoptee and the latter's offspring. The relationship with the blood relations remains in existence, § 1770 BGB.

II. Spousal Inheritance Rights

369.

(1) The spouse is not related to the decedent and, therefore, his or her right to inherit is subject to special rules. In all legal systems, an effort is made to ensure provision for the surviving spouse after the death of the decedent and to take into account the personal and economic unity of the married couple. A prerequisite for the spouse's inheritance rights is a valid marriage at the time of death. Even before a divorce decree, the right to inherit is extinguished if the deceased has either applied for a divorce or agreed to it, § 1933 sent. 1 BGB.

(2) The size of the share left to the surviving spouse depends on the matrimonial property regime chosen by the married couple and on which other heirs the spouse is in competition with.

A. *Community of Accrued Gains*

370.

(1) The spouse inherits a quarter alongside children according to § 1931 I BGB and in addition receives another quarter as a lump sum to equalize accrued gains, §§ 1931 III, 1371 I BGB. This amounts to a total of one-half. This is the solution provided by the law of succession (*erbrechtliche Lösung*).

---

403. *Zweites Gesetz zur erbrechtlichen Gleichstellung nichtehelicher Kinder, zur Änderung der Zivilprozessordnung und der Abgabenordnung* of 12 Apr. 2011 (BGBl. I 615).

404. *Mitzinger v. Germany*, No. 29762/10, §§ 42–43, Eur. Ct. H.R. 9 Feb. 2017.

Next to secondary relatives and grandparents, the spouse inherits three quarters. If there are no primary or secondary relatives or grandparents, the surviving spouse takes as sole heir, § 1931 II BGB. The spouse also inherits in place of grandparents who have passed away, taking their share, § 1931 I 2 BGB. Consequently, the spouse has a dominant position. Nevertheless, he or she must share with children and parents, which can lead to difficulties concerning maintenance and housing. For that reason, many couples appoint each other as sole heirs in their wills and their children only as heirs of the spouse who is the last to die, cf. § 2269 BGB.

In cases of gains acquired through succession, the lump sum awarded to equalize accrued gains is not considered an acquisition *mortis causa* for the purposes of inheritance tax (§ 5 I ErbStG).

(2) The spouse's position is further strengthened by preferential rights to the matrimonial home, § 1932 BGB, and the thirty days' maintenance rule, § 1969 BGB, according to which a member of the decedent's family and household can claim maintenance from the heir for the first thirty days after the death. The thirty days' maintenance rule expressly includes the use of the home and household supplies, unless the deceased has provided differently in a will. Nevertheless, there are proposals to expand the rule to a general claim for maintenance against the estate. This could consume the entire estate. Both the claim for the preferential advance and the one for thirty days' maintenance are treated as legacies, cf. §§ 1932 II, 1969 II in connection with § 2174 BGB.

(3) Potentially, the spouse can improve his or her position by waiving the inheritance and claiming the exact amount due to him or her under the rules governing equalization of accrued gains (in accordance with §§ 1373 et seq. BGB) (*güterrechtliche Lösung*) along with the compulsory portion under § 1371 III BGB. The equalization of accrued gains should then be in excess of three-sevenths of the estate if there are children or two-thirds of the estate if there are secondary heirs. If the spouse does not take under the will, he or she can claim the exact amount of the equalization claim and the compulsory portion. In that case, the intestate share used to determine the size of the compulsory portion is not increased by one quarter ('small compulsory portion'), § 1371 II BGB. According to some, the spouse may alternatively claim the 'augmented compulsory portion' (which is calculated on the basis of an augmented intestate share). This is called the election theory. However, it is not compatible with the wording of § 1371 II BGB and the legislative intent.

B. Separate Property

371. If the couple has agreed upon separate property (§ 1414 BGB) in a matrimonial property agreement (§ 1408 BGB), the accrued gains are not equalized and, therefore, the share of the inheritance is not increased pursuant to § 1371 I BGB. Instead, it remains regulated by § 1931 I, II BGB. If the deceased is succeeded by his or her spouse and one or two children, they each take equal shares of the estate, § 1931 IV BGB.

The spouse's preferential right to an advance (§ 1932 BGB) and the thirty days' maintenance rule (§ 1969 BGB) remain applicable, however.

C. *Community Property*

372. If the spouses have chosen a community property regime, the surviving spouse only inherits one-quarter of the estate if there are children, one-half if there are parents, § 1931 I, II BGB. The spouse is provided for out of the share of the community property, which he or she holds, independently of his or her share in the decedent's estate (§§ 1416 I, 1419 BGB):

(1) The decedent's death ends the community property regime. The dead spouse's share of the community is part of the estate. Who inherits it is determined by the general rules, § 1482 BGB.
(2) If the surviving spouse is the sole heir, there is no need for a division. However, if there are several heirs, the community has to be distributed according to §§ 1471 et seq. BGB. The spouse is entitled to half after making adjustments for liabilities, § 1476 I BGB. The estate to be allocated consists of the other half as well as the deceased's special and separate property, §§ 1417, 1418 BGB.
(3) Finally, the married couple can arrange to continue the community between the surviving spouse and the children, § 1483 BGB. Because of the restrictions attached to it, however, such an arrangement is exceptional.

III. The Registered Partner's Right to Inherit

373. According to § 10 LPartG, the surviving registered partner has a legal right to inherit. This right is the mirror image of the spousal right to inherit in § 1931 BGB. If the partners live in a community of accrued gains (§ 6 LPartG), the share of the surviving partner is increased by one quarter to at least one-half.

IV. The State's Right to Succeed

374. If there is neither a spouse nor registered partner nor relatives, the state of the decedent's last residence is legal heir, § 1936 BGB. This is also the case where the legal heirs have waived the inheritance (e.g., because of excessive debts) or where distant family members cannot be located (§ 1964 BGB). However, the probate court has to search for possible relatives (§ 1964 BGB) first and publicly summon them to claim their inheritance (§ 1965 BGB).

The state inherits like a private person. However, because of the purpose of the fiscal right of inheritance, the state cannot, like other heirs, refuse to accept the inheritance, § 1942 II BGB. Therefore, the right to limit its liability is always reserved to the state by virtue of the law, § 780 II ZPO.

§2. TESTATE SUCCESSION

I. Testamentary Freedom

A. Constitutional Guarantees

375. Testamentary freedom is an essential component of the German legal system of succession. It is part of individual autonomy as it pertains to the law of succession. According to the principle of testamentary freedom, the testator may make dispositions as he or she sees fit in order to change the intestacy rules. Testamentary freedom is constitutionally guaranteed not only by Article 2 I GG, which protects individual freedom in general, but also by the more special Article 14 I GG, which enshrines the right of succession.

Testamentary freedom arises indirectly from §§ 1937–1941 BGB.

The Civil Code also protects testamentary freedom in § 2302 BGB. According to this provision, any contract which obliges the testator to make, revoke or not to revoke a will is null and void.

B. No Will-Making by Proxy

376. A disposition *mortis causa* can only be made in person. The testator must make the will or conclude the contract of inheritance formally and in person, §§ 2064, 2274 BGB. He or she must also personally determine the document's substantive content.

According to § 2065 BGB, the testator may not leave it up to a third party to decide whether a disposition *mortis causa* should be valid or who should receive specific sums of money. This rule causes problems especially when determining the successor to a business. Therefore, in practice, the testator is permitted to lay down objective criteria for establishing a successor. However, what must be decided then are the identity of the successor, the form in which he or she should be appointed, and the time limit for the person who has to make the final decision to establish a successor.[405]

C. Revocation of a Will

377. Testamentary freedom is further ensured by the fact that unilateral dispositions *mortis causa* are freely revocable at any time (§ 2253 BGB) and that a contract by which a person promises to make or not to make a disposition *mortis causa* is void (§ 2302 BGB). Although inheritance contracts meeting the requirements of §§ 2274 et seq. BGB do bind the testator, he or she can always challenge them on the grounds of mistake or undue influence, § 2281 BGB, rescind them pursuant to §§ 2293 et seq. BGB or cancel them by a new agreement pursuant to §§ 2290 et

405. BGHZ 15, 199.

seq. BGB. In a joint will, the testator is only bound to the reciprocal provisions (§ 2270 BGB). However, these, too, may be revoked in accordance with § 2271 BGB, challenged under § 2281 BGB, and cancelled according to §§ 2292 et seq. BGB. Whoever interferes with the testator's testamentary freedom intentionally and unlawfully is not eligible to take under the will, § 2339 BGB, and can be declared unworthy of inheriting (§ 2342 BGB).

D. Illegality of the Will

378. Like every legal transaction, a last will can be unlawful or immoral and hence void, §§ 134, 138 BGB. It is not permissible, e.g., for a care home (*Heimträger*) or its manager (*Heimleiter*) to become a beneficiary of the home's residents, § 14 HeimG.[406]

According to the prevailing opinion, immorality is determined at the time of the drawing up the will,[407] not the time at which the inheritance takes place. The basis of any vetting of the contents of a will is the principle of testamentary freedom. Furthermore, it is to be kept in mind that the closest family members are, in principle, protected by the 'compulsory portion'. A will is only immoral, therefore, when the overall character of the provisions is immoral in terms of content, effects, and motive.[408]

The appointment of a mistress or lover as heir is, therefore, only immoral where sexual services alone are rewarded, but not where there is a long-term relationship (involving housekeeping, care when sick or help in a profession, etc.).

It is a moot point whether the testator may favour male issue (the prevailing opinion is: yes)[409] and whether marriage clauses (stipulating for marriage within the same class, etc.) are permissible. The Federal Constitutional Court and the Federal Supreme Court decided in 1999 that such clauses were valid if the testator is pursuing a legitimate aim.[410] In the 'Hohenzollern'-case, however, the BVerfG required a comprehensive consideration of all facts at the time of death and a balancing of testamentary freedom with freedom of marriage.[411]

The Federal Supreme Court also held that a testator may impose restrictions on the inheritance of a handicapped child in the child's favour, preventing public authorities from recovering care expenditures.[412]

---

406. BayObLG FamRZ 2003, 1882; BayObLG FamRZ 2005, 142.
407. BayObLG FamRZ 1997, 656, 661.
408. BGHZ 53, 369, 375.
409. BGHZ 140, 118; BayObLG FamRZ 1997, 705. Opposing opinion: OLG Stuttgart, FamRZ 1998, 260.
410. BVerfG FamRZ 2000, 945; BGHZ 140, 118.
411. BVerfG ZEV 2004, 241.
412. BGHZ 111, 36 = NJW 1990, 2055; BGHZ 123, 368 = NJW 1994, 248.

II. Competence to Make a Will

A. *Full Capacity*

379. A person who has come of age has full testamentary capacity. Those placed in the care of others remain competent to make a will as well, § 1903 II No. 2 BGB, as long as they can be considered legally competent.

B. *Capacity of Minors*

380. A minor who has turned 16 has limited testamentary capacity. He or she can make a will, but only in the form of a public will by means of an oral declaration or by handing over an open document, § 2233 I BGB. A holographic will made by a minor is not valid, § 2247 IV BGB.

Minors under the age of 16 are not competent to make a will, § 2229 I BGB. They can also not make one through a representative since a will can only be made in person, § 2064 BGB.

C. *General Incapacity*

381. Those who lack contractual capacity also lack testamentary capacity, § 2229 IV BGB. Rudimentary intellectual capability is insufficient.[413] Substantively, § 2229 I BGB corresponds to §§ 104 No. 2, 105 II BGB. Thus, a valid will may be made in a *lucidum intervallum.* In case of dispute, the probate court has to resolve the issue of the testator's capacity, §§ 26, 29 FamFG. The person disputing the testator's lack of testamentary capacity carries the burden of proof.[414]

D. *Restrictions on the Handicapped*

382. Illiterate persons can only make a will by means of an oral declaration before a notary (§§ 2233 II, 2247 IV BGB). In the past, difficulties arose where deaf, mute or blind persons tried to draw up wills. If they were unable to write or speak, they could not make a will. The Federal Constitutional Court, however, found this rule to be unconstitutional.[415] The legislature reacted by setting out in §§ 22 et seq. BeurkG, effective from 1 August 2002, how the public will of a person suffering from such disabilities may be drawn up (if necessary by calling in a third person who is able to communicate with the handicapped testator).

A will that is ineffective at the time it is made remains null and void, even if the testator subsequently acquires testamentary capacity.

---

413. BayObLG ZEV 2005, 348.
414. OLG Hamm FamRZ 1997, 1026; for alcohol excess *see* BayObLG FamRZ 2003, 121, 125 et seq.
415. BVerfGE 99, 341.

III. Creation and Revocation of a Will

A. *Creation*

383. A will can only be made in notarial or holographic form, § 2231 BGB. Additionally, an emergency will can be made in accordance with §§ 2249 et seq. BGB.

1. Holographic Will

384. A holographic will must be written in the testator's hand and signed by him or her, § 2247 I BGB. The deceased must have written the entire text himself or herself. References to texts that are not written in the testator's own hand are only permissible where they serve to explain the will's content, but not where important provisions are affected. A typed will that has only been signed by hand is invalid. Likewise, a will that is signed with a facsimile stamp or not signed at all is invalid. The identity of the testator, his or her intention to make a will, and the fact that the declaration is meant to be final are sought to be ensured by requiring a handwritten text and signature. The signature should include the first name(s) and surname, but other ways of signing are permissible, if they are unambiguous, § 2247 III BGB. Stating the time and place makes it easier to establish a will's validity, but a will that does not include these details may still be valid, § 2247 V BGB.

The will does not have to be described as 'a will' or in similar ways. It is sufficient that the piece of writing contains *earnest provisions* for the event of death. A machine-written heading reading 'testament' does not hinder validity if the text itself is handwritten.[416] A letter can also be considered a holographic will if it contains the provisions and does not simply allude or refer to them.[417]

Codicils and additions must be signed separately. As a conclusion to the document, the signature has to be placed underneath the text, to create a visual closure. Signing at the top or in the margins is insufficient, unless it is due to lack of space and, therefore, still serves as a visual closure. A signature on a closed envelope entitled 'Will' is likewise insufficient.[418] An envelope can, in exceptional circumstances, be considered the 'conclusion' of a testamentary document consisting of several parts. Where it is such a conclusion, it may bear the signature.[419] In case of several single sheets of paper, a connection has to be discernible through either the wording or pagination.[420] In any case, the signature has to be so closely connected to the rest of the text that it may be regarded as an outward continuation and conclusion of the declaration.[421]

416. BayObLG ZEV 2005, 348.
417. OLG Köln FamRZ 1995, 1301.
418. Different opinion BayObLG Rpfleger 1986, 294.
419. BayObLG ZEV 2003, 26.
420. LG München I FamRZ 2004, 1905.
421. Cf. BayObLG FamRZ 2003, 966.

2. Public Will

385. The testator must declare his or her intentions for the notary to write down. This is recorded in the form of notarial certificates according to the law governing documentation. The last will and testament are usually declared orally to the notary (after previous discussion and consultation), § 2232 sent. 1 Alt. 1 BGB. The testator can also hand over an open or closed writing and, in doing so, state that it contains his or her last will, § 2232 sent. 1 Alt. 2 and sent. 2 BGB. The writing does not need to be in the testator's own hand. It is sufficient that the notary's recording is approved and signed, § 13 I BeurkG.

3. Wills Made in an Emergency

386. Those finding themselves in acute mortal danger can also make a will orally before the mayor in the presence of two witnesses, § 2249 BGB. Those finding themselves in an inaccessible place (at least for the notary) can likewise make a will orally before the mayor or, in cases of acute mortal danger, before three witnesses, § 2250 BGB.[422] The same is possible on board a German ship at sea, § 2251 BGB. A will made in an emergency becomes invalid three months after its creation, § 2252 BGB.

4. Official Custody of Wills

387. Any will recorded by a notary shall be put in official custody at the local court, §§ 344, 346 FamFG. A holographic will is also taken into official custody upon demand by the testator, § 2248 BGB. The testator may demand the return of his or her will at any time, § 2256 II BGB. Where a public will is returned, it is deemed to have been revoked by the testator, § 2256 I BGB. Since 2012, the Federal Chamber of Notaries Public has maintained the central register of wills (§ 78c BNotO). To ensure that a will is found after the death of the testator, all wills put into official custody are listed there. On receiving an official notice of death, a clerk of the Federal Chamber checks the register to see if a will of the deceased is listed and communicates the result of his or her search to the competent probate court, §§ 78c et seq. BNotO.

Furthermore, whoever has a will in his or her possession must deliver it to the probate court after the death of the testator, § 2259 BGB.

422. Cf. KG FamRZ 2016, 1966; OLG Bremen FamRZ 2016, 1968.

B. Revocation of a Will

388. Basically, a will can be revoked at any time, in whole or in part, without any reason, § 2253 BGB. The fact that a third party knows about (and potentially has relied on) the will or that the testator has promised to appoint specific heirs does not prevent revocation.

However, whoever relies to his or her detriment on a promise of an inheritance has a restitutionary claim under § 812 I BGB if the promise is not honoured. The claim is directed against the testator and after his or her death against the heirs as a liability of the estate.[423]

A will may also be revoked by making a new one, § 2254 BGB, or by destroying or altering the testamentary document with the intention to revoke it, § 2255 BGB. A public will is also revoked when it is removed from official custody, § 2256 BGB. By creating a new will, the earlier will is revoked to the extent that it is inconsistent with the later will, § 2258 BGB. If the revoking will is revoked, then, in case of doubt, the earlier will is valid again, § 2257 BGB. However, a will that has been torn up with the intention to revoke it does not become valid again merely by glueing it back together.[424]

Since the revocation cancels the provisions made for the event of death, the testator has to have legal capacity, § 2229 BGB. This is also true where the testamentary document is destroyed or taken from official custody.

C. Challenging the Will

389. If a testator makes a will on the basis of a mistaken assumption, he or she can correct his or her error by revoking the will if he or she notices the mistake during his or her lifetime. This being so, the testator does not need to challenge his or her own will.

Things are different where an error or coercion only comes to light after the testator's death. In that case, the testator can no longer put his or her true intention into effect. However, third parties are protected from the testator's defective provisions by the right to challenge the will.

A will contest on the grounds of error or coercion only comes into play where the presumed true intention of the testator (absent the error or coercion) cannot be given effect through interpreting the will:

(1) Provisions made for the event of death can be challenged in accordance with §§ 2078, 2079 BGB. These provisions extend the right to contest the will beyond the scope of §§ 119, 123 BGB. Since there is no protection for reliance with respect to wills as opposed to contracts, a will can be contested on the grounds of any 'mistake of motive', according to § 2078 II BGB. It is also possible to challenge a will on the grounds of unlawful threats or coercion.

---

423. BGHZ 44, 321.
424. BayObLG FamRZ 1996, 1113.

Since a will may be challenged for any mistake of motive, there is no need for a special provision allowing a challenge for fraud.

(2) § 2079 BGB contains a special case of mistake of motive. According to this provision, a disposition can be challenged where the testator has failed to include someone entitled to a compulsory portion whose existence was either not known to him or her when making the disposition or who was born or became entitled to a compulsory portion after that date.
There is no basis for the challenge if it can be shown that the testator would have disposed of his or her estate in the same way even with full knowledge of all relevant facts, § 2079 sent. 2 BGB.

(3) The successful challenge of the will results in its retrospective annulment, § 142 I BGB. In the case of challenge under § 2079 BGB, it is contentious whether the entire will is annulled or whether the will is annulled only insofar as it deprives the person the testator has overlooked of his or her intestate share.[425]

(4) A right to challenge the will is, according to § 2080 BGB, given to those who would be entitled to succeed if the will in question did not exist. If several people have a right of challenge, each of them may contest the will independently. A challenge made by one will be for the benefit of all. In the case of § 2079 BGB, only those entitled to a compulsory portion can contest, § 2080 II BGB. If the error as to content is limited to one specific person, only that person is entitled to challenge the will, § 2080 II BGB. A minor can challenge a will without parental consent since such a challenge is an entirely advantageous legal action (§ 107 BGB).[426]

According to § 2082 I BGB, the challenge must be made to the probate court (§ 2081 I BGB) within one year of the person becoming aware of the grounds for it (§ 2082 II 1 BGB).

The right to challenge the will lapses thirty years after the testator's death, § 2082 III BGB.

IV. Contents and Interpretation of Wills

A. Permissible Contents

390. The testator has wide discretion in organizing his or her will as regards content, but must observe the formal requirements dictated by law. A will may contain the following:

(1) The appointment of an heir or heirs; the disinheritance of a legal heir or heirs (§ 1938 BGB), the appointment of preliminary and reversionary heirs (§§ 2100 et seq. BGB) as well as substitute heirs (§ 2096 BGB). To carry on

---

425. Cf. OLG Schleswig NJW 2016, 1831; Dieter Leipold, *MünchKommBGB* § 2079 para. 28 (8th ed. 2020).
426. Jacob Joussen, *Die erbrechtliche Anfechtung durch Minderjährige*, ZEV 2003, 181.

a business or to ensure that his or her estate is used for a certain purpose, the testator may also order that a foundation shall be established *mortis causa* (§ 83 BGB).

(2) Legacies (§§ 1939, 2147 et seq. BGB) and testamentary burdens (§§ 1940, 2192 et seq. BGB).
(3) Provisions for dealing with the estate, dividing it up (§§ 2048, 2049 BGB); handling differences of opinion (§ 2044 BGB); ordering or excluding an obligation to compensate (§§ 2050 et seq. BGB); appointing an executor (§§ 2197 et seq. BGB).
(4) Rules about the compulsory portion: withdrawal of the compulsory portion (§ 2333 BGB) or limiting the legal share to the compulsory portion.
(5) Revocation of a previous will.
(6) Decisions relating to family law, e.g., appointment of guardians, § 1777 III BGB; restriction of parents' legal rights with regard to property given to a child, § 1638 BGB,[427] declaration as to reserved goods in accordance with § 1418 II No. 2 BGB.
(7) The choice of the *lex patriae* as general law of succession, Article 22(1) European Succession Regulation. A choice of law restricted to real property in a particular state is no longer possible.

In practice, children often receive substantial donations from their parents *inter vivos*. These donations are only deducted from their share if the testator so ordered when making the donation, § 2050 BGB. A subsequent instruction in the will is ineffective.

B. Interpretation of Wills

391. Most disputes in the law of succession relate to the correct interpretation of wills. Holographic wills are frequently drawn up by laymen. Problems can also arise where the interpretation of public wills is concerned.[428] The notary can miss the testator's intention; a large period of time can pass between the drawing up of a will and death and relationships may have altered to such an extent that it is difficult to derive any sensible meaning from the text under the changed circumstances. For example, what exactly does 'Should we pass away at the same time … ' signify?[429] Or: what are 'my, your and our children' in patchwork families?[430]

Wills, as unilateral declarations of will, are as a rule interpreted according to the real intention of the deceased, § 133 BGB. The position of the recipients and the principle of protecting expectations are irrelevant and are usually not considered. When in doubt, the words are to be understood in their general, everyday meaning.

427. Cf. BGH NJW 2016, 3032.
428. BayObLG FamRZ 1997, 1243.
429. *See* OLG Düsseldorf FamRZ 2016, 408; OLG Frankfurt FamRZ 2016, 748; OLG München FamRZ 2011, 504; OLG Hamm FamRZ 2011, 1428.
430. Cf. Susanne Kappler & Tobias Kappler, *Patchworkfamilie und Erbrecht*, ZEV 2015, 437.

The fundamental basis for interpretation is the principle of benevolent interpretation, § 2084 BGB: an interpretation is to be preferred if it gives practical effect to the provisions.

Circumstances external to the will can also be taken into account in the interpretation if/when they permit conclusions about the testator's intention. Admittedly, there must be some indication of this intention in the will (the intimation theory – *Andeutungstheorie*) because otherwise the rules for will formation could be evaded.[431]

If circumstances have changed since the making of the will in a way that was not contemplated by the testator, it must be checked whether the gap can be closed through interpretation. The aim is to give effect to the intentions of the testator. The question is what the testator would have wanted if he or she had contemplated the intermediate event. Such a problem can concern either the beneficiary or the object being bequeathed. The testator's hypothetical intention has to be derived from the will. According to the prevailing opinion, the will must contain some indication that the change would have been acceptable to the testator.[432]

Interpretation may also be used to turn a void provision into a valid one, § 140 BGB.

Legal rules for interpretation:

(1) *Appointment of an heir.* Laymen use the terms 'inheriting' and 'bequeathing' interchangeably or as non-technical terms. Whether someone is appointed as heir is therefore not determined by the expression the testator used, but by the contents of the will. Whoever receives the estate in its entirety or a fraction thereof is an heir.[433] Whoever is granted individual objects is not an heir, but a legatee, § 2087 BGB, unless the object in question represents virtually all of the estate.[434] If the testator divides his or her entire estate into different groups of objects, the beneficiaries can be regarded as joint heirs subject to a division arrangement (§ 2048 BGB).

(2) *Doubts as to the beneficiary.* §§ 2066 et seq. BGB contain various, more or less important rules in the event of doubt as to the beneficiary. Whoever appoints his or her future heir in indefinite terms has, in case of doubt, appointed those who are the statutory heirs at the time of the testator's death, § 2066 BGB. Whoever appoints his or her children or offspring who subsequently die is deemed, in cases of doubt, to have appointed his or her grandchildren as well, §§ 2068, 2069 BGB.[435] If the testator has named his or her

431. For the prevailing opinion, cf. Dieter Leipold, *MünchKommBGB* § 2084 paras 16 et seq., 35 et seq. (8th ed. 2020); for a differing view: Hans Brox & Wolf-Dietrich Walker, *Erbrecht* § 16 para. 4 (29th ed. 2021).

432. Kurt Kuchinke, *Der hypothetische Wille als Instrument zur Durchsetzung des vom Erblasser wirklich Gewollten, in Festschrift für Hans Friedhelm Gaul* 357 (Eberhard Schilken, Ekkehard Becker-Eberhard & Walter Gerhardt eds, 1997).

433. Cf. BayObLG FamRZ 1997, 1242.

434. OLG Schleswig FamRZ 2016, 406.

435. OLG Köln FamRZ 1992, 475.

spouse as a beneficiary, the provision is nullified, in cases of doubt, if the marriage was void or dissolved, prior to the testator's death, § 2077 BGB. The termination of a registered partnership has the same effect, § 10 V LPartG.[436] § 2077 BGB does not apply where children-in-law have been appointed[437] or where a non-matrimonial relationship fails.[438] A final heir is, in doubt, also a substitute heir.[439] If the spouse is named as a beneficiary in a life insurance policy of his or her partner, the right is not automatically extinguished on divorce.[440] Between the spouses inter se, however, the basis for the transaction is usually negated. Hence the heirs can seize the money held by the surviving ex-spouse, provided that it was not the testator's intention that the former spouse should keep the insurance money regardless.

(3) *Lack of clarity about the size of the portion of the inheritance.* §§ 2088 et seq. BGB contain procedural rules for cases where the will allocates some of the estate or more than the estate or where the inheritance portions are imprecise. If the testator has excluded intestate succession by appointing several heirs, intestate succession will not occur where one of the chosen heirs does not succeed. Instead, that person's portion of the inheritance will be used to increase the remaining ones proportionally, § 2094 I 1 BGB. Admittedly, such an increase is ruled out where the testator has appointed a substitute heir, § 2099 BGB, either expressly or by interpretation (especially in accordance with § 2069 BGB).

(4) *Interpretation of Conditions, cf. §§ 2074, 2075 BGB.*

V. The Joint Will of Spouses

A. The Object and Purpose of a Joint Will

392. A life spent in common frequently results in a wish to regulate the financial position after the death of the first and second spouse through mutually agreed provisions. The law accommodates this practical need on two levels:

(1) It simplifies the formal requirements for a joint will (*see supra* paragraph 391).

(2) In the case of reciprocal provisions, whoever lives longer is compelled to obey the provisions of the first to die. The practical result of this is that a joint will caters for the death of both spouses. In practice, the joint will is of great significance.

---

436. Through marrying again the provision does not become operative again, BayObLG NJW 1996, 133.
437. BGH FamRZ 2003, 870.
438. OLG Celle ZEV 2003, 328.
439. OLG Frankfurt FamRZ 1996, 829.
440. BGHZ 157, 79 = NJW 2004, 767, 768.

In European cases, the joint will should be treated as a contract of inheritance (Article 25 European Succession Regulation).[441]

B. The Creation of a Joint Will

393.

(1) Spouses (§ 2265 BGB) and registered partners (§ 10 IV LPartG) can make a joint will, § 2265 BGB. While engaged couples can enter into a prenuptial agreement and inheritance contract, §§ 1408 I, 2274 BGB, a joint will can only be drawn up after marriage.

(2) A joint will can be made before a notary or as a holographic will. Since the spouses create the will jointly, each spouse must be aware of the provisions of the other.
In practice, holographic wills in the spouses' own hand are the most frequent. For them, § 2267 BGB introduces a simpler form. It is sufficient for one spouse to write the will and sign it and for the other spouse simply to add his or her signature.

(3) The joint character of the will's creation can also arise from other circumstances, e.g., mutual provisions or provisions referencing each other in the same piece of writing. Thus, two separate documents might constitute a joint will.[442]

(4) If only one spouse has written the will in his or her own hand and signed it while the other spouse's signature is missing, the writing is considered a draft. Nevertheless, it may be a valid single will of the person who wrote and signed it if such an intention can be found.[443]

(5) A divorce or the testator's filing for divorce renders the joint will invalid, § 2268 I BGB. Nevertheless, a contrary intention may be found on interpretation, § 2268 II BGB.

C. Contents of the Joint Will

394. A married couple can use a joint will to dispose of their respective estates independently of each other. Their provisions may, however, also be legally dependent upon each other. In that case they are called reciprocal provisions, § 2270 I BGB. Whether a provision is reciprocal is to be established by interpretation.[444]

---

441. Cf. Dieter Leipold, *Das Europäische Erbrecht (EuErbVO) und das deutsche gemeinschaftliche Testament*, ZEV 2014, 139; only in case of no single document: Friedrich Nordmeier ZEV 2012, 513, 514.

442. OLG Zweibrücken FamRZ 2003, 1415.

443. Cf. BGH NJW-RR 1987, 1410.

444. For the individual cases cf. Maximilian Zimmer, *Aktuelle Entwicklungen im Bereich wechselbezüglicher Verfügungen beim gemeinschaftlichen Testament*, ZEV 2015, 450; Gerhard Pfeiffer, *Das gemeinschaftliche Ehegattentestament*, FamRZ 1993, 1266.

Reciprocity or interdependency is presumed according to § 2270 II BGB:

- where each spouse bequeaths something to the other (as heir, legatee, etc.); or
- where one spouse makes a financial contribution to the other, who, in his or her turn, provides a benefit for a third party who is related or close to the contributing spouse.[445]

The third party can but does not have to be related to the other spouse. If spouses appoint each other and stipulate that after the death of the surviving spouse the estate should go to their children, it cannot be said that each spouse makes a provision in favour of the children only because the other does so.[446]

Reciprocity has significant legal consequences:

(1) If a reciprocal provision is void or repealed, the other spouse's provision is also ineffective, § 2270 I BGB. This legal consequence applies only to the appointment of future heirs, legacies, and testamentary burdens, according to § 2270 III BGB. Other provisions, like naming an executor, arranging for the division of the estate, disinheriting a relative or withdrawing a compulsory portion still remain valid where the provision of the other spouse becomes void, insofar as the existence of the other's provisions has not been a condition for their validity. If a joint will also contains unilateral provisions, the nullity of the reciprocal provisions only invalidates the rest where it can be assumed that the unilateral provisions would not have been made without those with interdependent content, § 2085 BGB.

(2) A reciprocal provision cannot be revoked during the other spouse's lifetime by a unilateral provision, § 2271 I 2 BGB. A revocation is only possible in accordance with the provisions for the rescission of an inheritance contract, i.e., by bringing the revocation to the other spouse's notice in notarial form, §§ 2271 I 1, 2296 II BGB. This also holds in the case of § 2268 II BGB.[447]

(3) On the death of the other spouse, the right to revoke is extinguished; the surviving partner can only revoke his or her own dispositions if he or she refuses everything bestowed on him or her, § 2271 II 1 BGB. The only exception to this rule is where the surviving spouse is authorized by the will to amend or revoke the will (reserved right of amendment or exemption clause).

(4) A binding reciprocal provision does not prevent the disposal of the estate during the lifetime of the parties. This is laid down expressly for inheritance contracts in § 2286 BGB but also applies to joint wills. Only in the case of gifts made with the intention of interfering with the will does the heir affected have a claim for restitution against the beneficiary in analogy with § 2287 BGB.

Spouses frequently appoint each other as heirs and stipulate that after the death of the last to die the children should receive the property. Legally, this final result can be achieved in two ways:

---

445. *See* BayObLG FamRZ 1997, 1241; Hans-Joachim Musielak, *MünchKommBGB* § 2270 paras 11 et seq. (8th ed. 2020).
446. BayObLG FamRZ 1985, 1287.
447. BGH ZEV 2004, 423.

(1) The surviving spouse becomes the preliminary heir of the first to die, while the children are appointed reversionary heirs of the first spouse and full heirs of the surviving spouse. This is called the principle of separation (*Trennungslösung*).
(2) The surviving spouse becomes full heir of the first spouse to die. The children only inherit from the survivor. The children are thereby excluded from the inheritance of the first to die. This is called the unity principle or *Berlin Testament*.[448] In accordance with the rules of interpretation in § 2269 BGB, this principle of unity applies in cases of doubt. The disadvantage of this construction is that the children can demand their compulsory portion on the death of the first spouse, § 2303 BGB. To get around this, it is common practice to insert a *penalty clause* providing that a child who demands the compulsory portion should be excluded from the inheritance of the last to die as well.

A remarriage clause can frequently be found in joint wills, according to which the surviving spouse must give the estate to the children in case of remarriage. In cases of doubt, this means that the full inheritance of the surviving partner may potentially be annulled, §§ 158 II, 2075 BGB. At the same time, a preliminary and reversionary heir-solution enter into operation, but only if the condition (remarriage) occurs. It is only established on the death of the surviving spouse whether he or she has become a full heir or not.[449] According to the opposing view, the survivor must observe the rules and restrictions placed on a preliminary heir, but of one exempted from certain statutory restrictions and obligations, while it is still possible for the spouse to remarry. This view treats the survivor as a preliminary heir (subject to a resolving condition of non-remarriage) and a potential full heir (subject to condition precedent of non-remarriage).[450]

Compulsory portion penalty clauses are quite common. By them, a child appointed as reversionary heir is disinherited if he or she demands the compulsory portion upon the death of the first parent to die.[451]

D. Challenging a Joint Will

395. If a reciprocal provision has become binding by the death of the first spouse, the surviving spouse must be able to contest the will if he or she has grounds for challenge. Rules catering for this scenario only exist for inheritance contracts, §§ 2281 et seq. BGB. However, these rules are applied to binding joint wills by analogy.[452] The right of third parties (according to §§ 2078, 2079 BGB) to contest

448. Cf. Rainer Kanzleiter, *Das Berliner Testament: immer aktuell und fast immer ergänzungsbedürftig*, ZEV 2014, 225.
449. Cf. BGHZ 96, 198.
450. Cf. Hans-Joachim Musielak, *MünchKommBGB* § 2269 paras 54 et seq. (8th ed. 2020), who nevertheless agrees with the conclusions of the prevailing opinion.
451. BayObLG ZEV 2004, 202.
452. BayObLG FamRZ 1995, 1024.

a joint will is not precluded in analogy to § 2285 BGB, even if the testator had lost his or her right to contest the will at the time of his or her death.[453]

VI. The Inheritance Contract

A. *Contractual Dispositions* Mortis Causa

396. The testator can dispose of his or her assets *mortis causa* by contractual means, §§ 2274 et seq. BGB. This contract only takes effect after death, but binds the testator so that the provisions in the contract may no longer be unilaterally revoked, § 2289 I BGB. The purpose of the inheritance contract is to bring about this commitment, mainly for the benefit of the contractual partner.

The inheritance contract is a regular contract. However, to protect the testator from entering into it in haste, it must be recorded by a notary, § 2276 BGB.

The testator is bound by the provisions in the contract, but can dispose of his or her wealth freely during his or her lifetime, as long as he or she does not make gifts in bad faith, §§ 2286 et seq. BGB. The person due to inherit under the contract, therefore, has no legally ensured interest in an estate of a specific size, but only a prospect of acquisition. This expectation cannot be secured by a priority notice in the land register.

B. *Concluding an Inheritance Contract*

397. The testator must conclude an inheritance contract in person, § 2274 BGB and must have it authenticated by a notary. For this, both parties must be present before the notary at the same time, § 2276 BGB.

Since the inheritance contract is a contract, the rules on contractual capacity apply, § 2275 I BGB.

C. *Contents of the Inheritance Contract*

398.

(1) The testator may appoint heirs, leave legacies, impose testamentary burdens, and (since 2015) choose the applicable law in a contractually binding manner; other dispositions remain unilateral, § 2278 BGB. For contractually binding dispositions, the testamentary rules apply correspondingly, § 2279 I BGB, but with some exceptions and modifications.
Unilateral dispositions in an inheritance contract are governed by the general rules on wills, § 2299 BGB.

453. BGH NJW 2016, 2566.

(2) The contents of an inheritance contract may vary. One or both contractual parties can make dispositions *mortis causa*. They can also appoint each other as beneficiaries. Several persons can enter into inheritance contracts with each other.
In the case of a bilateral inheritance contract, the nullity of a reciprocal disposition will invalidate the corresponding provision of the other partner, § 2298 BGB. A reserved right to withdraw will also lead to the revocation of the entire contract, if exercised, § 2298 II 1 BGB.
(3) As a rule, the appointment of an heir in an inheritance contract is meant to reward some past or future performance of that party. However, the inheritance contract is not a reciprocal agreement. Still, if the person appointed in the inheritance contracts fails to meet his or her contractual obligations under a contract to maintain or care for the testator, the latter may renounce the inheritance contract, § 2295 BGB.

D. Obligations Arising from an Inheritance Contract and Their Extinction

399. By concluding the inheritance contract, the testator becomes bound to his or her contractual dispositions *mortis causa*. Earlier wills are revoked to the extent that they impair the rights of the contractual beneficiaries, § 2289 I 1 BGB. Later testamentary dispositions will be invalid to the same extent, § 2289 I 2 BGB. Any legal or economic infringement of any of the contractual heirs' rights will suffice. A disposition of this nature can only be valid if the other contractual partner consents to it, which requires the form of a contract of rescission, § 2290 BGB.

The inheritance contract (like other contracts) can lack a beneficiary because of his or her predecease, etc. In such cases, a previous or later disposition will be valid.

Basically, the testator can only dispose of his or her assets in conflict with the inheritance contract if he or she has reserved a right to do so.[454]

The effect of the inheritance contract can be extinguished:

(1) By mutual consent, § 2290 BGB, expressed in the form of an inheritance contract, § 2290 IV BGB. Spouses can also do so through a joint will, § 2292 BGB. As a matter of course, it is possible for the parties to change or amend the contract of inheritance.[455]
(2) After the death of one contractual party, the inheritance contract can no longer be revoked, § 2290 I 2 BGB. A third-party beneficiary can, therefore, not conclude a contract terminating the inheritance contract. However, he or she may declare his or her intention to waive the inheritance, §§ 2346, 2348, 2352 BGB, thereby restoring the testator's freedom of disposition.

---

454. Hans-Joachim Musielak, *Zur Bindung an den Erbvertrag und zu den rechtlichen Möglichkeiten einseitiger Änderungen*, ZEV 2007, 245.
455. Hilmar Keller, *Aufhebung, Änderung und Ergänzung eines Erbvertrags durch die Vertragspartner*, ZEV 2004, 93.

(3) Contractual bequests, testamentary burdens or a choice-of-law clause can be revoked by a simple will with the consent of the other contractual partner. The consent has to be recorded by a notary, § 2291 BGB.
(4) The testator can rescind the inheritance contract unilaterally:
   - if he or she has reserved the right to do so, § 2293 BGB;
   - because of serious misconduct by the beneficiary, § 2294 BGB; and
   - where the contractual obligations of the other party (e.g., under a nursing contract) are terminated, § 2295 BGB.

   In each case, the declaration to rescind has to be made to the other contracting party and recorded by a notary, § 2296 II BGB. After the death of the other contracting party, it may be included in a will, § 2297 BGB.
(5) Finally, the testator can challenge the contractual dispositions in accordance with the requirements of § 2281 BGB. The challenge must be made in personal. It requires official authentication, and must be declared within a year of the grounds for challenge coming to the testator's knowledge. While the other contracting party is still alive, the challenge has to be declared to him or her, § 143 II BGB. After the death of that party, the disposition in question can be challenged in the probate court, § 2281 II 1 BGB. Persons entitled to challenge a will (according to §§ 2078, 2079 BGB) are precluded from contesting the inheritance contract if the testator had lost his or her right to do so at the time of his or her death, § 2285 BGB.

If the inheritance contract is rescinded, any unilateral dispositions become null and void as well. This is the default rule, § 2299 III BGB. In the case of a bilateral inheritance contract, the entire contract is annulled on rescission, § 2298 II 1 BGB. A challenge to an individual contractual disposition in such a contract will, in case of doubt, cause the entire contract to become invalid in the same way, § 2298 I, III BGB.

The inheritance contract only precludes inconsistent dispositions *mortis causa*. By an *inter vivos* transaction, the testator remains able to dispose of his or her assets freely, § 2286 BGB. Only gifts made with the intention of interfering with the will can be impugned; the beneficiary may demand the return of the gift from the recipient according to the law of unjust enrichment, § 2287 BGB. The term 'gift' takes its meaning from § 516 BGB. Unnamed donations (*unbenannte Zuwendungen*) between spouses that arise from the marital relationship are, within the scope of § 2287 BGB, to be treated as gifts.[456] An intention to interfere can only be shown where the testator has no legitimate personal interest in making the donation. The intention to interfere with the rights of the contractual heirs does not have to be the main motive for the gift.[457]

456. BGHZ 116, 167 = NJW 1992, 564.
457. BGHZ 59, 343.

§3. The Right to a Compulsory Portion

400. In accordance with the principle of testamentary freedom, the testator can also disinherit his or her relatives. The right to a compulsory portion secures a minimum share in the estate to the closest relatives. This minimum share is protected by the guarantee of the right of inheritance in Article 14 I 1 in connection with Article 6 I GG.[458] According to German law, those entitled to a compulsory portion are not compulsory 'statutory heirs', but only have an in personam claim against the heir or heirs. The personal claim for the compulsory portion is an estate liability, § 1967 II BGB. The compulsory portion is rooted in the idea that the estate belongs to the family. As 'starting capital', the compulsory portion nowadays often comes too late for children. Furthermore, children today usually accumulate their own assets and savings.

I. The Compulsory Portion

A. Persons Entitled

401. Those entitled to a compulsory portion are the descendants, the parents, and the spouse or registered partner of the deceased, but not siblings, § 2303 BGB, § 10 VI LPartG. More distant descendants and parents are not entitled to a compulsory portion if a closer descendant can claim the compulsory portion or accepts what has been left to him or her, § 2309 BGB.[459]

The right to the compulsory portion comes into existence on the death of the deceased. It is hereditable and transferable, § 2317 BGB.

Generally, a person is only entitled to a compulsory portion if he or she has been completely excluded from the succession by a disposition *mortis causa*. However, an heir appointed subject to restrictions and a legatee may claim a compulsory portion if they turn down the inheritance or legacy, §§ 2306 I, 2307 I 1 BGB. Another option is contained in § 1371 III BGB for a spouse who refuses the inheritance. A person appointed as revisionary heir can also reject this position and claim the compulsory portion, § 2306 II BGB.

The decision to claim the compulsory portion is in the free discretion of the person entitled to it. A third party can only seize the claim to the compulsory portion after its existence has been acknowledged by the heir or if proceedings are pending concerning it (§ 852 I ZPO). In contrast, a social security agency can attach the claim to a compulsory portion without the consent of the person entitled, § 93 SGB XII.[460]

458. BVerfGE 112, 332 = NJW 2005, 1561.
459. Cf. BGHZ 193, 369 = FamRZ 2012, 1379.
460. BGH ZEV 2005, 117.

B. Debtor of the Compulsory Portion

402. The heir is the debtor of the compulsory portion, § 2303 I 1 BGB. Several heirs are liable jointly, §§ 2058 et seq. BGB. After the estate has been divided up, a co-heir who is entitled to a compulsory portion can refuse to pay others entitled to a compulsory portion, in order to keep his or her own compulsory portion, § 2319 BGB.

C. Size of the Compulsory Portion

403. The compulsory portion amounts to one-half of the value of the intestate share, § 2303 I 2 BGB.[461] When calculating this share, those who disclaim or reject their inheritance have to be included, § 2310 BGB. The value of the legacy at the time of succession is determinative, § 2311 BGB. Charges on land do not reduce the value, as long as it is uncertain whether the charge will be realized, § 2313 II 1 BGB.[462] Since those entitled to a compulsory portion have no knowledge of the size of the estate, they have a right to demand information against the heirs, § 2314 I 1 BGB.[463] By the same token, the heir can demand information from the compulsory taker about any gifts received from the deceased, which are to be taken into account when calculating the size of the compulsory portion.[464]

D. Donations to Be Deducted from the Compulsory Portion

404. If the testator has made a payment during his or her lifetime and stipulated for it to be deducted from the compulsory portion, this will be binding on the claims of those involved, § 2315 BGB. Likewise, the legal obligation to deduct prior donations by the testator or the value of special services or care provided in his or her favour according to §§ 2050 et seq. BGB or § 2057a BGB is to be taken account of in calculating the compulsory portion.[465] Expenses towards an adequate old-age pension for a spouse are not regarded as a donation.[466]

E. Statutory Bars

405. The claim for a compulsory portion becomes statute-barred three years after the discovery of the disposition that infringes the rights of those entitled and

461. Cf. BGH FamRZ 2015, 1284.
462. BGHZ 187, 304 = FamRZ 2011, 105.
463. Cf. OLG Schleswig FamRZ 2011, 1821.
464. OLG Koblenz FamRZ 2016, 662.
465. The heir's right to information is discussed by Claus-Henrik Horn, *Auskunftsrechte des Erben gegen den Pflichtteilsberechtigten*, NJW 2016, 2150.
466. OLG Stuttgart FamRZ 2011, 1823.

after thirty years at the latest, § 199 IIIa BGB. The statutory period of limitation expires regardless of whether the compulsory taker has knowledge about the composition and the value of the estate.[467]

F. Respite from Paying Out the Compulsory Portion

406. Any heir can demand a delay in paying over the compulsory portions to avoid extraordinary hardship, § 2331a BGB.

II. Protection of the Compulsory Portion

407. The compulsory portion is meant to ensure a minimum share in the estate for those entitled to it. If, considered in economic terms, the testator has left those entitled to the compulsory portion with less, they can make supplementary claims or waive their testamentary share so as to be able to claim the compulsory portion.

A. The Claim for the Remainder of the Compulsory Portion

408. If those entitled to a compulsory portion are left a share of the inheritance that is less than one-half of the intestate share, they can make a residual claim to the difference pursuant to § 2305 BGB. They cannot reject the inheritance and claim the full compulsory portion instead.

B. Protection from Liabilities

409. A share of the inheritance may be subject to bequests, a testamentary burden, the appointment of a reversionary heir or other things of this nature. In that case, the person entitled to a compulsory portion has a choice. He or she can either accept the testamentary share or waive it and claim the compulsory portion instead, § 2306 BGB. If a person entitled to a compulsory portion only receives a legacy, he or she can reject it and claim the full compulsory portion instead, § 2307 I 1 BGB. If he or she does not reject the legacy, he or she must allow its value to be deducted from his or her compulsory portion, § 2307 I 2 BGB. A spouse who has lived under the statutory matrimonial property regime (community of accrued gains – *Zugewinngemeinschaft*) can, if he or she accepts the legacy, claim the full compulsory portion (calculated according to the augmented share envisaged by § 1371 I BGB). If he or she rejects the legacy, he or she can only claim the small compulsory portion and, in addition, the exact amount due as an equalization of accrued gains (*see supra* paragraph 370).

---

467. BGH FamRZ 2013, 539.

C. Right to a Supplement to the Compulsory Portion

410.

(1) Testators could undermine the claims for compulsory portions by giving away a substantial part of their assets during their lifetime. To prevent this, those entitled to a compulsory portion may have a right to supplementary portion. The right to a supplement is determined by the amount by which the compulsory portion would be increased if gifts made by the testator in the last ten years of his or her life were included in the calculation of the total estate, § 2325 I BGB. According to a reform of 2009, a gift made in the last year before death is calculated with the full value. For gifts made earlier, 10% of their value is deducted for any year which has passed since it was made, § 2325 III 1 BGB. A gift in discharge of a moral debt is not to be included, § 2330 BGB. The concept of a gift takes its meaning from § 516 I BGB. If one spouse has paid the complete price for the family home and the other spouse becomes co-owner, the value of the co-ownership is regarded as a gift.[468]

In case of life insurance payable on death, there is a long-standing debate about what value should be the basis for calculating the supplement: the full amount of the insurance payment or the premiums paid within the last ten years?[469] The Federal Supreme Court steered a middle course in 2010. It decided that both positions are incorrect. The value has to be calculated according to the market price of the insurance immediately before the death, i.e., the surrender value.[470] In the case of mixed donations, the unremunerated part must be included in the adjustments.[471] Donations going back ten years and more are not included, except for gifts made to the testator's spouse, § 2325 III 2, 3 BGB. Donations for a special purpose to foundations are also considered gifts.[472]

(2) The right to have one's compulsory portion supplemented is independent of the claim for the compulsory portion itself. The only prerequisite is that the person making the claim should in theory be entitled to a compulsory portion. The supplement to the compulsory portion can also be claimed when more than the compulsory portion was donated, but the surplus value of the share nevertheless remains smaller than the claim to a supplement, § 2326 sent. 2 BGB. A supplement can be claimed not only by those already entitled to do so when the donation was made but also by persons entitled to the compulsory portion at the time of the testator's death.[473]

(3) Usually, the claim for a supplement is directed against the heir (§ 2302 I 1 BGB). The supplement is treated like the compulsory portion. Thus, the heir

468. OLG Schleswig FamRZ 2014, 1740.
469. Cf. Claus Elfring, *Die Lebensversicherung im Erbrecht*, ZEV 2004, 305, 309 (full amount); RGZ 128, 187, 190 (only the premiums).
470. BGHZ 185, 252 = FamRZ 2010, 1071.
471. Adolf Pentz, *Pflichtteilsergänzung bei 'gemischten' Schenkungen*, FamRZ 1997, 724.
472. BGHZ 157, 178 = ZEV 2004, 115.
473. BGHZ 193, 260 = FamRZ 2012, 1383 breaking with BGHZ 59, 210 and BGH NJW 1997, 2676.

has to provide information on relevant, even indirect gifts, § 2314 BGB.[474] If he himself or she herself is entitled to a compulsory portion, he or she can refuse to pay over the supplement to the extent that his or her own supplemented compulsory portion would be affected, § 2328 BGB.

The recipient of the gift is only secondarily liable, i.e., only if the heir is not obliged to supplement the compulsory portion, § 2329 BGB. If the recipient gives the gift away, the new owner becomes liable, § 822 BGB.[475] The sole heir can also claim a supplement to his or her compulsory portion, § 2329 I 2 BGB.

III. Exclusion of the Compulsory Portion

A. *Loss of the Right to Inherit*

411. Those who have been declared unworthy of taking under a will or who have waived their right to inherit[476] have no right to a compulsory portion, §§ 2345 II, I, 2346 I 2 BGB. If the person entitled to a compulsory portion, but unworthy to inherit, has been disinherited without also expressly withdrawing the compulsory portion, the heir can assert the disqualification, § 2345 II, I 2 in connection with §§ 143, 142 BGB. The waiver of a right to inherit can also be confined to the compulsory portion, § 2346 II BGB. Such a restricted waiver can only be agreed during the lifetime of the testator.[477] As a consequence, the person waiving the right to a compulsory portion does not get any compulsory portion, if disinherited, but could be a regular heir if the deceased did not provide otherwise.

B. *Divestment of the Compulsory Portion*

412. A breakdown in family relations between the testator and the person entitled to a compulsory portion due to serious crimes on the part of the latter gives the testator the right to withdraw the compulsory portion in his or her last will, §§ 2333, 2336 BGB.[478] By a law of 24 September 2009, the grounds for withdrawal were reformed.[479] Now, the testator may withdraw the compulsory portion, if a child, a spouse, father or mother has committed a crime resulting in a prison sentence of at least one year and if, in consequence, it cannot reasonably be expected for the testator to accept that the wrongdoer participates in his or her inheritance. The same is true if the wrongdoer is detained in a psychiatric hospital or detoxification centre due to an equivalent crime, § 2333 I No. 4 BGB. The compulsory portion is only withdrawn, according to § 2333 No. 1 BGB, if the person

474. BGH FamRZ 2015, 318.
475. BGHZ 199, 123 = FamRZ 2014, 200.
476. Cf. OLG Frankfurt FamRZ 1995, 1450.
477. BGH NJW 1997, 521.
478. Cf. OLG Düsseldorf FamRZ 1995, 1299.
479. *Gesetz zur Änderung des Erb- und Verjährungsrechts* of 24 Sep. 2009 (BGBl. I 3142).

entitled committed a deliberate, but not necessarily a culpable action.[480] The withdrawal of the compulsory portion extends to all claims for it and also implies a disinheritance.

The person entitled to a compulsory portion can, even in the testator's lifetime, bring an action to determine that the withdrawal of the compulsory portion in a will is invalid.[481]

C. Unworthiness to Receive the Compulsory Portion

413. Those unworthy to inherit are also unworthy to receive the compulsory portion, § 2345 II BGB. While this unworthiness is not established by law, enforcement via legal action is not necessary, either. A challenge by the person benefiting from the claimant's unworthiness is sufficient, §§ 2345 I, 2341 BGB.

D. The Bona Fide Limitation to the Compulsory Portion

414. The testator can limit the right to a compulsory portion for a wasteful descendant or one with too many debts by appointing the issue of the descendants as reversionary heirs or reversionary legatees. An administrative executor can also be appointed, § 2338 BGB.

§4. Legal Transactions on Succession

I. Power of Attorney

415. Since the power of attorney is not extinguished by the death of the grantor, §§ 168 sent. 1, 672 sent. 1 BGB, the testator can provide for his or her estate to be dealt with after his or her death and for urgent business with banks and insurance companies to be carried out, without the heirs having to be identified or granted a certificate of inheritance. A power of attorney can also be granted as a *post-mortem* authorization, even with regard to dispositions on real property.[482] The agent does not need to wait for any instructions from the heirs. His or her competence is limited, however, by the rules on the misuse of the power of agency.[483]

480. BVerfGE 112, 332, 358.
481. BGH ZEV 2004, 243.
482. Dietmar Weidlich, *Grundstücksverfügungen mittels Vollmachten über den Tod hinaus*, ZEV 2016, 57; Maximilian Zimmer, *Die postmortale (Vorsorge-)Vollmacht als Ersatz für den Erbschein im Grundbuchrecht*, NJW 2016, 3341; but *see* OLG München ZEV 2016, 659.
483. Cf. BGH NJW 1995, 215; OLG Frankfurt ZEV 2015, 648; OLG Düsseldorf FamRZ 2016, 329; Dietmar Weidlich, *Grundstücksverfügungen mittels Vollmachten über den Tod hinaus*, ZEV 2016, 57; Barbara Grunewald, *Die Verwendung post- und transmortaler Vollmachten zum Nachteil des Erben*, ZEV 2014, 579.

After the death of the testator, the agent represents the heir or heirs so that each heir can revoke the power of attorney with respect to himself or herself. The executor and the estate administrator also have a right to revoke.[484]

II. Donations *Mortis Causa*

A. *Formal Requirements for Promises* Mortis Causa

416. A promise to make a gift on death is only valid if it is carried out by means of a disposition *mortis causa*, § 2301 I 1 BGB.

B. *Donations Executed* Inter Vivos

417. An *inter vivos* gift, by contrast, is valid in accordance with the general rules on gifts, § 2301 II BGB. This means, above all, that even an informal gift is effective upon execution, § 518 II BGB:

(1) The gift is only executed when the donor has diminished his or her estate in his or her lifetime. It is sufficient for the beneficiary to receive a future interest in rem, which protects him or her from its unilateral withdrawal by the donor. It is not a sufficient execution for the testator to empower the beneficiary to appropriate the object in question on his or her death.[485]
(2) If the donor involves a third party, there is no requirement that the execution be complete at the time of death. According to the prevailing opinion, it is sufficient that the beneficiary has attained a future interest in rem in the sense that he or she can receive the donated object without any further acts by the donor.

It is sufficient for the third party to carry out the necessary act of execution after the death of the donor.[486] It is only if the heirs have revoked the power of attorney before the execution that the third party is unable to make the necessary declarations.[487]

484. Walter Zimmermann, *MünchKommBGB* Vor § 2197 paras 14 et seq. (8th ed. 2020). Differing opinion, accepting only a revocation by all joint heirs: Stephan Madaus, *Der Widerruf trans- oder postmortaler Vollmachten durch einzelne Miterben*, ZEV 2004, 448.
485. BGHZ 87, 19.
486. According to the now prevailing opinion, cf. Hans-Joachim Musielak, *MünchKommBGB* § 2301 paras 24 et seq. (8th ed. 2020); for a different view RGZ 83, 223.
487. BGH NJW 1995, 953.

III. The Contract for the Benefit of a Third Party Effective on Death

A. *Admissibility*

418. §§ 328, 331 BGB expressly provide that performance towards a third party on the death of the promisee can be stipulated for by contract. By virtue of the contract, the third party receives a claim against the promisor. The most frequent application of this principle is the capital life insurance contract payable on death. A third party (revocably) nominated as beneficiary acquires the right to payment against the insurer on the death of the testator and policy holder, § 159 II VVG. Arrangements with banks, by which the testator leaves claims from a savings agreement or deposit contract to a third party, also have practical significance and are treated accordingly.

The underlying contract between the promisee and the promisor follows normal contractual rules.

B. *Relation Between Testator and Beneficiary*

419. It is a moot point whether the donation by the testator to the third-party beneficiary must be made in the form of a testament and according to the formality requirements contained in § 2301 BGB. According to the prevailing opinion, what is involved is a gift between living persons.[488] The failure to meet the formality requirements for a gift becomes irrelevant, according to § 518 II BGB, on the death of the testator because the contract is thereby carried into execution. If the beneficiary does not know of his or her good fortune, the contract of gift can be concluded even after the death of the testator. In that case, the insurer or bank passes on the offer of gift (§ 516 BGB), which continues to be valid despite the testator's death (§§ 672, 130 II BGB), to the beneficiary, who can accept it without notice to the heirs (§§ 153, 151 BGB). Nevertheless, the heirs can prevent the contract from coming into existence by revoking the insurer's or the bank's power of attorney.[489] They then have a restitutionary claim against the third-party beneficiary.[490]

If the gift is valid, the heir who would be entitled to a compulsory portion can demand a supplement pursuant to § 2325 BGB (*see infra* paragraph 410).

C. *Taxation and the Obligation to Set Off Against the Compulsory Portion*

420. Since the insurance sum is usually an indirect donation, it is to be set off against the compulsory portion if the testator has provided for this at the time of the appointment (§ 2315 I BGB). It is also subject to inheritance tax and capital transfer tax.[491]

---

488. BGH ZEV 2004, 118.
489. BGH NJW 1975, 382.
490. OLG Hamm ZEV 2005, 126.
491. *See* Dieter Gebel, *Mittelbare Schenkung einer Versicherungssumme durch unentgeltliche Einräumung eines Bezugsrechtes aus einer Kapitallebensversicherung*, ZEV 2005, 236.

IV. Succession Clauses in Partnership Contracts

A. *Consequences of the Death of Partner*

421. A partnership is dissolved on the death of a partner, unless otherwise agreed in the partnership contract, § 727 I BGB. Since the commercial law reform of 1998, however, this rule is no longer valid for the general partnership and for the limited partnership, both of which are regulated by the German Commercial Code (HGB). Here, the partnership remains in existence on the death of a personally liable partner, unless the dissolution is agreed upon in the contract (§ 131 III No. 1 HGB). The dead partner is excluded; the compensation due to him or her forms part of the estate (§ 105 III HGB; § 738 BGB).

B. *Continuation Clauses*

422. Even in partnership contracts governed by the BGB, the partners can agree that the partnership should remain in existence among the remaining partners, § 727 BGB. A possible claim for a lump sum settlement (§ 738 BGB) forms a part of the deceased partner's estate.

C. *Succession Clauses*

423. A continuation can also be agreed upon with the heir or heirs of the deceased (succession clause). According to prevailing opinion, each heir becomes a partner who, in accordance with the succession clause and on account of his or her right to inherit, succeeds the testator. A succession clause purely according to company law is rejected because of the liability for debts that comes with it. A non-heir can, therefore, only be given an option to enter the partnership (partnership agreement as a contract for the benefit of a third party).[492]

Because of the liability structure of the partnership, the joint heirs receive independent parts of the original share of the deceased in proportion to their shares under the law of succession ('special succession').

D. *Qualified Succession Clauses*

424. If the partnership is meant to be continued with only one or some heirs (qualified succession clause), only those nominated become partners on the testator's death.

492. BGHZ 68, 255 = NJW 1977, 1339.

In cases of doubt, it is to be assumed that the testator's share should go entirely to the successor.[493] Nevertheless, the share forms part of the estate, at least in terms of its value, and also with regard to liability for debts.

If a single joint heir receives more from the estate through his or her share in the partnership than he or she is entitled to as heir, he or she is obliged to compensate the other heirs.[494] However, the testator can exclude this obligation within the limits of the right to a compulsory portion.[495]

E. Anticipated Succession

425. An anticipated succession due to age or illness has to be agreed upon between the partners. The duty of loyalty may oblige a partner to give his or her consent if the arrangement furthers the continuation of the enterprise.[496]

V. Contracts Relating to the Estate of a Living Third Party

426. Contracts concerning the estate of a living third party are void, § 311b IV BGB. This rule is meant to protect possible heirs or legatees from selling their future inheritance at a discount. It is also meant to protect the freedom of the future testator. The future heir can, however, contract about specific items of the future estate.

Future statutory heirs may also enter into a contract relating to their share or compulsory portion with the intention of fixing the distribution of the future estate by mutual consent, § 311b V BGB.

VI. Renunciation of Future Inheritance

427. Relatives, the spouse, and the registered partner may renounce the future inheritance by contract (in notarial form, § 2348 BGB) by an agreement with the future deceased, § 2346 I 1 BGB, § 10 VII LPartG. Such a waiver may be restricted to the compulsory portion, § 2346 II BGB. The effect is to exclude the person renouncing from legal succession as if he or she was no longer alive at the time of the death of the deceased, § 2346 I 2 BGB. The renunciation, however, does not prevent the testator from appointing this person as heir or legatee in his or her will.[497]

In practice, such contracts of waiver are often part of an anticipated succession agreement. One child receives assets, which correspond to his or her future inheritance, and waives future inheritance rights so that, in the end, all children will be

493. BGHZ 68, 225.
494. BGHZ 68, 225.
495. Thomas Gergen, *MünchKommBGB* § 2032 para. 77 (8th ed. 2020).
496. BGH ZEV 2005, 71.
497. BGHZ 30, 261, 267.

treated equally. In such a case, the parties conclude an indemnity contract in addition to the renunciation contract, both in notarial form (§ 2348 BGB). This instrument is also used to avoid conflict between children by different spouses.

The waiver can be made in favour of a specific person. In such a case, the renunciation is conditional and only valid if this person becomes heir, § 2350 I BGB. If a child waives his or her position as legal heir, this renunciation is only effective with respect to brothers and sisters as well as the spouse or registered partner of the deceased, § 2350 II BGB.

As in any contract, a renunciation may violate public policy and hence be void (§ 138 BGB). However, the waiver of the compulsory portion by a handicapped child, who lives on social security, was accepted (*see supra* paragraph 378).[498]

498. BGHZ 188, 96.

Chapter 3. The Legal Position of the Heir

§1. Devolution of the Inheritance and Legal Position of the Heir

I. Devolution of the Inheritance, Waiver and Acceptance

A. Devolution of the Inheritance

428. The heir receives the inheritance immediately and directly on the death of the testator, § 1922 BGB. He or she is treated as possessor of the estate, § 857 BGB. By contrast, an heir in Austria only receives the inheritance after an allocation by the probate court. In common law countries, the estate goes to the personal representative first, who has to pay the estate liabilities. It is only after he or she has done that he or she can distribute the net estate to the heir or heirs. In German law, the discharge of the estate liabilities is the duty of the heirs themselves. They can avoid this duty by waiving the inheritance.

B. Waiver of the Inheritance

429.

(1) Heirship is automatic, but one may also waive the inheritance and thus annul the devolution, § 1953 I BGB. Often, the reason for the waiver is that the estate is insolvent. However, a waiver can also allow the inheritance to be distributed to other persons, § 1953 II BGB. Even a pauper (welfare recipient) may turn down an inheritance, even one of several millions.[499]
A waiver by a parent for his or her minor child must be approved by the family court, unless the child only became heir as a result of a waiver by his or her parent, § 1643 II BGB. A waiver by a protector or carer must be approved by the guardianship court, § 1908i and § 1822 No. 2 BGB.

(2) The waiver must be declared within six weeks of learning about the succession and the legal basis of the appointment, § 1944 BGB. It has to be expressed to a probate court, § 1945 BGB.[500] An inheritance can only be waived after the testator's death, § 1946 BGB. Before the testator's death, it is possible to relinquish the legal right to the future inheritance through a contract with the testator pursuant to §§ 2346 et seq. BGB.

The probate court has to inform the next in line of the waiver, § 1953 III BGB. For this person, a new six-week period starts, during which the inheritance may be waived, § 1944 BGB.

---

499. BGH FamRZ 2011, 472.
500. In European cases there is jurisdiction under Art. 13 European Succession Regulation.

C. Acceptance of the Inheritance

430.

(1) The heir cannot waive the inheritance once he or she has accepted it. The acceptance can be declared expressly or by implication to the creditors of the estate or the court (e.g., by application for a certificate of inheritance, disposing of items belonging to the estate). The inheritance is also accepted when the deadline for waiving it has passed, § 1943 Hs. 2 BGB.

(2) If an inheritance is accepted or waived by mistake, this declaration can be rescinded according to §§ 119, 123 BGB, even if the waiver was not declared in time due to error.[501] Contesting for mistake as to the contents of the inheritance (§ 119 II BGB) is of special importance. Mistake as to future political and legal developments, e.g., the continued existence of the German Democratic Republic (East Germany), and the depreciation of assets located there, does not result in an entitlement to contest.[502] Should someone waive his or her inheritance 'on any and all grounds, irrespective of the value of the inherited share', this waiver cannot be challenged because of an error as to the value of the inherited share.[503]

In order to avoid legal uncertainty, acceptances and waivers can only be contested within six weeks from learning of the grounds for challenge or from the point at which the coercion is no longer present, § 1954 BGB. If the challenge was made in error, the new challenge must be declared without delay, § 121 BGB.[504] Contesting the acceptance is considered a rejection of the inheritance, and contesting the rejection amounts to an acceptance, § 1957 I BGB. Contesting, therefore, does not only annul the former declaration but also contains the opposite declaration. The heir is not allowed a new period for consideration.

*D. The Legal Position of the Provisional Heir (*Vorläufiger Erbe*)*

431.

(1) The provisional heir is the owner of the estate from the devolution of the inheritance, § 1922 I BGB, and can dispose of it, § 2112 BGB. If he or she turns down the inheritance later on, his or her dispositions are considered to have been made by an unauthorized person, but they can be valid according to § 932 BGB. On waiving the inheritance, the estate will go to the next in line (with retroactive effect). Notwithstanding, the items/objects disposed of will be lost because the provisional heir was the real and rightful owner at the time of the

501. BGH FamRZ 2016, 210.
502. Cf. Barbara Grunewald, Die *Auswirkungen eines Irrtums über politische Entwicklungen in der DDR auf Testamente und Erbausschlagungen*, NJW 1991, 1208.
503. OLG Düsseldorf ZEV 2005, 255.
504. BGH FamRZ 2015, 1383.

disposal.[505] Urgent dispositions by the provisional heir are always valid irrespective of the good faith of those involved, § 1959 II BGB. Transactions that must be undertaken in relation to the heir (e.g., the termination of a lease) also remain valid after the inheritance is rejected, § 1959 III BGB.

(2) The provisional heir is also liable for the debts of the estate, § 1967 I BGB, although these cannot be pursued in court before his or her acceptance, § 1958 BGB. Before the acceptance, a judgment against the testator can only be enforced against the estate and not against the personal assets of the provisional heir, § 778 I ZPO. Personal creditors of the provisional heir, in their turn, are not permitted to enforce their claims against the estate, § 778 II ZPO. A creditor who urgently wishes to enforce his or her rights during the provisional heirship must apply to the probate court for an order to appoint a provisional administrator, §§ 1960, 1961 BGB.

(3) If the provisional heir has done anything before waiving the inheritance, he or she is treated as a *negotiorum gestor* (i.e., a person performing a service for or acting on behalf of another without authority to do so) in relation to the final heir, § 1959 I BGB.

II. Waiver of Future Inheritance

432. Those who have waived their future legal right to inherit (with or without consideration) in a (notarized) contract with the testator are excluded from legal succession. The waiver can be limited to the compulsory portion, § 2346 BGB. Its effect extends to the offspring of the person signing the waiver, § 2349 BGB. Even a handicapped person living on social security benefits may waive his or her right to the compulsory portion (*see supra* paragraph 378).[506] For a contract obliging the party to sign such a contract of waiver in the future, the same formal requirements (§ 2348 BGB) apply.[507] The waiver may be challenged for mistake after the devolution of the inheritance.[508]

In the same way, a beneficiary under a will or an inheritance contract can relinquish his or her interest through a contract with the testator, § 2352 BGB. Such a relinquishment also extends to the offspring of the relinquishing person, §§ 2352 sent. 3, 2349 BGB.

III. Disqualification to Inherit

433. Those guilty of particularly serious offences against the testator are disqualified from inheriting, § 2339 BGB.[509] The testator can disinherit them, § 1938

505. Dieter Leipold, *MünchKommBGB* § 1953 para. 4 (8th ed. 2020); differing view: Heinrich Lange & Kurt Kuchinke, *Erbrecht* § 8 V 2 n. 110 (5th ed. 2001).
506. Cf. BGH FamRZ 2011, 472.
507. Cf. Hilmar Keller, *Die Form des Erbverzichts*, ZEV 2005, 229.
508. Differently OLG Celle ZEV 2004, 156.
509. Cf. BGHZ 204, 258.

BGB, and have them stripped of their compulsory portion, §§ 2333 et seq. BGB. However, frequently he or she is no longer in a position to do so or does not learn about these offences during his or her lifetime. Therefore, those who would benefit from the disqualification of this person can bring an action for this person's claims to be set aside, §§ 2341, 2342 BGB. Once the judgment comes into force, the person disqualified is no longer eligible to be an heir. The inheritance descends to whoever would have been entitled had the person disqualified predeceased the testator, § 2344 BGB. Previous dispositions made by the disqualified heir remain valid.[510]

The unworthiness of legatees and those entitled to a compulsory portion does not need to be established in a legal action. It may be established by contesting their eligibility by a declaration directed at them, §§ 2345, 143 BGB.

IV. The Claim for the Inheritance

434. An inheritance may initially come into the possession of a putative heir. In that case, the real heir has individual claims to all the individual items in the estate, e.g., a claim in accordance with § 985 BGB, claims arising from dispossession, §§ 861, 857 BGB, from unjust enrichment, §§ 812 et seq. BGB, from the owner-possessor relationship, §§ 987 et seq. BGB, or a claim for rectification of the land register, § 894 BGB.

A. Special Claim for Restitution

435. In addition to these individual claims, the heir also has a special overall claim for the surrender of the entire inheritance, the so-called claim for the inheritance, §§ 2018 et seq. BGB (*Erbschaftsanspruch*). This claim covers not only the original assets of the deceased but also all substitutes acquired by means of the estate, § 2019 BGB, and all produce of a thing or right belonging to the estate, § 2020 BGB. Individual and overall claims exist alongside each other. The extent of the overall claim determines the extent of the individual claims, § 2029 BGB. Moreover, the law facilitates the heirs' legal pursuit of the overall claim by obliging the person in possession of the inheritance to disclose relevant information, §§ 2027, 2028 BGB. Procedurally, the heir can, therefore, take legal action against the person in possession of the inheritance in stages, § 254 ZPO. In addition, the overall claim can be sued for in the court having jurisdiction over claims against the successor, § 27 ZPO, whereas, usually, the competent court is determined by the location of the real estate, § 24 ZPO.

---

510. Karlheinz Muscheler, *Erbunwürdigkeitsgründe und Erbunwürdigkeitsklage*, ZEV 2009, 101, 107.

B. Persons Subject to the Claim

436. The claim for the entire inheritance can be enforced by the true heir against the person in possession of the inheritance. A joint heir can only claim performance in favour of all joint heirs, § 2039 sent. 1 BGB.

The party subject to the claim is the person in possession of the estate. This is anyone who has received something from the estate because of a putative or assumed right to succeed. The claim can be directed against another joint heir if he or she has assumed the status of sole heir and thus sole possession of an asset without being entitled to do so. According to § 2030 BGB, the claim is also directed against those who have received the inheritance from the person originally in possession of it.

By contrast, this claim cannot be directed against a third party who has individual items from the estate in his or her possession, but who does not claim to hold them by any right of succession.

C. Assets to Be Restituted

437. The claim contains the items that the putative heir has received and what he or she has acquired by means of the inheritance (*surrogatio in rem*), § 2019 BGB. The use of the item and any benefits received from it must be returned, § 2020 BGB. If this is no longer possible, the person in possession of the inheritance must refund its value according to the law of restitution, §§ 2021, 818 II, III BGB. Where the action is pending or where the possessor is in bad faith, he or she cannot defend himself of herself by claiming that he or she is no longer enriched, §§ 2023, 2024 BGB. In these cases, the person in possession of the inheritance is liable according to §§ 987 et seq. BGB. Conversely, the person in possession of the inheritance can claim compensation for his or her expenses, § 2022 BGB.

§2. The German and the European Certificate of Inheritance

I. The Function of the Certificate of Inheritance

438. On applying to the probate court, the heir will receive a certificate detailing his or her inheritance rights, § 2353 BGB (*Erbschein*). This certificate provides information about the identity of the heir, the extent of his or her inheritance rights, and also any arrangements for the succession of a reversionary heir or the execution of the will. The certificate establishes a presumption of legality and completeness, § 2365 BGB. Due to the irrebuttable presumption that the certificate of inheritance is accurate, it protects bona fide third parties who contract with those identified in the certificate, §§ 2366, 2367 BGB. Thus, the inheritance certificate authorizes the heir named in it to enter into legal relations, i.e., in relation to private persons, authorities, and courts.

In his or her dealing with the land registry, the heir must prove his or her right of succession by means of an inheritance certificate unless the right arises from a public will, § 35 I GBO. This is also true if the deceased was a partner of a non-commercial partnership.[511] In all other cases, the heir is not obliged to prove his or her right of inheritance through a certificate of inheritance. Presenting a public will[512] or even an unambiguous holographic will that was formally opened is sufficient.[513] A bank cannot stipulate for a certificate of inheritance in its standard terms.[514]

There are individual and joint certificates of inheritance corresponding to the various inheritance rights. In case of joint heirs, a joint certificate may be granted. Regularly, the shares of the heirs are stated in the certificate, unless the heirs waive these details, § 352a II FamFG. If part of the estate is located abroad, the certificate of inheritance can be restricted to assets located in Germany, § 352c FamFG.

II. Procedure for Issuance of the Certificate of Inheritance

A. *Jurisdiction of Probate Court*

439. When it comes to issuing the German certificate of inheritance, the local court of the testator's last habitual residence in Germany has jurisdiction as probate court, § 343 I, II FamFG. If the testator was a German national or a foreigner with assets in Germany and has never had a habitual residence in Germany, jurisdiction lies with the local court of Schöneberg in Berlin, § 343 III FamFG. The certificate is issued by the court clerk; where there is a will or where foreign law applies, the certificate is issued by a judge, §§ 3 No. 2 lit. c, 16 I No. 6 RPflG.

With regard to the European certificate of inheritance, the local court also has jurisdiction as probate court, § 34 III IntErbRVG. The local competence is determined by Article 64 European Succession Regulation and §§ 2, 34 I 1 IntErbRVG. In general, § 2 IV IntErbRVG refers to the court of the district where the deceased had his or her last habitual residence.[515]

B. *Application*

440. Both certificates are only issued on application.[516] The application and the affidavit may be made either before the probate court or before a notary. German State Laws, however, may direct that both can only be made before a notary (Article 239 EGBGB).

---

511. Johannes Weber, *Grundbuchberichtigung nach dem Tod eines GbR-Gesellschafters*, ZEV 2015, 200.
512. BGH NJW 2005, 2779.
513. BGH FamRZ 2016, 1073.
514. BGHZ 198, 250 = FamRZ 2014, 120; BGH NJW 2016, 2409.
515. Cf. KG FamRZ 2016, 1203.
516. § 2353 BGB; Art. 65(1) European Succession Regulation.

The necessary statements to be included in the application for the German certificate are listed in § 352 FamFG; for the European certificate, they are listed in Article 65 European Succession Regulation. The court can only issue the particular certificate applied for. A different certificate, in particular a less comprehensive one, cannot be issued. In these cases, the probate court will, through an interim order, give the applicant an opportunity to make the correct application.

The probate court examines – factually and legally – whether the alleged right to succeed exists, §§ 26, 29 FamFG. The parties have a right to be heard, Article 103 I GG. The certificate of inheritance may only be issued if the court is convinced that the inheritance right exists, § 352e I 1 FamFG.

The duty of examination is limited to the contents of the particular certificate applied for.

C. Declaratory Decision on Applications

441. Before 2009, if there was a dispute between several parties concerning the right of succession, the probate court granted an interim order (*Vorbescheid*). This was an announcement, capable of being contested, that the court intended to issue a particular certificate of inheritance if no objection was raised within a certain period. The parties could then have the legal situation clarified on appeal, without any party being able to dispose of the estate since the certificate had not yet been issued. This kind of interim order was abolished by the new FamFG. Now the probate court decides by court order (*Beschluss*) whether the requirements for issuing the certificate are met, § 352e I 2 FamFG. If this order conflicts with the will of any interested party, the order must be made known to that party, § 352e II 1 FamFG. At the same time, the court must suspend the effect of the order and postpone the issuance of the certificate until the order has become final and absolute, § 352e II 2 FamFG.

This procedure also applies where the parties seek a European certificate of inheritance, § 35 I IntErbRVG.

A German certificate may be issued by the delivery of the original or of a certified copy.[517] A European certificate is handed over as a certified copy only, Article 70(1) European Succession Regulation.

D. Withdrawal of the Certificate

442. The German certificate of inheritance is evidence of the right of succession. It does not, however, have the force of a final decision on that question. If the certificate issued is incorrect (no time limit!),[518] the probate court has to ask for its return.[519] If it is not returned to the court, it can be declared invalid, § 353 FamFG.

517. Cf. BayObLG NJW 1960, 1722.
518. Cf. BayObLG FamRZ 1997, 136.
519. § 2361 BGB.

The same is true for the European certificate. If it appears that the certificate is wrong, whether completely or in part, it has to be taken back, Article 71(2) European Succession Regulation and § 38 IntErbRVG.

E. Ordinary Proceedings with Regard to Succession Rights

443. The parties can also bring ordinary civil claims against each other for the determination of their succession rights, § 256 ZPO. A judgment of this nature only binds the parties and the probate court. Optional local jurisdiction lies with the court of the district where the deceased had his or her last domicile (*Wohnsitz*), § 27 I ZPO. In European cases, jurisdiction primarily lies with the courts of the Member State where the deceased had his or her last permanent residence, Article 4 European Succession Regulation. If the deceased has chosen the law of a specific Member State in his or her will, the parties may agree on jurisdiction in the courts of that Member State, Article 5 European Succession Regulation.

III. The Effects of the Certificate of Inheritance

A. Presumption of Accuracy

444. For as long as it is in existence, the German certificate is presumed to contain accurate information about the heir, the specified right of inheritance and the lack of any restrictions on that right, § 2365 BGB. The presumption is rebuttable, however, § 292 ZPO.

The European certificate is also meant to help (1) the heirs and legatees prove their status and their share of the estate, Article 63(2)(a); (2) an heir or legatee prove the attribution of specific assets, Article 63(2)(b); and (3) an executor or administrator prove his or her power, Article 63(2)(c) European Succession Regulation. The European certificate is presumed accurately to evidence these rights, with no conditions or restrictions other than those contained in the certificate, Article 69(2) European Succession Regulation.

B. Good-Faith Protection

445. Whoever acquires an item from the person named as heir on the German certificate of inheritance, confers a benefit on him or her or enters into another legal transaction with him or her with reference to the inheritance, may rely on the accuracy of the certificate so long as he or she does not know of its inaccuracy or that the probate court has demanded the return of the certificate on account of its inaccuracy, §§ 2366, 2367 BGB. Both rules fully correspond with the good-faith protection in real estate transactions under §§ 892, 893 BGB. The protective effect of the aforementioned rules can also be combined. For movables, the certificate of inheritance enables good-faith acquisition according to § 2366 BGB in connection with §§ 932 et seq. BGB. § 935 BGB applies. These rules are designed to protect third parties. Therefore, they do not apply to transactions among co-heirs.[520]

A priority notice protecting a claim to transfer of the ownership in land (*Auflassungsvormerkung*) forming part of the estate can also be acquired in good faith from those who are legitimated by the certificate of inheritance.[521]

446. Similar rules apply where a transaction is made with a person authorized by a European certificate, Article 69(3), (4) European Succession Regulation. The European certificate is also a valid document for recording succession to property in the relevant register of a Member State, in particular in the German land register, Article 69(5) European Succession Regulation. The European certificate does not, however, prove a specific right in rem or the due recording of such a right, Article 1(2)(k) European Succession Regulation. Whereas the German certificate protects the good faith of anyone who does not have *positive* knowledge that the certificate is wrong, § 2366 BGB, the European certificate's protective effect is more limited. It does not protect parties who are unaware of the certificate's inaccuracy due to gross negligence, Article 69(3) European Succession Regulation.

C. German or European Certificate

447. The European certificate is created for use in other Member States, but the use is not mandatory, Article 62(1), (2) European Succession Regulation. It does not take the place of national documents issued for similar purposes. However, once it has been issued, it may also be used in the Member State where it was issued, Article 62(3) European Succession Regulation.

Persons entitled to apply for a certificate are consequently free to apply for the one or the other instrument (Recital 69). For practical reasons, an applicant can apply for both certificates at the same time. As the applicant for a European certificate has to explain why he or she needs the certificate for use in another Member State (Article 63(1), 65(3)(f) European Succession Regulation), a European certificate cannot be issued for succession cases that are purely national in scope.[522]

The European certificate is effective in all Member States without any special procedure, Article 69(1) European Succession Regulation, or any formal legalization being required, Article 74 European Succession Regulation. On the other hand, it is uncertain whether a national certificate is recognized as an authentic instrument in other Member States according to Article 59 European Succession Regulation. A certified copy of the European certificate is only valid for six months, Article 70(3) European Succession Regulation. It is only in exceptional cases that the court may endow it with a longer period of validity, Article 70(3) European Succession Regulation. Once the period has elapsed, the person in possession of the copy may apply for an extension, Article 70(3) European Succession Regulation.

520. BGH FamRZ 2015, 1025.
521. BGHZ 57, 341.
522. Cf. Arts 65(3)(f), 63(1) European Succession Regulation.

§3. CONSTRAINTS ON THE HEIR

I. Estates of the Preliminary and Reversionary Heir

A. *Preliminary and Reversionary Heir*

448. The usual heir is the final heir or the sole heir. He or she can dispose of the inherited estate freely. But the testator can also stipulate that someone is heir for a limited time only and that after a certain time or the occurrence of an event, another person becomes heir, § 2100 BGB.

The first heir is called the 'preliminary heir' (*Vorerbe*) and the heir who follows him or her is called the 'heir in reversion' or 'reversionary heir' (*Nacherbe*). Both are heirs of the testator, but in chronological order.

The purpose of the appointment of a reversionary heir is to maintain the estate as one unit and to restrict the heir's power of disposition over the estate.

B. *Time of the Reversionary Heir's Succession*

449. Upon the devolution of the inheritance, the preliminary heir becomes heir under a condition subsequent. On the reversionary heir's succession, the preliminary heir ceases to be heir and the inheritance devolves on the reversionary heirs, § 2139 BGB. The testator can set a time for this to occur or stipulate a condition.[523] If the testator does no more than appoint a preliminary and a reversionary heir, the reversionary heir succeeds on the death of the preliminary heir, § 2106 I BGB. If a *nondum conceptus* is appointed as reversionary heir, he or she succeeds on his or her birth, § 2106 II BGB. Whoever is appointed as reversionary heir is also, in cases of doubt, appointed as substitute heir, § 2102 I BGB. If the testator has appointed someone as preliminary heir without specifying the reversionary heir, the intestate heirs are the reversionary heirs, § 2104 BGB. If he or she has named the reversionary heirs, but not the preliminary heirs, the intestate heirs are the preliminary heirs, § 2105 BGB. Should the appointed preliminary heir die before the reversionary heir is born, the legal heirs take the place of the preliminary heir in the interim according to § 2105 BGB.

C. *The Legal Position of the Preliminary Heir*

450.

(1) The preliminary heir is the first heir to succeed and may dispose of the items belonging to the estate, § 2112 BGB. In the interests of the reversionary heir, however, there are limitations on the right to dispose of land and on dispositions for which no consideration is given, §§ 2113, 2114 BGB. Enforcement

523. BayObLG ZEV 2005, 27.

of judgments by personal creditors is also not permitted against the preliminary heir, § 2115 BGB. Enforcement by creditors of the estate remains possible.
Whoever acquires any part of the estate from the preliminary heir in good faith is protected in the same way as when acquiring from a non-owner, § 2113 III BGB in connection with § 932 and § 892 BGB, respectively.
The testator may, however, free the preliminary heir from some or all of these restrictions, but not from the restriction on gratuitous dispositions, § 2136 BGB.

(2) The reversionary heir is protected by the principle of substitution according to § 2111 BGB: assets which have been acquired by means of the inheritance form a part of the inheritance. The use or enjoyment of the inheritance remains with the preliminary heirs for the time of their limited succession.

D. Relationship of Preliminary and Reversionary Heir

451. If the time of the preliminary heirship has expired or the condition subsequent has been met (*Nacherbfall*), the inheritance devolves on the reversionary heir, § 2139 BGB. The reversionary heir can ask for the properly administered inheritance to be turned over to him or her, § 2130 BGB. The preliminary heir has to draw up a register of the estate (§ 2121 BGB) and provide information if there is cause for concern about considerable infringements (§ 2127 BGB). The preliminary heir has to make compensation for damage to the estate (§ 2130 BGB), but his or her duty of care is limited to *diligentia quam in suis*, §§ 2131, 277 BGB. If the preliminary heir has used some of the estate for his or her own purposes in breach of his or her legal duties, he or she must pay compensation, § 2134 BGB.

By contrast, the preliminary heir can demand reimbursement for extraordinary expenses incurred for the upkeep of the property and in repairing or improving it, §§ 2124 II, 2125 BGB. Ordinary maintenance costs and burdens are borne by the preliminary heir, § 2124 I BGB. Extraordinary burdens must be refunded to the preliminary heir, § 2126 BGB.

The preliminary heir's dispositions after the devolution of the inheritance to the heirs in reversion are valid until he or she actually becomes aware or is held to have become aware of it, i.e., until he or she has at least constructive notice of the devolution, § 2140 BGB.

E. The Legal Position of the Preliminary Heir Exempted from a Number of (Otherwise Applicable) Statutory Restrictions

452. The testator can grant the preliminary heir a greater freedom of disposition, § 2136 BGB. He or she cannot exempt the preliminary heir from the prohibition on gratuitous dispositions, however, from the invalidity of enforcing judgments against him or her, and from the principle of substitution. The exempted heir, therefore, remains trustee for the reversionary heir, but may dispose of land and does not need to compensate for possible losses. He or she only has to hand over what is left of the inheritance to the reversionary heir, cf. §§ 2137, 2138 BGB. Even the exempt preliminary heir can be subject to an executorship.[524]

F. The Legal Position of the Reversionary Heir

453. On the reversionary heir's succession, he or she becomes the heir of the testator, § 2139 BGB. Before his or her succession, the reversionary heir has an inchoate right to the inheritance. This inchoate right is hereditary, § 2108 II 1 BGB.[525]

The reversionary heir can immediately dispose of his or her inchoate right and make use of his or her legal position. Creditors can also levy execution against the reversionary heir's right.

The reversionary heir can give up the inchoate right by transferring it to the preliminary heir or by waiving the reversionary inheritance after the first succession, § 2142 I BGB. However, the deadline for expressing such a waiver set out in § 1944 BGB only runs from the reversionary heir's succession.

II. The Legacy (*Vermächtnis*) and the Testamentary Burden (*Auflage*)

A. Legacy

454.

(1) The legacy gives a claim against those charged with payment of the legacy (*Beschwerte*) for release of the items bequeathed, § 2174 BGB. The claim is usually directed against the heir, but can also be directed against another legatee, § 2147 BGB.
Whether someone is an heir or a legatee is determined, in cases of doubt, according to § 2087 II BGB.[526]

(2) The legacy can be of any benefit relating to assets. If in doubt, the legacy of a specific item will be assumed to include appendages or accessories, § 2164 I BGB, but is invalid if the item does not belong to the estate. There is no warranty against defects. An unspecified legacy (*Gattungsvermächtnis*, § 2155 BGB), an alternative legacy (*Wahlvermächtnis*, § 2154 BGB), and a legacy of a thing to be acquired (*Verschaffungsvermächtnis*, § 2170 I BGB) are also possible. The legacy may also consist in the obligation to free any legatee from debts.
In the case of the legacy of a specific item, those charged with payment of the legacy can claim compensation for the expense incurred with respect to the item, § 2185 BGB.

(3) Anyone can be a legatee, even an heir, § 2150 BGB. The legacy given to an heir in advance (*Vorausvermächtnis*) has to be distinguished from directions

---

524. OLG Bremen ZEV 2005, 26.
525. For the reversionary heir's claim to disclosure, *see* BGH FamRZ 1995, 158.
526. BayObLG FamRZ 1997, 641.

given by the testator on how to divide up the estate: a *Vorausvermächtnis* can be received by the joint heir in addition to his or her share of the inheritance.

(4) The legatee becomes entitled to the legacy on the testator's death, § 2176 BGB, or on the fulfilment of a posterior condition, § 2177 BGB. He or she can either accept or waive the legacy by making a declaration to that effect to the obligor (the heir or another legatee). There is no deadline for the waiver, § 2180 BGB.

B. The Testamentary Burden

455. By means of a testamentary burden, an obligation can be imposed on a legatee or heir without giving the beneficiary a corresponding right to performance, § 1940 BGB. The burden can consist in any act or omission. Examples of testamentary burdens include: caring for the testator's grave, for animals, making donations to the poor, etc. Since the burdens affect the heir in a similar way as a legacy, the rules applicable to legacies apply to burdens as well, § 2192 BGB.

If the obligor (the heir or legatee) does not discharge the burden imposed on him or her, joint heirs or other persons benefitting from the obligor's elimination from the succession can demand that it be carried out.[527] Where there is a public interest in the discharge of a burden, public authorities have a right of action, too, § 2194 BGB.

If the required performance is impossible, the burden is null and void, §§ 2192, 2171 BGB. Generally, the testamentary benefit conferred on the obligor is not affected by this fact, § 2195 BGB. If the discharge of the burden becomes impossible due to the obligor's fault, the person who would be entitled to the inheritance in the obligor's stead may demand the return of the benefit in accordance with the rules of unjust enrichment, § 2196 I BGB.

III. The Executor

A. Purpose of Appointing an Executor

456. What happens to the estate after the death of the testator depends largely on the parties involved. They can divide up the estate by mutual agreement or otherwise override the arrangements envisaged by the testator. If the testator wishes to ensure that his or her arrangements are carried out, or if he or she wants to keep the estate as one unit for a certain time (e.g., until the majority of his or her children) or until the reversionary heir succeeds to it, he or she can appoint an executor in his or her will or in an inheritance contract, §§ 2197 I, 2299 I BGB. The testator can specifically name the executor, but he or she can also leave the choice to a third party or the probate court, §§ 2198, 2200 BGB, albeit not to the decision of the

527. OLG Karlsruhe ZEV 2004, 331.

notary who has recorded the will, § 7 No. 1, § 27 BeurkG.[528] A joint heir can also be an executor. The sole heir can be the executor for a legatee.[529]

The service provided by an executor is not considered legal advice. It can consequently be performed by a bank.[530] According to § 5 II No. 1 RDG, the executor may give legal advice in connection with the executorship.

B. Types of Executors

457. The executor of the will is usually an executor in charge of settling the estate (*Abwicklungsvollstrecker*). He or she has to carry out the testator's testamentary dispositions, to distribute the estate among the heirs, and to administer everything up to that point, §§ 2203 et seq. BGB.

However, the testator can also arrange for an executorship with long-term estate maintenance (*Dauervollstreckung*) or an executorship involving administration (*Verwaltungsvollstreckung*) where, e.g., he or she does not want to entrust the administration of the estate to an inexperienced sole heir or where he or she wishes to appoint an agent on behalf of the preliminary heirs, cf. § 2209 BGB. The long-term estate maintenance (*Dauervollstreckung*) usually ends thirty years after the testator's death. However, the testator may provide that it should not end until the death of the heir or the executor, § 2210 BGB.

The executor enters upon his or her duties after the succession and after accepting the position by an official declaration to the probate court, § 2202 BGB. It is not commonplace for someone to be compelled to carry out the duties of an executor. The executor receives a certificate (*Testamentsvollstreckerzeugnis*) on application, § 2368 BGB. Its legal effects correspond to those of the certificate of inheritance.

His duties are terminated by death, the loss of legal capacity or by becoming a ward of court, § 2225 BGB. In addition, the executor's duties end if he or she gives notice to the probate court, § 2226 BGB. His or her office is also terminated by a dismissal by the probate court following an application by one of the parties for good cause, § 2227 BGB. The office is terminated by a completion of all duties.

C. Duties of the Executor

458. The executor has to take possession of the estate and can make dispositions with respect to it, § 2205 sent. 1 and 2 BGB. He or she is not permitted to make gratuitous dispositions, § 2205 sent. 3 BGB.[531] Transactions carrying out the will are for valuable consideration.[532] In acting for a minor heir, the executor does not need the permission of the family court.[533] The heir cannot dispose of the items

528. BGH FamRZ 2013, 32; but *see* OLG Bremen ZEV 2016, 273.
529. BGH ZEV 2005, 204.
530. BGH ZEV 2005, 122.
531. BGH FamRZ 2015, 1284 and FamRZ 2016, 808.
532. OLG München FamRZ 2015, 1833.
533. OLG Karlsruhe FamRZ 2015, 2086.

of the estate within the executor's competence, § 2211 BGB. An acquisition from the heir by a third party in good faith is possible, however, § 2211 II BGB. The executor can incur liabilities within the confines of proper administration, § 2206 BGB.

D. Civil Proceedings with Regard to Assets

459. Assets within the administration of an executor can only be claimed by the executor, § 2212 BGB. Claims against the estate can be brought not only against the heir but also against the executor, § 2213 I 1 BGB, with the exception of claims for payment of the compulsory portion; these must be brought against the heirs, § 2213 I 3 BGB. In order to make an execution against the estate, an enforceable judgment for forbearance (*Duldungstitel*) against the executor is required in any case, § 2213 III BGB. Claims against the executor himself or herself as debtor of the estate can be brought by the heir.[534]

The executor can (in cases of doubt) sue a person claiming to be an heir (*Erbprätendent*) to establish whether or not he or she is the heir.[535]

According to the prevailing opinion, the executor, like a receiver in bankruptcy proceedings (*Insolvenzverwalter*), acts not as the heirs' agent, but as a party by virtue of office (*Partei kraft Amtes*) in his or her own name, but with economic consequences for others (called the *Amtstheorie*). Any natural or legal person can be an executor. Acting as an executor is regarded as a free service. The executor may handle legal affairs as a supplementary service, § 5 II No. 1 RDG.[536]

E. Position of Executor with Regard to Commercial Enterprise

460. If a commercial enterprise forms part of the estate, the executorship plus the heir's limited liability would result in the principle of the sole trader's unlimited personal liability being undermined. Therefore, according to the prevailing opinion, an executor can only carry on a sole trader's business in one of two ways:

(1) He or she can carry on the business in his or her own name, being comprehensively liable himself or herself, as a trustee for the heir.
(2) He or she can act as the heir's agent, with the heir granting him or her the power of attorney.[537]

Being an executor for a limited partner is less problematic (§§ 161, 171 HGB). In case of a long-term executorship, the executor can be entered in the company register.[538]

534. BGH FamRZ 2003, 307.
535. OLG Karlsruhe ZEV 2005, 256.
536. *Rechtsdienstleistungsgesetz* (RDG) of 12 Dec. 2007 (BGBl. I 2840).
537. BGHZ 12, 100.
538. BGH FamRZ 2012, 706.

F. Relationship Between Heir and Executor

461. The executor receives remuneration for his or her work, § 2221 BGB. He or she is obliged to administer the estate properly, § 2216 I BGB. To the extent that he or she does not need assets for proper administration, he or she has to leave them to the heir for the heir's free disposition, § 2217 I BGB. In case of a long-term executorship, the executor has to provide the heir(s) with the use of the estate.[539] For culpable breaches of his or her duties, the executor is liable in accordance with § 2219 BGB.

The relationship to the heir is similar to that between principal and agent (*Auftragsverhältnis*). The executor has a duty to disclose and a duty to hand over the estate, but also a claim for expenses. By contrast, a right to give detailed instructions does not exist; the probate court can only discharge the executor for a good reason on the application of one of the parties, § 2227 I BGB.

§4. The Heir's Liability

I. Unlimited Liability Which Is Capable of Being Limited

462. On the occurrence of the succession, the heir immediately becomes liable for the debts of the testator, § 1967 I BGB. His or her liability is unlimited, to be paid for out of the estate and his or her own assets, but is capable of being limited. This possibility is restricted to debts inherited from the testator or arising from the succession and does not include debts incurred by the heir himself or herself.[540] Using a condominium after accepting the estate creates debts of the heir.[541]

A. Possibilities of Limiting Liability

463. The heir has the possibility of limiting his or her liability to the estate by asking for its administration or for bankruptcy proceedings, §§ 1975 et seq. BGB. The liability is not limited by operation of law, but can be directed to be so limited by the probate or insolvency courts respectively on the application of the heir. If the estate is so small that the costs of the administration or the administration in bankruptcy would not be covered, it is not necessary for the estate to be officially set apart (*Nachlassabsonderung*). The heir can plead directly that there are insufficient assets in the estate, i.e., *plene administravit* (*Dürftigkeitseinrede*), § 1990 I BGB, but he or she must then surrender the estate to the creditors, § 1990 I 2 BGB.

---

539. Wolfgang Reimann, *Muss der Testamentsvollstrecker die Erträge des Nachlasses an die Erben ausschütten?*, ZEV 2010, 8.
540. AG Köln FamRZ 2016, 578.
541. BGH FamRZ 2013, 1476.

B. *Loss of Possibility to Limit Liability*

464. The heir loses the possibility of limiting liability in relation to all the estate creditors if he or she does not draw up an inventory within a time limit set by the court, § 1994 I 2 BGB, or if he or she intentionally draws up this list incorrectly, cf. § 2005 I 1 BGB. He or she loses his or her limited liability in relation to individual creditors where he or she refuses to swear to the correctness of the inventory, § 2006 III BGB, or where he or she waives limited liability.

C. *Public Citation of Creditors*

465. In order to allow the heir to get an idea of the possible estate debts, he or she can request the general estate creditors to file their claims by way of a public summons (*Aufgebotsverfahren*), §§ 433 et seq., 454 et seq. FamFG. Those not filing their claim in time can be excluded by an order of the court (*Ausschließungsbeschluss*), § 439 FamFG. The heir can refuse to satisfy creditors who have been excluded if the estate has been depleted by satisfying creditors who are not excluded, § 1973 I 1 BGB. The heir has the same right in relation to estate creditors, who only validate their claim five years after the succession, § 1974 BGB (called concealment, *Verschweigung*).

D. *Debtor of Estate's Liabilities*

466. The debtor of the estate liabilities is the heir, § 1967 I BGB. The heir is liable for:

(1) the debts of the testator. Those include alimony for the surviving spouse according to § 1586b I 1 BGB. A judgment against the testator can be changed to name the heirs;[542] for the liability cap of § 1586b I 3 BGB, the fictitious claim to supplement the compulsory portion of the surviving spouse is to be set off;[543]
(2) the debts arising from the succession, i.e., claims for a compulsory portion, legacies and burdens, a preferential right in advance in respect of the matrimonial household (*Voraus*), the thirty days' maintenance for a member of the heir's family (*Dreißigster*), the funeral costs, a claim for equalization of accrued gains (*Zugewinnausgleichsforderung*), and the duty to maintain the mother of an unborn child. The costs for the settlement and administration of the estate also fall into this category;
(3) the debts of the estate heir, i.e., for the liabilities that arise from the legal acts of the heir on administering the estate; the estate is liable for the latter, but also

542. BGH ZEV 2004, 429.
543. BGHZ 153, 372.

the heir personally since he or she has incurred these debts himself or herself. The personal liability of the heir continues even after limiting liability;

(4) any welfare (§ 102 SGB XII) benefits the testator received up to the total value of the estate. This rule is based on the conviction that the rules on protected assets are not intended for the benefit of heirs.[544]

If the heir continues a commercial enterprise belonging to the estate, he or she is liable according to §§ 27 I, 25 I HGB for all business liabilities of the former owner. He or she can exclude liability by making an entry in the register of companies, §§ 27 I, 25 II HGB. If he or she does not continue the firm, he or she is only liable according to the law of succession, §§ 27 I, 25 III HGB.

If the heir becomes a partner in a general partnership (*OHG-Gesellschafter*) on the basis of a succession clause (*Nachfolgeklausel*), he or she is liable according to § 130 I HGB for all the existing liabilities of the OHG without limit, to the extent that he or she does not turn his or her interest into a limited partnership interest (*Kommanditgesellschaft*) in accordance with § 139 HGB or drop out of the company.

E. Determining and Executing the Estate Liabilities

467.

(1) Public summons, §§ 1970 et seq. BGB (*see supra* paragraph 465).

(2) As long as the heir can still waive the inheritance, the above-mentioned debts cannot be pursued against him or her, § 1958 BGB. The liability will only materialize once the heir has accepted the inheritance. Before that, a creditor must apply for a provisional administrator to be nominated, § 1961 BGB.

(3) After the inheritance has been accepted, the estate liabilities can be recovered. However, the three-month plea in § 2014 BGB (*Dreimonatseinrede*) and the plea relating to the public summons to assert claims (*Aufgebotseinrede*), § 2015 BGB, are available to the heir. Neither plea leads to a dismissal of the claim against the heir. Rather, he or she is sentenced to perform his or her obligations subject to the limitation of liability, §§ 305 I, 782, 780 ZPO. He or she can assert his or her limited liability by way of a counterclaim in the execution, §§ 782, 785, 767 ZPO. The pleas have no substantive effect and, therefore, do not exclude the heir's default.

II. Possibilities of Restricting the Liability to the Estate

468. Under the German Civil Code, there are several possibilities of restricting the heir's liability.

544. Wolfgang Conradis, *'Sozialhilferegress': Kostenersatz durch den Erben, § 102 SGB XII, § 35 SGB II*, ZEV 2005, 379.

*A. Administration of the Estate (*Nachlassverwaltung*)*

469. The heir can restrict his or her liability for good by applying for the administration of the estate, §§ 1975 et seq. BGB:

(1) The administration of the estate is ordered on the application of the heir, § 1981 I BGB, if the estate is not too heavily in debt, but the heir wants to avoid the trouble of effecting the settlement and taking on the risk of his or her own assets being claimed. If the heir's liability has already become unlimited, he or she can no longer apply for the administration of the estate, § 2013 I 1 BGB.
(2) The administration of the estate can also be ordered on the application of one of the estate creditors if there is reason to believe that the heir is jeopardizing the estate creditor's claim to satisfaction, § 1981 II BGB. When the order is made, the heir loses the right to administer and dispose of the estate, § 1984 BGB. The estate and the heir's own assets are separated; the administration of the estate is transferred to the estate administrator, § 1985 BGB. Dispositions by the heir, which are made after the order, are void, § 1984 I 2 BGB in connection with §§ 81, 82 InsO.
(3) As a result of the separation of the heir's own assets and the estate, claims between the heir and the testator continue in existence, § 1976 BGB. An estate creditor cannot offset his or her own claims against the heir against the testator; any setoff declared beforehand will become void, § 1977 BGB.
(4) Before administration of the estate is directed, the heir is liable in the same way as an agent, § 1978 I 1 BGB, and for the time before accepting the inheritance like an agent without authority (*negotiorum gestor* or *Geschäftsführer ohne Auftrag*), § 1978 I 2 BGB.
(5) According to the prevailing view, the estate administrator takes action as an office holder in his or her own name. Procedurally, he or she is a party by virtue of his or her office. A legal relationship exists between the estate administrator and the heir (*gesetzliches Schuldverhältnis*). The administrator is liable to the heir for culpable breaches of duty, §§ 1985 I, 1975, 1915 I, 1833 I BGB. He or she is also liable to the creditors, § 1985 II BGB. The main task of the estate administrator is the administration of the estate and the satisfaction of the estate creditors, § 1985 I BGB. The surplus is to be handed over to the heir, § 1986 I BGB.
(6) If a creditor (who has not been excluded) makes himself or herself known after the administration of the estate has ended, the heir can, according to the prevailing view, refer the creditor to the remainder of the estate (corresponding to §§ 1992, 1990 BGB) without having to apply for the estate to be administered anew.

*B. Proceedings on an Insolvent Estate (*Nachlassinsolvenzverfahren*)*

470. If the estate is heavily in debt or insolvent, the heir has to apply for estate insolvency proceedings immediately, § 1980 I 1 BGB (§§ 315 et seq. InsO).

Estate insolvency can be established even if the heir has not yet accepted the inheritance or has unlimited liability for estate debts, § 316 I InsO. The proceedings can also begin after apportioning the estate if there are several heirs, § 316 II InsO. The right to make an application is granted to any heir, to the estate administrator (*Nachlassverwalter*), to the provisional administrator (*Nachlasspfleger*), to the executor, and to any of the estate creditors, § 317 InsO. Grounds for opening proceedings are insolvency or that the estate is too heavily in debt. The heir, the estate administrator, a provisional administrator, or an executor can also start proceedings in the case of imminent insolvency, § 320 InsO. The estate insolvency administrator (*Nachlassinsolvenzverwalter*) must settle the estate debts and in addition convert the estate into cash.

The funeral costs, the costs for obtaining a death certificate, the opening of a disposition *mortis causa*, the securing of the estate, the liabilities from provisional administrators' and executors' transactions etc., are additional priority debts (*Masseverbindlichkeiten*) and, therefore, must be settled in full, § 324 InsO. Only estate liabilities can be invalidated in the proceedings, § 325 InsO. Claims for the compulsory portion, legacies, and burdens are only met when the other liabilities have been paid off, § 327 InsO.

After the estate insolvency proceedings have come to an end, the competence to make dispositions is retransferred to the heirs. If the process is stayed because of a lack of funds in the estate, the heir can refer the estate creditors to the estate in accordance with § 1990 BGB. If the proceedings are completed after distribution, the heir is only liable to the extent of the value of the estate, which has been handed over to him or her, according to the law of unjust enrichment, §§ 1989, 1973 II 1 BGB. If the estate insolvency is ended by an insolvency plan, the creditors can only claim satisfaction from the heir's own assets if the heir has unlimited liability with respect to them or has personally committed himself or herself to fulfil the composition quota (*Vergleichsquote*) in the plan.

C. Limiting Liability When the Estate Is Meagre

471. If there is not enough in the estate to cover the costs of estate administration or estate insolvency proceedings, the heir can refuse to satisfy the creditors out of the assets he or she has apart from the estate, without any special direction, § 1990 BGB. If the excessive debts are due to legacies and testamentary burdens, the heir can refuse to fulfil them to the extent that the estate is insufficient, § 1992 BGB.

§5. The Community of Heirs (*Erbengemeinschaft*)

I. Joint Commitment and Joint Share in an Inheritance

A. *Estate as Common Asset*

472. On succession, the estate in its entirety devolves on the joint heirs, § 1922 I BGB and becomes their joint property, § 2032 I BGB. Until partition (sharing), the heirs can only jointly dispose of the individual estate items, § 2040 I BGB. Each joint heir can only dispose of his or her own share of the estate, § 2033 I 1 BGB.

B. *Joint Ownership*

473. The community of heirs is not a fractional ownership in common (*Bruchteilgemeinschaft*), but a community of joint ownership (*Gesamthandsgemeinschaft*). The estate is treated as a special fund. The community of heirs is an involuntary association, however, and is geared towards its liquidation. It is not a partnership because it lacks a common purpose. If the joint heirs continue a business belonging to the estate, an ordinary partnership does not arise by implication. Rather, the community of joint heirs carries on the enterprise as long as no formal transfer takes place.[545] In contrast to the civil law partnership, the community of heirs does not have legal capacity.[546]

C. *Joint Disposition of Items*

474. Items in the estate may only be disposed of by all joint heirs acting together, § 2040 I BGB. If an individual joint heir makes a disposition, the disposition is void if the others do not agree to or approve of it. The special assets of the community of joint heirs are legally independent. Therefore, a debtor cannot set off a claim belonging to the estate with claims against an individual joint heir, § 2040 II BGB.

D. *Surrogatio In Rem*

475. To guarantee that the substance of the estate is maintained, everything acquired by means of the estate becomes a part of it, § 2041 BGB (*surrogatio in rem*). The surrogation extends to items that have been replaced as well as to new acquisitions, whether they have been acquired by operation of law or by means of the estate itself.

545. BGHZ 92, 259.
546. BGH NJW 2002, 3389.

E. Disposition Shares in the Estate

476. The individual joint heir can dispose of his or her share of the inheritance or raise a charge on it, § 2033 I 1 BGB. Such dispositions require notarial authentication, § 2033 I 2 BGB. After the share is transferred, the transferee remains as member of the joint ownership of co-heirs.[547] Therefore, he or she steps into the shoes of the disposing joint heir.

F. Right of First Refusal of Joint Heirs

477. Since the administration and settlement of the estate might become more difficult as a result of the involvement of a third party, the joint heirs have a right of first refusal (*Vorkaufsrecht*) where one of them disposes of his or her share, §§ 2034 et seq. BGB. The right of first refusal only arises in the case of a sale and not on donation to a third party, etc. Neither will a right of first refusal arise on the compulsory partition by public auction (*Teilungsversteigerung*, § 180 ZVG) for the purpose of settlement.[548] The right of first refusal also does not arise if the share of the joint heir passes on death. The right of first refusal cannot be exercised by a single joint heir, but must be exercised by all remaining co-heirs jointly, § 2034 I BGB. Once the share has been transferred to the buyer, the right of first refusal may be exercised against the buyer, § 2035 I 1 BGB.

II. Administration of the Estate

A. Internal Management

478. Internally, the principle of joint administration (*gemeinschaftliche Verwaltung*) applies, § 2038 I 1 BGB. Any heir is obliged to cooperate with the others with regard to regular administrative measures, § 2038 I 2 BGB. This includes the duty to consent to a profitable or necessary sale of particular items. If the heir refuses his or her consent, he or she is liable for all damage caused:[549]

(1) According to §§ 2038 II 1, 745 I BGB, the joint heirs can decide on general administrative measures by a majority vote. Hence, for other administrative measures, which are more unusual, the joint heirs must act unanimously. In cases where emergency administrative decisions must be made (*Notverwaltung*), any joint heir can act alone, § 2038 I 2 Hs. 2 BGB.

547. BGH FamRZ 2016, 212; FamRZ 2016, 464.
548. BGH NJW 1972, 1199.
549. BGH ZEV 2006, 24.

What is proper or 'conventional' administration is determined by the nature of the estate and by the interests of the joint heirs.[550] Substantial changes to the estate do not fall within that category and, therefore, require unanimity.[551]

(2) There is no general duty of disclosure among the joint heirs regarding the estate. A claim for disclosure can only arise between them in individual instances from the duty of good faith.[552]

(3) If the joint heirs have directed individual joint heirs to become administrators, the latter can claim reimbursement for their expenses, § 670 BGB, or ask for an advance, § 669 BGB. However, the administrating joint heir must deduct the share corresponding to his or her own portion, §§ 2038 II, 748 BGB.
The internal distribution of costs and burdens for the administration is determined in proportion to the sizes of the co-heirs' shares, §§ 2038 II 1, 748 BGB.

(4) Likewise, the usufruct of the estate property is due to the joint heirs in proportion to their shares, but is not distributed among the heirs before settlement, § 2038 II 2 BGB. If the settlement is excluded for a period longer than one year, each co-heir can claim the net proceeds at the end of the year, § 2038 II 3 BGB.

B. *External Management*

479. Contractual obligations (*Verpflichtungen*) must be differentiated from dispositions having an immediate in rem effect (*Verfügungsgeschäfte*):

(1) As regards *contractual obligations*, everything depends on the type of administrative measure involved. If the joint heirs have agreed on a regular administrative measure (unanimously or by majority vote), the majority or one of the appointed joint heirs can represent the community externally.[553] If a share of a company with limited liability (GmbH) is part of an estate, the co-heirs can appoint a representative to act for them in the shareholders' meeting by majority vote.[554]
The legal transactions concluded result in rights and obligations for the estate and in estate liabilities for all the joint heirs.
For irregular or unusual administrative measures, all joint heirs must join in the act.
A statutory power of attorney for the community of heirs follows from § 2038 I 2 Hs. 2 BGB, for measures of *Notverwaltung*, i.e., that cannot be postponed. If the prerequisites for representation in emergencies are not present, the individual heir acts without power of attorney. He or she is thus liable as a *falsus procurator* (i.e., as a representative with no power of attorney) § 179 BGB.

550. Thomas Gergen, *MünchKommBGB* § 2038 para. 31 (8th ed. 2020).
551. Cf. §§ 2038 II 1, 745 III 1 BGB.
552. OLG Koblenz FamRZ 2013, 976.
553. BGHZ 56, 47.
554. OLG Nürnberg MDR 2014, 1097.

(2) *Dispositions* can only be made by all co-heirs jointly, § 2040 I BGB. To the extent that an administrative measure leads to a disposition, but can be decided upon by a majority vote or can be carried out by individuals, the disposition can also be made by the majority or individual. Besides, co-heirs may also act as deputies for the others with their explicit or implied consent.[555] The minority are sufficiently protected through the principle of substitution in § 2041 BGB.

(3) If the estate includes any claims, each joint heir can call for payment to all the heirs. The debtor, on the other hand, can only perform for the benefit of all heirs jointly, § 2039 BGB. If an individual heir asserts a claim on behalf of the other joint heirs, he or she acts as a *Prozessstandschafter*, i.e., a person with capacity to sue or be sued in his or her own name. The judgment for or against the individual heir will have no legal effect for or against the other joint heirs.[556]

III. The Dissolution of the Community of Heirs

A. Possibility to Dissolve

480. The community of joint heirs is an arrangement which arises by chance. It is one the participants are compelled to be in (*Zwangs- und Zufallsgemeinschaft*). It should not exist any longer than necessary. Therefore, in principle, any joint heir can demand partition at any time, § 2042 I BGB. However, the testator can exclude this right in his or her will wholly or partly or otherwise condition it. However, he or she cannot exclude it for longer than thirty years after the succession, § 2044 II BGB.

None of this means that the joint heirs *have* to distribute the assets, however. Rather, they can choose to let their community continue. In case of a secession by some joint heirs, the shares of the remaining heirs are increased.[557]

The right to demand partition is not subject to any statutory limitation.[558]

B. Rules for Partition

481. On distributing the estate, liabilities must be paid first, § 2046 BGB: next, the surplus is to be distributed to the heirs in proportion to their shares in the inheritance, § 2047 BGB. When apportioning the estate, the rules on a fractional ownership in common (*Bruchteilgemeinschaft*) apply, § 2042 II BGB, so that the items are to be distributed in their natural state, or, if necessary, liquidated, §§ 752, 753 BGB.

---

555. BGHZ 56, 47.
556. Thomas Gergen, *MünchKommBGB* § 2039 para. 22 (8th ed. 2020).
557. BGHZ 138, 8; BGHZ 187, 132.
558. Jan Holtmeyer, *Die Verjährung von Ansprüchen im Recht der Erbengemeinschaft*, ZEV 2013, 53.

C. Partition Contract

482. The actual means of partition are not determined officially. Rather, the heirs must agree among themselves and conclude a partition contract (*Auseinandersetzungsvertrag*). As of 1 September 2013, the exclusive competence to arrange such a contract lies with notaries public, § 23a III GVG, § 344 IVa FamFG. They can only help by acting as an intermediary, §§ 363 et seq. FamFG. If the joint heirs do not come to an agreement, one of them can file a claim against the others asking that they consent to a partition plan established according to the statutory rules.

The partition is to be effected according to the general law of property after the agreement is concluded. To avoid conflict, the testator can name an executor in the will or inheritance contract to effect the partition, § 2204 I BGB. However, he or she is obliged to listen to the views of the heirs before he or she acts, § 2204 II BGB.

In addition, the testator can lay down rules on whom the partition is to be effected. He or she may also call on a third party to settle the estate as appears just and fair, § 2048 BGB.

D. Compensation for Advancements

483. On the partition, the obligation to bring into account any sum paid or settled by way of advancement (*gesetzliche Ausgleichungspflicht*) must be observed, §§ 2050 et seq. BGB. Likewise, there is an obligation to make adjustments for special assistance or care given to the testator during his or her lifetime, § 2057a BGB. These rules operate on the assumption that the descendants should inherit equal shares:

(1) If one of the heirs has received substantial advancements from the testator within the latter's lifetime, these are to be taken into account on settlement, § 2050 I BGB. In doing so, the law seeks to carry out the testator's presumed intentions. In an intestate succession, the testator's descendants are obliged to make payments to balance their shares. Any advancements a descendant has received and any extraordinary subsidies to his or her income are taken into account, § 2050 II BGB. The same is true for educational expenses. Other transfers are only considered if the testator so directed on making them, § 2050 III BGB. A later direction in a testament is invalid.

(2) The value of the shares of those joint heirs who are not involved in the balancing process is calculated in advance. Balancing the shares (*Ausgleichung*) then takes place between the joint heirs with a right to have their shares balanced (*ausgleichsberechtigte Miterben*). The value of all relevant transfers is added to the estate, § 2055 I 2 BGB and then the value of the shares is calculated. The sum each individual has to balance out must be set off against the share of that individual, § 2055 I 1 BGB. However, there is no duty to repay advancements, § 2056 BGB. To make equalizing easier, there is a duty of disclosure on every joint heir, § 2057 BGB.

Special assistance or care, for which the carer did not receive consideration within the testator's lifetime, is also considered when equalizing, § 2057a BGB. This is the case even if the assistance was provided without any loss of professional income, i.e., by a housewife.[559]

E. Assignment of the Share of the Inheritance

484. The community of heirs can also be dissolved by an assignment of all shares to one of the joint heirs by a notarized contract (§ 2033 I BGB). It is also possible to withdraw informally from the community of heirs (in return for consideration) by means of detachment (*Abschichtung*).[560] The share is then given to the remaining joint heirs in proportion to their shares.

IV. The Joint Heirs' Liability for Estate Debts

A. Liability Before Partition of the Estate

485.

(1) Before dividing the estate, the estate and the personal assets of the individual heirs are strictly separate. Creditors can access either the joint assets (*Nachlass*) of the inheritance or the personal assets of the individual joint heirs. The creditor, therefore, has the choice of whether to bring his or her claim against the undivided estate by means of a collective action (*Gesamthandsklage*) or against the (individual) joint heirs as joint debtors (*Gesamtschuldner*), §§ 2058, 421 BGB. The title certificate (*Titel*) from the collective action allows him or her to seize the undivided estate, § 747 ZPO. A judgment against the individual heirs as joint debtors (*Gesamtschuldtitel*) allows him or her to proceed against the individual heirs and their personal assets.

(2) Nevertheless, the individual joint heir can limit his or her personal liability to his or her share of the estate until the estate is divided up, § 2059 I 1 BGB. This right to refuse satisfaction out of his or her personal assets has no substantive legal effect. It does not prevent the adjudication and only gives the joint heir the right (and only in case of a reservation in the judgment, § 780 ZPO) to object to the execution by bringing a defensive legal action ('*Vollstreckungsabwehrklage*', §§ 781, 785, 767 ZPO).

(3) However, the estate creditor can in this case seize the share of the joint heir, § 2033 I BGB; §§ 859 II, 857 I ZPO, and force a partition. The remaining joint heirs are treated as third-party debtors within the meaning of § 829 III ZPO.

---

559. Gerrit Langenfeld, *Das Gesetz zur Änderung des Erb- und Verjährungsrechts – Inhalt und Praxisfolgen*, NJW 2009, 3121, 3125.

560. BGHZ 138, 8 = NJW 1998, 1557; BGH ZEV 2005, 22.

(4) The collective action (*Gesamthandsklage*) must be brought against all joint heirs collectively. They are joint litigants by necessity (*notwendige Streitgenossen*), § 62 I Alt. 2 ZPO.

(5) If a joint heir is also an estate creditor, he or she can proceed against the other joint heirs with a claim against the joint heirs as joint debtors (*Gesamtschuldklage*) as well as with a collective action (*Gesamthandsklage*). He or she must take his or her own share into account (including an obligation to bring into account sums paid in advance (*Ausgleichspflicht*)) when proceeding against the joint heirs as joint debtors. The *Gesamthandsklage* or collective action for performance from the estate does not lead to the claim being reduced. However, before partition, the claim may be contrary to good faith in some cases. For execution against the estate, an enforceable legal document against the remaining joint heirs suffices.

B. The Heirs' Joint Liability after Partition of the Estate

486.

(1) After the division, there are no changes in terms of the joint heirs' personal liability. Each individual is still liable as a joint debtor, §§ 2058, 421 BGB. The possibility of protecting his or her personal assets from being used to meet his or her liabilities is no longer open to him or her, however (cf. § 2059 I 1 BGB).

(2) A collective action (*Gesamthandsklage*) can no longer be brought after dividing up the estate. Whether each individual heir can limit his or her liability to his or her share in the estate depends on the general rules. Administration of the estate can only be applied for before partition, § 2062 BGB. However, estate insolvency proceedings can still be started after the estate has been divided up, § 316 II InsO. These proceedings also lead to the heir's liability being limited to the estate, § 1975 BGB.

(3) In some special cases, the joint heir is not liable as a joint debtor after the partition, but only as a partial debtor (*Teilschuldner*). These cases are specified in §§ 2060, 2061 BGB. In these cases, orders can only be made against the joint heir on a pro rata basis. If the conditions for partial liability do not arise until after the court has passed judgment, the joint heir must assert them in a special action objecting to the execution, § 767 ZPO.

Selected Bibliography

Family Law

Textbooks

Andrae, Marianne. *Internationales Familienrecht*. 4th ed. 2019.
Dethloff, Nina. *Familienrecht*. 32nd ed. 2018.
Gernhuber, Joachim & Dagmar Coester-Waltjen. *Familienrecht*. 7th ed. 2020.
Henrich, Dieter. *Internationales Scheidungsrecht*. 4th ed. 2017.
Muscheler, Karlheinz. *Familienrecht*. 4th ed. 2017.
Rauscher, Thomas. *Familienrecht*. 2nd ed. 2008.
Schlüter, Wilfried. *BGB-Familienrecht*. 14th ed. 2012.
Schwab, Dieter. *Familienrecht*. 28th ed. 2020.
Wellenhofer, Marina. *Familienrecht*. 5th ed. 2019.

Handbooks and Commentaries

Bamberger, Heinz Georg, Herbert Roth, Wolfang Hau & Roman Poseck. *Bürgerliches Gesetzbuch*. Vol. 4. 4th ed. 2020.
Bergschneider, Ludwig (ed.). *Familienvermögensrecht*. 3rd ed. 2016.
Bergschneider, Ludwig. *Verträge in Familiensachen*. 6th ed. 2018.
Borth, Helmut. *Praxis des Unterhaltsrechts*. 3rd ed. 2016.
Borth, Helmut. *Versorgungsausgleich*. 8th ed. 2017.
Börger, Ulrike & Lutz Engelsing. *Eheliches Güterrecht*. 2nd ed. 2005.
Ehinger, Uta, Ingeborg Rasch, Alexander Schwonberg & Walter Siede. *Unterhaltsrecht*. 8th ed. 2018.
Erman, Walter. *Bürgerliches Gesetzbuch*. 16th ed. 2020.
Eschenbruch, Klaus, Heinrich Schürmann & Martin Menne (eds). *Der Unterhaltsprozess*. 7th ed. 2020.
Göppinger, Horst & Peter Wax. *Unterhaltsrecht*. 9th ed. 2008.
Göppinger, Horst & Ingeborg Rakete-Dombek. *Vereinbarungen anlässlich der Ehescheidung*. 11th ed. 2018.
Grziwotz, Herbert. *Nichteheliche Lebensgemeinschaft*. 5th ed. 2014.
Hausmann, Rainer & Gerhard Hohloch (eds). *Das Recht der nichtehelichen Lebensgemeinschaft*. 2nd ed. 2004.
Hauß, Jörn. *Elternunterhalt*. 6th ed. 2020.
Helms, Tobias, Jörg Kieninger & Christian Rittner. *Abstammungsrecht in der Praxis*. 2010.

Hepting, Reinhard & Anatol Dutta. *Familie und Personenstand*, 3rd ed. 2019.
Hoffmann, Birgit, *Personensorge*. 3rd ed. 2018.
Jauernig, Othmar. *Bürgerliches Gesetzbuch*. 18th ed. 2021.
Johannsen, Kurt Herbert, Dieter Henrich & Christoph Althammer. *Familienrecht*. 7th ed. 2020.
Kaiser, Dagmar, Klaus Schnitzler, Roger Schilling & Anne Sanders. *NomosKommentar Bürgerliches Gesetzbuch: Familienrecht*. 4th ed. 2021.
Koch, Elisabeth (ed.), *Handbuch des Unterhaltsrechts*. 13th ed. 2013.
Langenfeld, Gerrit & Lutz Milzer. *Handbuch der Eheverträge und Scheidungsvereinbarungen*. 8th ed. 2019.
Lipp, Martin & Thomas Wagenitz. *Das neue Kindschaftsrecht*. 1999.
Löhnig, M., A. Gietl & M. Preisner *Das Recht des Kindes nicht miteinander verheirateter Eltern*. 3rd ed. 2010.
Münch, C. *Ehebezogene Rechtsgeschäfte*. 5th ed. 2020.
Münchener Kommentar zum Bürgerlichen Gesetzbuch. Vols. 9–10. 8th ed. 2020.
Niepmann, Birgit & Christian Seiler. *Die Rechtsprechung zur Höhe des Unterhalts*. 14th ed. 2019.
Palandt, Otto. *Bürgerliches Gesetzbuch*. 80th ed. 2021.
Prütting, Hans, Gerhard Wegen & Gerd Weinreich (eds). *Bürgerliches Gesetzbuch*. 16th ed. 2021.
Schulz, W & J. Hauß. *Vermögensauseinandersetzung bei Trennung und Scheidung*. 6th ed. 2015.
Schulz, Werner & Jörn Hauß. *Familienrecht, Handkommentar*. 3rd ed. 2018.
Schwab, Dieter & Rüdiger Ernst. *Handbuch des Scheidungsrechts*. 8th ed. 2019.
Soergel, Hans-Theodor. *Bürgerliches Gesetzbuch*. Vols. 17–20. 13th ed. 2000–2017.
von Staudinger, Julius. *Bürgerliches Gesetzbuch*. New ed. 2010–2020.
Wendl, Philipp & Hans-Joachim Dose. *Das Unterhaltsrecht in der familienrichterlichen Praxis*. 10th ed. 2019.
Wagenitz, Thomas & Heinrich Bornhofen. *Handbuch des Eheschließungsrechts*. 1998.
Wagenitz, Thomas & Heinrich Bornhofen. *Familiennamensrechtsgesetz*. 1994.
Wever, Reinhardt. *Vermögensauseinandersetzung der Ehegatten außerhalb des Güterrechts*. 7th ed. 2018.
Zorn, Dagmar. *Das Recht der elterlichen Sorge*. 3rd ed. 2015.

Specialized Law Journals

Das Jugendamt (JAmt).
Das Standesamt (StAZ).
Der Familienrechtsberater (FamRB).
Familie und Recht (FuR).
Forum Familienrecht (FF).
Neue Zeitschrift für Familienrecht (NZFam).
Recht der Jugend und des Bildungswesens (RdJ).
Zeitschrift für das gesamte Familienrecht (FamRZ).
Zeitschrift für Kindschaftsrecht und Jugendhilfe (ZKJ).
Zentralblatt für Jugendrecht (ZfJ).

Selected Bibliography

Succession Law

Textbooks

Brox, Hans & Wolf-Dietrich Walker. *Erbrecht*. 29th ed. 2021.
Frank, Rainer & Tobias Helms. *Erbrecht*. 7th ed. 2018.
Gursky, Karl-Heinz & Saskia Lettmaier. *Erbrecht*. 7th ed. 2018.
Harder, Manfred & Inge Kroppenberg. *Grundzüge des Erbrechts*. 5th ed. 2002.
Herberger, Maximilian et al. (eds). *Juris Praxiskommentar BGB*. Vol. 4. 9th ed. 2020.
Lange, Knut Werner. *Erbrecht*. 2nd ed. 2017.
Lange, Heinrich & Kurt Kuchinke. *Erbrecht*. 5th ed. 2001.
Leipold, Dieter. *Erbrecht*. 22nd ed. 2020.
Löhnig, Martin. *Erbrecht*. 3rd ed. 2016.
Michalski, Lutz & Jessica Schmidt. *BGB-Erbrecht*. 5th ed. 2019.
Muscheler, Karlheinz. *Erbrecht*. 2 Vol., 2010.
Obergfell, Eva Inés. *Erbrecht*. 2013.
Olzen, Dirk & Dirk Looschelders. *Erbrecht*. 6th ed. 2020.
Röthel, Anne. *Erbrecht*. 18th ed. 2020.
Schellhammer, Kurt. *Erbrecht*. 3rd ed. 2010.
Schmoeckel, Mathias. *Erbrecht*. 6th ed. 2020.
Zimmermann, Walter. *Erbrecht*. 5th ed. 2019.

Handbooks and Commentaries

Bamberger, Heinz Georg, Herbert Roth, Wolfang Hau & Roman Poseck. *Bürgerliches Gesetzbuch*. Vol. 5. 4th ed. 2020.
Bengel, Manfred & Wolfgang Reimann (eds). *Handbuch der Testamentsvollstreckung*. 7th ed. 2020.
Burandt, Wolfgang & Dieter Rojahn (eds). *Erbrecht*. 3rd ed. 2017.
Damrau, Jürgen & Manuel Tanck (eds). *Praxiskommentar Erbrecht*. 4th ed. 2020.
Dutta, Anatol & Johannes Weber (eds). *Internationales Erbrecht*. 2nd ed. 2021.
Erman, Walter. *Bürgerliches Gesetzbuch*. 16th ed. 2020.
Ferid, Murad, Karl Firsching, Heinrich Dörner & Rainer Hausmann. *Internationales Erbrecht*. 117th ed. 2021.
Firsching, Karl & Hans Lothar Graf. *Nachlassrecht*. 11th ed. 2019.
Frieser, Andreas, Ernst Sarres, Wolfgang Stückemann & Ursula Tschichoflos (eds). *Handbuch des Fachanwalts Erbrecht*. 7th ed. 2019.
Groll, Michael & Anton Steiner (eds). *Praxis-Handbuch Erbrechtsberatung*. 5th ed. 2019.
Hausmann, Rainer & Gerhard Hohloch (eds). *Handbuch des Erbrechts*. 2nd ed. 2010.
Herberger, Maximilian et al. (eds). *Juris Praxiskommentar BGB*. Vol. 5. 9th ed. 2020.
Jauernig, Othmar. *Bürgerliches Gesetzbuch*. 18th ed. 2021.
Kroiß, Ludwig, Christoph Ann & Jörg Mayer (eds). *NomosKommentar Bürgerliches Gesetzbuch: Erbrecht*. 5th ed. 2018.
Münchener Kommentar zum Bürgerlichen Gesetzbuch. Vol. 11. 8th ed. 2020.

Selected Bibliography

Nieder, Heinrich, Reinhard Kössinger & Winfried Kössinger. *Handbuch der Testamentsgestaltung*. 6th ed. 2020.
Palandt, Otto. *Bürgerliches Gesetzbuch*. 80th ed. 2021.
Prütting, Hans, Gerhard Wegen & Gerd Weinreich (eds). *Bürgerliches Gesetzbuch*. 16th ed. 2021.
Reimann, Wolfang, Manfred Bengel & Florian Dietz (eds). *Testament und Erbvertrag*. 7th ed. 2020.
Scherer, Stephan (ed.). *Münchener Anwaltshandbuch Erbrecht*. 5th ed. 2018.
Soergel, Hans-Theodor. *Bürgerliches Gesetzbuch*. Vols. 32–33. 14th ed. 2021.
von Staudinger, Julius. *Bürgerliches Gesetzbuch*. New ed. 2016–2021.

Specialized Law Journals

Zeitschrift für das gesamte Familienrecht (mit Erbrecht) (FamRZ).
Zeitschrift für die Steuer- und Erbrechtspraxis (ZErb).
Zeitschrift für Erbrecht und Vermögensnachfolge (ZEV).

Index

The numbers here refer to paragraph numbers.

Index

www.ingramcontent.com/pod-product-compliance
Ingram Content Group UK Ltd.
Pitfield, Milton Keynes, MK11 3LW, UK
UKHW020142290926
15471UKWH00004B/646

9 789403 542522